We Make Our Own History

We Make Our Own History

Marxism and Social Movements in the Twilight of Neoliberalism

Laurence Cox
Alf Gunvald Nilsen

WE MAKE OUR OWN HISTORY
Laurence Cox and Alf Gunvald Nilsen

First Indian Edition 2017

ISBN 978-93-5002-472-2

Published in agreement with Pluto Books, London for publication and sale only in the Indian Subcontinent (India, Pakistan, Bangladesh, Nepal, Maldives, Bhutan & Sri Lanka)

Published by
AAKAR BOOKS
28 E Pocket IV, Mayur Vihar Phase I, Delhi 110 091
Phones : 011 2279 5505, 2279 5641
aakarbooks@gmail.com; www.aakarbooks.com

Printed at
Mudrak, 30A, Patparganj, Delhi 110 091

Contents

Preface: About This Book

Human beings make their own history, but they do not make it just as they please; they do not make it under self-selected circumstances, but under circumstances existing already, given and transmitted from the past.[1]

Karl Marx, *The Eighteenth Brumaire of Louis Bonaparte*

We make our own history. Social movements know this: it is why we struggle, sometimes against seemingly overwhelming odds, to make a different world. It is hard to recognise in the present, which is one reason activists often read movement history and the biographies of earlier generations of organisers: looking back, it is far clearer just how much movements have shaped the world we live in. The end of monarchies and empires, freedoms of assembly and expression, wage raises and weekends, the development of welfare states, the end of fascism and apartheid, equal rights legislation, the legalisation of homosexuality, the fall of dictatorships, defeats of environmentally destructive projects, and so on: with all their geographical restrictions, practical limitations and disappointments, all the backlash and vitriol, social movements from below have shaped the modern world. They have not done so alone, but in conflict with massively powerful movements from above: successive forms of capitalist accumulation, new types of state and hegemony, racist mobilisations and patriarchal movements, new forms of 'common sense' and brute force which have all attempted, often effectively, to reinforce existing structures of power, exploitation and sociocultural hierarchies.

Today, at this point in its complex history, neoliberalism – a *social movement from above* that sought to restore profitability through market-oriented economic reforms pursued both against the popular gains that were institutionalised in state-centred forms of capitalist accumulation after 1945 in the global North and South, and against the movements of 1968 and after – is facing ever-deeper crisis. With declining popular support, geopolitical reach and economic effectiveness, the neoliberal project is confronted with a growing wave of movements from below in much of the world. This book is written with the conviction that we need to understand both sides of this equation. If we see neoliberalism purely as system – often with a dystopian or paranoid angle – we fail to see that it, too, is a human product, often held together with duct tape and sailing on increasingly stormy waters. If we see our movements purely through the spectacles of celebration or disappointment, we fail to see what we can do to take them further.

We are living in the twilight of neoliberalism – but not necessarily of capitalism. Movements from below have sustained a remarkably long cycle of resistance to neoliberalism, and may be in a position to shape what comes afterwards, in a way that they were not after the defeat of 1968 and the collapse of organized capitalism (see Chapter 4). If we are not acting under circumstances of our own choosing, we none the less make our own history. Understanding how we do that – and seeing the circumstances as the results of other people's collective action – is an important part of what can help us make our own history in a direction that is more in line with the needs expressed by our movements.

History of this Book

This book is the fruit of over a decade of joint work. As activists looking for understanding, perspectives and strategy on our own struggles, we became aware of each other's work around a 2002 conference on social movements and the British Marxist historians, and realised that we were both working on the same problem from different angles. Alf, looking at rural struggles against dispossession in India, and Laurence, looking at anti-capitalist organising and working-class community activism in Ireland, saw the importance and potential power of a Marxist approach, but also the feebleness of existing Marxist theorisations of popular agency in relation to the situations we knew. All too often, the question 'What would a Marxist say about this?' was not one to which we could find existing answers. At the same time, both Ireland and India were rife with institutionalised and state-centric forms of Marxism which relegated human beings making their own history to an unimportant back place, far behind the 'real' concerns of economic theory and the desperate search for political parties to identify with, at home or abroad. We thought that another Marxism was possible.

By 2005–06, we had presented working versions of the chapters of this book to activist gatherings and social movement conferences and were busy contacting possible publishers: activist presses, left intellectual houses, university publishers and commercial academic presses. Between

2005 and 2009 we contacted 19 publishers, all of whom either turned it down, or failed to reply. The book provoked a serious division on one editorial board, and in another case convinced the editors that there was a need for a book on Marxism and social movements, but that this wasn't it.

Some publishers rejected the idea of a Marxist book as outdated by definition; others were committed to a different version of Marxism, autonomism or anarchism; others again felt that no-one would be interested in a Marxist reading of social movements – and there the book languished, condemned 'to the gnawing criticism of the mice' as two mightier authors once said. We turned our attention to making the case for serious reflection on Marxism and social movements, particularly the book of that name which we co-edited with British socialist Colin Barker and North American Marxist John Krinsky; to setting up the journal *Interface*, which develops dialogue between movement participants and activist researchers; and to our own writing on the Narmada movement in India and European social movements.

What a difference a recession makes.

With the rise of anti-austerity movements in Europe, movement-linked states in what was once the US' backyard in Latin America, popular uprisings in the Arab world and 'Occupy' in the Anglophone world, the connection between movement and inequality is once again visible to all. Books on movements proliferate, as do books on Marxism, though books which reflect on both remain rare. Over the last few years, Marxists have seen their own political organisations fall into (even further) disarray and 'Marxist celebrity' has proliferated as a result, while at the same time the anarchist and autonomist perspectives dominant in many movements in the mid-2000s have found it hard to offer strategic ways forward beyond the ritual celebration of movements. We share that celebration in some ways; but to agree that we need movements, even movements independent of political parties, is not the end of a discussion but the start of one – *what should we do? How can we win?*

Our Politics

We did not come to these questions, as the received wisdom in social movement studies has it, as Marxist intellectuals looking for an agent of social change. We came to them as movement activists seeking to understand the deeper structural reasons for the inequalities and oppressions we were fighting against and looking for perspectives that could help develop our movements' capacities. 'Marxism' and 'social movement research' were tools whose value for us lay in their potential to enable bottom-up social change. That remains our perspective today, although we have had to remake those tools considerably from the museum specimens of the one and the 'art for art's sake' versions of the other which we were initially directed to: our starting-points for approaching theory are activist experience and movement needs.

We have been involved in movements since our teens; between us, we have spent over forty years in movements in several different countries, including movements against dispossession, ecological campaigns, international solidarity, community organising, anti-war activism, radical media, workplace struggles, alternative education projects, organising against repression, social centres, anti-racism, the global 'movement of movements', and various left political formations. We have also been able to work together on occasion, in solidarity with campaigns each other was involved in. We have been ordinary foot soldiers and local organisers as much as spokespeople or intellectuals in any grandiose sense, and our perspectives are shaped by these personal experiences and, more fundamentally, by the other activists we have worked alongside, learned from, or collaborated with indirectly.

What this Book is, and What it is Not

We came to Marxism in large part because we were convinced of the need for what we would now call a 'critical realist' perspective. In our movements, we regularly experienced defeats or unexpected breakthroughs which could not be explained in surface terms, whether those of the play of discourses or organisational gaming, but had to be referred to underlying power structures, social and economic relationships, or cultural assumptions. A critical realist theory of society combines this recognition of underlying realities with a critical approach – one that does not reaffirm the necessity of how things currently are, but acknowledges its constructed character and hence the possibility of challenging and changing structures. We came to social movement studies from the angle of our collective action, particularly as we became more experienced and more aware of the long term and the big picture, and the need to reflect on it systematically, in ways which went beyond day-to-day polemics –

and the poorly informed journalistic clichés advanced by mainstream sociologists and political scientists.

Yet as we explored both these approaches we found some strange paradoxes. Although Marxism, as this book underlines, is a theory developed from and for social movements, and its critical perspective is regularly stressed, in practice most 'actually existing' Marxism has very little of theoretical substance to say about social movements (to the point that our co-edited book on the subject is literally the first sustained engagement we are aware of). In Leninist traditions, collective action has often been reduced to discussion of political parties, usually with no reference to the enormous distinction between what 'party' meant in the Communist Manifesto, what it meant in 1917, and what it means today. In what should be the more movement-relevant Gramscian tradition, popular agency is often reduced to consumption of commercially produced mass culture. The highest-status university Marxisms, however, mimic mainstream approaches by focusing on elaborate structural analysis, so that occasional moments of practical politics appear as a disconnected rhetorical flourish rather than integral to the overall picture. The result is a Marxism in which 'making our own history' has become almost entirely disconnected from serious intellectual reflection.

Conversely, social movement studies, particularly in its US variant, has become what Alain Touraine (1985: 769) calls 'a kind of spontaneous natural sociology of … [movement] elite groups' – mimicking, in its concern for organisational rationality, alliances with elites and the framing of media messages, the behaviour of the leaders of US movement organisations: stuck in a political context which makes alliances across movements very difficult, minimises the possibilities for movement-based parties and mass media, severely limits the scope for effective direct action or the changing of workplace and community power relations, and rules out wider-scale social change. Movements, in this analysis, can hardly *move*; all they can do is attempt to position themselves as best they can within a context whose ultimate rules are set by others.

As Europeans with a sense of global history, living in states shaped by social movements from above and below – peasant, democratic, nationalist, labour, fascist, Catholic, feminist, ecological and more – none of this makes sense. Our movement organisations come and go; the movements are sometimes massive, sometimes close to non-existent; the frontline of struggle is pushed backwards and forwards. Yet, undeniably,

Ireland and Norway – like India, and indeed the large majority of states in the world today – have been made and remade by social movements, not once but several times. An approach to social movement studies which excludes action on this scale – the scale that many social movements aim for, and often need to reach in order to win – is worse than useless, a sort of intellectual gloss on the forces that seek to integrate movement organisations into the institutional fabric at the expense of their ordinary participants and their wider goals.

This book thus attempts a rethinking of *both* Marxism and social movements research, aiming to explore how 'human beings make their own history', from above as well as from below, intentionally and unintentionally – and to do so in a way which might actually be useful to participants in contemporary movements from below. We situate social movements (from above and below) at the centre of an explanation of social change. Rather than a field-specific theory of social movements as a self-contained space, cut off from revolutions, radical parties, labour conflicts, community organising, popular subcultures, and so on, we treat these as interrelated aspects of popular agency, comparable to and in conflict with the collective action of elites (and on occasion being co-opted by them). It is only by managing to see the *relationships* between such things that movement participants themselves can get beyond fetishising one or another form of organising or field of conflict, and develop alliances which are sufficiently far-reaching, broad-based and strategically oriented to win.

Hence this book is not (as has become conventional) an exposition of Marxist takes on neoliberalism as structure, enlivened with a few journalistic accounts of our favourite struggles. Instead, it aims to analyse the collective agency of the movement from above which has successfully imposed neoliberalism (but is now struggling to maintain its viability and more importantly the alliance underpinning it) on the same level as the collective agency of movements from below seeking to overthrow it; and to theorise the nature of their interaction.

Nor is this book a celebratory account of recent movement waves which proposes (as has become equally conventional) that, if only they carry on accentuating our particular political preferences, all will be well. Too much blood has been spilt in the longer term, defeating waves of popular upsurge, for this kind of cheerleader role to be in any way responsible. Those who command the forces of repression (not to mention senior executives, political leaders, major media editors and the like) care little for radical intellectuals' preferences; it is by disaggregating the alliances which enable them to effectively deploy coercion that movements can hope to turn popular support into lasting social change.

Nor, finally, is this book an uncritical summary of 'the literature', as though an aggregation of summaries of high-status academic publications could remotely represent the existing state of human knowledge, as opposed to a rather banal orthodoxy reflecting institutionally determined academic status orders. We do on occasion draw on, engage with, or polemicise against particular writers, but not from a viewpoint in which the boundaries drawn around 'the literature' by those who seek to defend their private subfield are useful or significant ones.

On the positive side, one welcome effect of the revival of social movements and the crisis of neoliberalism has been the flourishing of new kinds of writing by movement participants who are not so deferential towards existing genres and field-specific orthodoxies. The study of social movements is no longer so conservative, nor is critical analysis so devoid of discussions of agency, as when we started thinking about these topics. The downside of this, as authors, is that it is impossible to keep up with, or even know about, everything that might be relevant. Thankfully, the same processes have undermined the top-down expectation that radical books, even Marxist ones, should claim to be a complete theory of everything – and, in some circles at least, undermined the sense of a monolithic 'literature' presenting the Sisyphean labour of constantly mastering and re-mastering. It is, we hope, now easier to write from a particular position which does not claim or imply universality, but nevertheless tries to say something useful in wider conversations within movements and engaged scholarship.

Because of this same opening-up of the field, and the range of fields we engage with, we have had to make particular choices about referencing, in order to avoid an infinite regression of references for each statement which might raise an eyebrow in a book whose central subject is contention. Where we mention widely-held positions, in academia or in movements, which are unlikely to be surprising to most readers, adding a reference would be a superfluous argument from authority, and it is better to offer a logical or empirical argument. Conversely, where an empirical area is likely to be unfamiliar or where it is important to avoid theoretical misunderstandings we provide references.

Chapter Overview

This book has five chapters. Chapter 1 discusses how theory can grow out of activist experience and discusses the implications for 'movement-relevant theory', identifying Marxism as one form of movement theorising, perhaps with particular advantages but with serious gaps at present. Chapter 2 discusses how a praxis-oriented Marxism can help activists change the rules of the socially constructed game to which social movement studies often confine them. Our third and pivotal chapter rereads Marxism as a theory of social movements, and shows what this means for movements from above and below. Chapter 4 extends the analysis to explore how movements have structured the historical development of capitalism, up to the crisis of neoliberalism. Finally, Chapter 5 discusses movements from below against neoliberalism, and what this book's analysis can contribute to such movements' strategies.

This is, in some ways, the best of times, the worst of times. In Europe, movements on a scale which might once have been seen as irresistible encounter the apparently immovable object of EU austerity policies – whose hegemonic reach in turn has never been feebler. In Latin America, a dramatic cycle of movements shaking states seems to be turning into a cycle of states disappointing movements. In North America, the re-establishment of wide-ranging alliances around Occupy and resistance to tar sands extraction seems powerless to affect wider change. Peasant uprisings in India and popular unrest in China also seem to break on the rock of state power. In the Middle East, the Arab Spring seems poised at the end of Act Two, waiting for a new cycle of struggle. Globally, the earth keeps warming and negotiators keep writing backroom trade deals, although their legitimacy has never been less. As Raymond Williams puts it, it is not in the 'detailed restatement of the problem' (1983: 268) that the chances shift in our favour – it comes down to movements, and struggle.

In our view, whether neoliberalism is ending is perhaps not the main question we should now be asking. Such hegemonic projects have relatively short shelf-lives, induced by their declining ability to meet the interests of the key members of the alliances which underpin them. The real question is more one of how much damage neoliberalism will do in its prolonged death agonies; and, even more importantly, what (or more sociologically, who) will replace it and how. This book is written as a contribution to the struggle of movements from below to make our own, common, history after the twilight of neoliberalism finally fades to black.

Acknowledgements

The arguments in this book developed out of presentations to the Alternative Futures and Popular Protest conference in Manchester and the 'Making global civil society' KnowledgeLab in Lancaster. Earlier versions of some of the material in this book were published as 'Why do activists need theory?' in the *Euromovements* newsletter (2005); as 'History does nothing' in *Sosiologisk Årbok* (1–2, 2007); as 'The authors and actors of their own drama' in *Capital and Class* (33/3, 2009); as 'What would a Marxist theory of social movements look like?' in Colin Barker, Laurence Cox, John Krinsky and Alf Nilsen (eds), *Marxism and social movements* (Brill 2013); as 'The bourgeoisie, historically, has played a most revolutionary part' in Colin Barker and Mike Tyldesley (eds), *Eleventh international conference on alternative futures and popular protest* (Manchester Metropolitan University); and as 'What should the movement of movements do if we want to win?' in the online wiki of the 'Making Global Civil Society' KnowledgeLab (2005). We are grateful to the conference organisers, publishers and editors for their permission to reuse material from these pieces.

1

'The This-Worldliness of their Thought': Social Movements and Theory

> *The question whether objective truth can be attributed to human thinking is not a question of theory but is a practical question. It is in practice that human beings must prove the truth – i.e. the reality and power, the this-worldliness of their thought.*
>
> Marx, *Theses on Feuerbach*

> In every country the process is different, although the content is the same. And the content is the crisis of the ruling class's hegemony, which occurs either because the ruling class has failed in some major political undertaking, for which it has requested, or forcibly extracted, the consent of broad masses … or because huge masses … have passed suddenly from a state of political passivity to a certain activity, and put forward demands which taken together, albeit not organically formulated, add up to a revolution. A 'crisis of authority ' is spoken of: this is precisely the crisis of hegemony, or general crisis of the state.

These are the words of the Italian revolutionary Antonio Gramsci (1998: 210), writing from behind the walls of Mussolini's prisons. The 'red years' of 1919–20, which saw north and central Italy swept by a wave of strikes, land and factory occupations and councils, had thrown liberal capitalism and parliamentary democracy into a systemic crisis, to which fascism had appeared as offering a way out. Such crises – organic in Gramsci's terms – are essentially those moments in modern history when economic growth grinds to a halt, when existing political loyalties wither away, and when dominant groups are confronted with the oppositional projects of subaltern groups – that is, *social movements from below* – which no longer accept the terms on which they are ruled and therefore strive to develop alternative social orders. Organic crises, in other words, are those moments when subaltern groups develop forms of collective agency that push the limits of what they previously thought it possible to achieve in terms of progressive change.

The present is just such a moment. The spectacular failure of neoliberalism as a global, elite-led project of market-oriented economic reforms is increasingly evident. Launched in the late 1970s as a response from above to the stagnation of post-war models of state-regulated capitalist development and to the movement wave of 1968 (Lash and Urry 1987, Wainwright 1994), the neoliberal project has produced an economic system that systematically privileges the needs and interests of an ever-narrowing segment of the global population. This was already evident long before the onset of the financial crisis of 2008.

Between 1960 and 1997, for example, the ratio between the share of income received by the richest 20 per cent of the world's countries to that received by the poorest 20 per cent increased from 30:1 to 74:1; the richest 20 per cent of humanity received more than 85 per cent of the world's wealth, while the remaining 80 per cent had to make do with less than 15 per cent of the world's wealth (UNDP 1999, 2000). The trend towards spiralling inequality has accelerated during the crisis: in 2013, 1 per cent of the world's families own 46 per cent of the world's wealth, while the bottom half of the global population owns less than the world's 85 richest people (Oxfam 2014, UNDP 2014). Behind these figures lie the poverty, unemployment and dispossession that result from how neoliberalism has concentrated wealth and resources towards global elites across the North-South axis over a 30-year period (Harvey 2005, McNally 2011). Importantly, the rewards offered to the northern service class and petty bourgeoisie in the early years of Thatcherism and Reaganism have dwindled away to the point where the 'death of the middle class' is regularly announced (see OECD 2008, 2011; West and Nelson 2013, Peck 2011). In other words, the key allies of the neoliberal project in its northern heartlands are being systematically disaffected.

Conversely, since the mid-1990s, we have seen the development of large-scale social movements from below across most regions of the world-system (Polet and CETRI 2003, Juris 2008, Zibechi 2010, Manji and Ekine 2011). While this development has unfolded according to specific rhythms and assumed specific forms in different countries and regions, it is increasingly clear that these protests, campaigns, movements and – in some cases – revolutionary situations, or even perhaps new state forms, are not isolated occurrences, but rather a historical wave within which we can see an emerging if complex 'movement of movements'. Indeed, the past two decades have witnessed an unprecedented degree of transnational coordination and alliance building between movements in different locales across the world, as well as the articulation of direct challenges to the global structures of economic and political power that have been entrenched in and through the neoliberal project (de Sousa Santos 2006, McNally 2013, Wood 2012).

In this book, we suggest that the current crisis can be thought of as the twilight of neoliberalism. Dramatic movements in Latin America and the Arab world have shown the limits of US geopolitical control of these once-crucial regions, while what once seemed an all-powerful New World Order has run into the sands of Afghanistan, Iraq and Syria. European anti-austerity struggles have pushed the EU to the limits of governability, while North American movements have started to rebuild the alliances broken apart by post-9/11 nationalism and repression. Indian and Chinese capitalism are both facing large-scale resistance in rural areas, India's 'special economic zones' and Chinese factories. The ability of neoliberal institutions to weather financial crisis, continue delivering the goods for their core supporters, maintain internal and international alliances and (literally) turn back the tide is increasingly feeble. In the absence of any capacity to develop alternative strategies, neoliberal actors are increasingly adopting a siege mentality, marked by a narrowing of public debate, the tightening of the screws of austerity and a quicker resort to repression. Indeed, 'neoliberalism' itself has become a dirty word in public, and its representatives now have to meet in remote locations protected by alpine mountains or deserts in order to be safe from their own publics.[1]

But it is not enough, we argue, to critique the nature of neoliberalism (Harvey 2005), celebrate the existence and practices of the movement (Maeckelbergh 2009), or proclaim a refusal to engage in traditional statist politics (Holloway 2002). Movement participants have already done their own thinking – on which much sympathetic academic writing relies, in a hall-of-mirrors relationship. It is certainly useful to movements to find books which articulate their current points of view well; it does not, however, help them think *forwards*, or more exactly, it does not take them beyond the belief that if only we keep on doing what we are doing, as we are doing it, hopefully with more participants and more adherence to our specific approach, we will win. As activists, we need something more from theory or research; we hope for the ability to think *beyond* our current understanding and identify perspectives that help us develop our practice, form alliances and learn from other people's struggles. Not all activists, of course, see things this way.

Why Do Activists Need Theory?

We start from the existential situation of activists as we understand and have experienced it. In this perspective, the process of becoming an activist is primarily a process of learning, which we describe in individual terms, though of course often this learning is that of a subaltern group, movement, or organisation (Vester 1975, Flett 2006, Raschke 1993). Initially, we become 'activists' because we find that something is not right in the world, and more specifically that it cannot be fixed within the normal channels. To become an activist, then, is to learn that the system does not work as it claims, and to move towards the understanding that to achieve change, we need to organise and create pressure.

For some, though not all, activists, this learning process continues, as we find that the system[2] is itself part of the problem, and that its resistance to our struggles for change is not accidental or contingent but, at some level, fundamental to its nature. Thus we come to connect our own issues with those of others, and to create solidarity in opposition to given power structures. This experience – of finding that we have to face off against a system, and that that system is both powerful and fundamentally opposed to us – raises some very large questions. The first, and most obvious, theoretical question that arises from this existential situation is simply 'What should we do?' (Barker and Cox 2002). Secondly, as we come to understand the agency of the various parts of the system, we ask 'How will the system react?' Thirdly, we have to ask ourselves, as struggle deepens and success does not seem easily within our grasp, 'What will work and how can we win?'

Laurence remembers very clearly the moment of realising that he had to think further than he had ever done before. It was early 1991, and the second Gulf War[3] was just about to start. As an activist researcher, he was spending the year in Hamburg, partly working with a local branch of the Green Party (going through its own convulsions), but becoming increasingly involved in a peace camp outside the US embassy in sub-zero temperatures. In Germany, as in several other countries, a massive movement had opposed the war, and the key arguments had apparently been won. Yet not only was the war going ahead, but opinion polls were suddenly swinging around in favour of it. Something was happening that was not caused by surface events; despite winning the public debates and on the streets, the movement was encountering hidden structures, and deeper resistances than could be explained by any conspiracy theory.

Focusing as it does on the structural nature of social problems and political issues, Marxism constitutes a particularly relevant resource when we seek answers to questions like these. This flows from the fact that Marxism is one among several bodies of theory that strive to go beyond everyday 'common sense' and ideological justifications of why things are as they are, by drawing on the knowledge built up by activists in movements grounded in communities in struggle. Such theories – movement theorising – are shaped very differently to the understandings of the world generated within the official institutions of 'intellectual production', such as universities, newspapers, government departments, or churches. They are grounded in the experience and activism of subaltern groups – working-class people, women, racial and ethnic minorities, gays and lesbians, indigenous peoples and others – who do not hold power, own the 'means of intellectual production', or benefit from high cultural status. Most fundamentally, the key goal of theories coming from such movements is not to reaffirm a given power structure but to change such structures, and their key resource is what activists have learned in their own lives and struggles, and from other movements, about how to do so (Eyerman and Jamison 1991, Conway 2005, Cox and Flesher Fominaya 2009, Choudry and Kapoor 2010, Hall et al. 2012, Cox 2014a).

This book is unashamedly based on this kind of activist theorising, whether it comes to us through our own lives and those of our friends and comrades, or through other writers who have attempted to articulate it. While we focus primarily on the example of Marxism, this is more because of our own familiarity with this body of thought than because we want to claim it as the only such kind of theorising.[4] Our concern is not to produce yet another defence of one activist theory *against* others. Rather, it is to show how we can reclaim activist knowledge – 'frozen' in the very specific form of Marxism – for our own movements and problems, and to encourage others to do the same with other forms of activist knowledge. The theoretical discourse of Marxism, in other words, has to show its 'this-worldliness' in practice, by offering something helpful to activists in terms of telling us what to do, what to expect, and how to win. What we have found, and what we want to discuss, then, is not a set of pre-packaged answers but rather a way of thinking about these issues.

Notoriously, classical Marxism offers relatively little in the way of explicit political prescriptions. Marx and Engels's own political practice and writings are 'multi-vocal' and have been interpreted and developed in many different ways through the Second (social-democratic), Third (orthodox communist) and Fourth Internationals (Mills 1962, Thompson 1997), to say nothing of the various council-communist, humanist, autonomist and non-dogmatic Marxisms which we find ourselves in closer alignment with politically (Gottlieb 1989, Jay 1984). What we are interested in here, however, is not so much the specific 'lines' developed in these traditions as a particular understanding of *what politics is*, and hence of the social situation we find ourselves in as activists.

We have developed this understanding (Cox 1999a, Nilsen 2007, 2009a) around the proposition that Marxism is, at its core, a theory of organised human practice, and thus an alternative theory of social movements, very different in its shape from the academic school of that name. In this chapter, we explore an outline of that understanding, to see what it can have to offer other activists, whether Marxists or not. Our hope is that others will be inspired to do something similar with whichever forms of frozen activist knowledge they are most familiar with: to break them free of the academy and its tendency to reward theoretical competition, and return them where they started, in the struggles of ordinary people not only to make sense of their world, but to change it.

Nothing is more urgent, within this kind of intellectual production, than to free activists from disempowering versions of 'theory' that tell them how impossible change is and how futile or impossible all activism is, and to 'reclaim, recycle and reuse' for our own purposes the precious learning of earlier generations of struggle. In our own exploration of Marxism, we start where activists start in our own learning processes: with human beings' experience of the world and ourselves, our understanding of this experience, and the ways in which we develop this understanding.

An Active Concept of Experience

What is experience anyway? As a point of departure, it is important to see experience as active rather than passive: experience is not just what happens to people, but also what people do with, and about, the things that happen to them (Thompson 1963). In this perspective, experience is the practical and tacit knowledge that we as human beings generate about the material (social and non-human) world, through our encounters with and interaction with this material world. In other words, experience is what we know about how we can meet our needs – of whatever kind – in the specific world that we inhabit. This practical-tacit knowledge is thus 'an attribute of individuals by reason of their social character, their participation, active or passive, in relations with others within inherited structures' (Wainwright 1994: 107). It is also, as William Blake knew, an attribute of our experience of *ourselves* as beings with needs and as agents engaging in struggles (Thompson 1998).

As Chapter 3 argues, experience is also the seedbed from which consciousness grows. Experience informs our consciousness of the world 'out there' and our place in it, and on the basis of this we choose to act – or not to act – in certain ways: '... human consciousness [is] produced by creative human beings trying to understand their existence so that they can purposefully choose how to better organise their efforts to fulfil their potentials' (Cole 1999: 250). This is central to what Marxist theory calls a materialist understanding of human consciousness: consciousness is fundamentally oriented towards real-world practical problems, not in the sense that all thought is explicitly concerned with practicalities, but that it is the problems that we encounter in our own lives which push us to think, and which push us to change how we think when our current way of thinking is not working for us (see Marx and Engels 1974).

Three key aspects of this notion of experience are worth noting:

1. This concept assumes epistemological realism; that is, it asserts that there is a world out there which exists independently of our perception of it, and which conditions our way of knowing. Our knowledge of this world in turn flows from the practical process of experience, the discovery of needs, and attempts to resolve problems.
2. It is a concept of experience which emphasises social change through human agency: the material and social world 'out there' is characterised by a constant process of people's *becoming* human beings, or *making themselves*, through reflecting on their social experience, developing their needs and capacities, and finding new ways of socially organising these needs and capacities and thus transforming their worlds.
3. It is a concept of experience that assumes *situatedness*: consciousness originates from experiences gathered through social practice that takes

> place within, and which is thus specific to, a given social, cultural, historical and spatial context. This context defines the parameters within which experience is formed.

Thus experience is engendered through the practices we engage in to make and change the particular worlds we inhabit, and the problems that we encounter as we go about the business of doing this. As we try to make sense of and move beyond these problems, we are forced to reflect on our problematic, changing and local experiences and develop a more thorough, articulated understanding of it. This is where theory enters the picture.

What is Theory?

We start by saying what theory is not: producing theory is not necessarily a scholastic exercise; theory is not necessarily produced within academia; the producers of theory are not necessarily academically trained or holders of qualifications as 'officially approved theorists'. Theory need not be a tool for intimidating others, displaying academic status, or dismissing struggles for change: these kinds of uses are parasitic on, and destructive of, what makes theory worthwhile (Horton and Freire 1990).

Positively, the building blocks of theory are ordinary people's efforts to make sense of and change their social experience; theory is produced wherever this happens. The producers of theory are – potentially – everyone who reflects on their experiences so as to develop new and improved ways of handling problematic aspects of that experience. Theory, in this perspective, is knowledge that is consciously developed out of experience, that has been worked through using experience as a touchstone, that has become explicit and articulate, and which has been brought to a level where it can be generalised.[5]

Gramsci phrased this insight as follows: 'All men [*sic*] are intellectuals, one could therefore say: but not all men have in society the function of intellectuals.' He goes on to say:

> When one distinguishes between intellectuals and non-intellectuals, one is referring in reality only to the immediate social function of the professional category of the intellectuals, that is, one has in mind the direction in which their specific professional activity is weighed, whether towards intellectual elaboration or towards muscular-nervous

> effort. This means that, although one can speak of intellectuals, one cannot speak of non-intellectuals, because non-intellectuals do not exist ... There is no human activity from which every form of intellectual participation can be excluded: *homo faber* cannot be separated from *homo sapiens*. Each man [*sic*], finally, outside his professional activity, carries on some form of intellectual activity, that is, he is a 'philosopher', an artist, a man of taste, *he participates in a particular conception of the world, has a conscious line of moral conduct, and therefore contributes to sustain a conception of the world or to modify it, that is, to bring into being new modes of thought*. (Gramsci 1998: 9; our emphasis)[6]

Here, as elsewhere in Gramsci, there is a strong developmental sense: knowledge is constructed or sustained, and the role of politics is in part structured around this. One example of this is highlighted by Stuart Hall's (1996) discussion of dominant, negotiated and oppositional 'readings' of texts (he gives the example of watching news about a strike). People caught within, or identifying with, the dominant reading will share the media 'message' both that strikes in general are a bad thing and that this particular strike is bad. By contrast, those who have developed a fully oppositional reading will be able both to criticise the assumption that strikes as such are bad, and to formulate solidarity with those actually out on strike.

However, many people may operate with a negotiated reading, unable (yet) to detach themselves from the general assumption that strikes are bad, but nevertheless making a particular exception in this case (perhaps because friends or family are involved). The problem with this, of course, is that the 'good sense' manifested around this particular strike is not extended into conflict with official 'common sense' about strikes in general; politically, it denies solidarity to those who are not already known, and isolates strikers, making it more likely that they will be defeated. It of course also makes it harder to articulate the possibility of an alternative world, closer to our practical-tacit experience.

The difference between Hall's dominant and negotiated readings is one of *experience*: the person who identifies with the dominant reading may not ultimately benefit from doing so (they may be an employee themselves, even a vulnerable one); however, they have not learned to experience themselves as producer rather than consumer, or to identify as employee rather than boss. Those who hold the negotiated reading are at least able to understand themselves, or those close to them, as employee/producers on strike – which cannot be taken for granted (see Fantasia 1988).

The difference between this negotiated reading and the oppositional one, however, is one of *theory*: the person who negotiates their reading has a sense of how things are for them, or for people close to them, but does not generalise this, see that others are in a similar situation, identify with those others, or draw more general conclusions about the world. The oppositional reading, in its ability to oppose the media message that strikes as such are bad, draws on a theoretical understanding of how the world is structured, of the general features of being an employee, and of the structural sources of conflict.

Theory and Struggle

Theory, in this sense, is a tool that we use to figure out what is happening to us, why it is happening, and what to do about it, by going beyond the immediacy and situatedness of a particular experience. It is this exercise of going beyond immediate surfaces and appearances that arguably defines theory. 'Going beyond' means trying to understand the wider ramifications of, and underlying processes that give rise to whatever we experience as problematic and frustrating in our everyday lives: 'Theory attempts to understand things not apparent on the surface, to find the inner connections … And the point of all this is to understand the real world – in order to change it' (Lebowitz 2003: 20).

Another way of expressing this is in the 'ABC' of organising practice (Cox 2010a), shared by radicals in many different contexts and traditions, which involves general principles like resisting alliances with the wealthy and powerful; trying to broaden out discussion about the issues a campaign is tackling, and linking to related groups; connecting with different movements; building a wider sense of identity; international solidarity around the issue – an ABC which of course embodies a whole theory of organising, as do more elaborated and specific approaches, from Alinsky (1971) to Starhawk (1988).

There are, of course, different types of movement knowledge (Cox and Flesher Fominaya 2009). Eyerman and Jamison (1991) and O'Sullivan (1999) have articulated broadly comparable typologies. Firstly, movements generate cosmological praxis (Eyerman and Jamison), or critiques (O'Sullivan): the structural aspects of Marxist, feminist, anti-racist, anti-imperialist, GLBTQ and other forms of knowledge clearly fit in here. In their original movement contexts, these serve the purpose of linking up specific issues, experiences and needs to a broader perspective which implies a coming together as a movement. Secondly, movements generate organisational praxis or resistance, knowledge of ways of acting here and now which enable the routinisation, coordination and understanding of collective action: these form the main topic of this book. Thirdly, movement knowledge has a technological or creative dimension, in the development of alternative institutions which foreshadow a different kind of society, build confidence and inspiration.

Two things are worth adding from a Marxist point of view. The first is the grounding of these processes in situated, materially structured social contexts. The needs and experiences woven together into a social critique, the forms of resistance and organising which make sense and the large and small utopias which people develop are all shaped by *who* is involved and the social relations which structure this – in particular, by the specific kinds of practical-tacit knowledge which are articulated and developed in these various processes.

Secondly, the 'dual-power' institutions which characterise revolutionary situations tend to combine *all* these aspects. At their best and within wider movements for social change, the council, the assembly, the occupied factory, the social centre, the self-organised neighbourhood, or the liberated zone can simultaneously prefigure a different way of living together, represent an effective means of organising here and now, and embody a critique of key social relationships and institutions. In more normal periods, of course, they often have to choose between these aspects because of the immense pressures on them.

The production of theory, then, is not detached from practical experience: 'Experience, rather than simply yielding facts which confirm or falsify general laws, provides clues to underlying structures and relationships which are not observable other than through the particular phenomena or events that they produce' (Wainwright 1994: 7). If theory is justified with reference to its ability to grasp the essential nature of social structures, then this endeavour in turn depends on the problematisation of those structures through social practice. Indeed, without this practice, those structures cannot become clearly visible to social actors. Theory, then, necessarily exists in dialogue with political praxis, whether that praxis is found here and now, or in some other context. In this dialogue, people can change society, but also themselves.

This is a transformational model of social activity (ibid.), which assumes that both the reproduction and the transformation of social structures are crucially related to how we understand these structures. It is at this point that the nexus between experience and theory converges with the character and dynamics of social movement practice. The aspiration of basing oneself in, but simultaneously also going beyond, existing human experience was central to the politics of the social movements of the 1960s and 1970s.

In Hilary Wainwright's analysis, much of the novelty of these movements can be attributed to the bottom-up politics of knowledge they articulated, characterised by a valuation of the experiential, practical tacit knowledge generated by humans through their being in – and acting in – the world: the 'hidden transcripts' of working-class, black, or women's experience, environmentalist groups challenging expert assurances of the safety of nuclear power, mental health patients talking back to psychiatry, communities resisting technocratic development and so on (Melucci 1989). This practical-tacit knowledge, limited though it is by the particular situatedness of a given 'knower' and by their degree of connectedness to other knowers, constitutes a valid source of insight into the workings of the social world with all its contradictions and constraints, and offers a touchstone which enables us to go beyond reshuffling ideological cards.

Particularly important for social movements is the experience of a situation as problematic, or of a way of doing things as not working. The relationship between experience and theory in this politics of knowledge is also a dialogical one, where the deepening of understanding that theory may bring about takes place through the socialisation of experiential common sense:

> Much of their practice indicates a belief in the possibility, through social organization, of extending and combining fragmented knowledge to gain not 'a complete picture', but rather a better understanding of the social mechanisms at work, so as to direct their efforts in order that their intentions might be more efficiently fulfilled. (Wainwright 1994: 107–8)

Movement Structures of Knowledge Production

The kinds of knowledge production discussed above are collectively produced rather than individual possessions; dialogical and contested rather than monolithic; and practice-oriented rather than narrowly cognitive or propositional. One particular form for these processes in recent movements consists of small, workshop-size gatherings of activists from different contexts and movements meeting on an equal plane, with some sharing how their campaign or group has learned to deal with a particular kind of problem (be it decision-making, repression, training, or whatever) and a general discussion in which wider principles – or differences between approaches – can be articulated. Such processes can be used for the creation of new knowledge, as ways to share existing knowledge internally, or indeed to articulate broader principles for movements – or society as a whole (Cox 2014a). Similarly, Gordon (2007), Maeckelbergh (2009, 2012) and Szolucha (2013) have all explored how recent movements have developed new forms of direct democratic and consensus decision-making processes from their multiple, historically specific roots in anti-authoritarian social movements, via the more standardised forms of the movement of movements to the mass-participation situations of *indignados* and Occupy movement events.

This book sets out to rethink Marxism in terms of this kind of knowledge production, especially in making sense of how the social movements of subaltern groups can, at times, develop forms of oppositional agency that join the dots between a conflict in a determinate locale and the wider structures of power that converge to generate this conflict. Moreover, the book seeks to interrogate how such achievements can enable social movements 'to shift gears, transcend particularities, and arrive at some conception of a universal alternative to that social system which is the source of their difficulties' (Harvey 2000: 241).

Barker and Cox (2002) argue for a distinction between movement and academic modes of organising intellectual practice (see Cresswell and Spandler 2012). They note 'An examination of activist theory shows that it is *dialogical* and *developmental*, as shifting groups of activists attempt to find answers to the question "what is to be done?" in situations which they do not fully control.' Our goal in this book is in part to reclaim (recycle, reuse) the 'good sense' and activist theorising frozen within academic Marxism, and restore them to movement modes – in terms of shape and purpose but also of distribution and audience: as analyses of collective agency, geared to the development of movement practice, and proving their 'this-worldliness' in the extent to which they enable this development.

Marxist Responses to the Current Conjuncture

Structuralist Responses

One particular strand of Marxist response to the current conjuncture consists of analyses that operate on a macro-structural terrain, empirically and conceptually. Typical of these types of analyses is a primary focus on the political economy of contemporary neoliberal capitalism, how this political economy emerged out of the crisis of post-war models of state-regulated capitalist development, and the ways in which neoliberal capitalism can be said to be crisscrossed by internal contradictions that in turn push towards the kind of crisis that we have been witnessing since 2007–08. Social movements are sometimes considered towards the end of these analyses, where authors discuss the ways in which the contradictions and crisis tendencies of neoliberalism have given rise to new rounds of struggle in the capitalist world-system (thus Petras and Veltmeyer 2001, Gill 2002, Silver 2003, McNally 2011).

For example, William Robinson's (2004) *A Theory of Global Capitalism: Production, Class, and State in a Transnational World* devotes three out of four chapters to a detailed exposition of a theory of globalisation as a distinct phase of capitalist development characterised by the emergence of a transnational capitalist class and a transnational state, before turning in the fourth chapter to an analysis of the emergence of 'a global counterhegemonic movement' from the contradictions of this phase of capitalist development. Similarly, half of Ray Kiely's (2005) *Clash of Globalisations: Neoliberalism, the Third Way, and Anti-Globalisation* is taken up by a detailed account of the transition towards neoliberalism across the global North and the global South, the reproduction of neoliberalism in Third Way politics, and the consequences of neoliberalism in terms of inequality and poverty, before turning to a discussion of different forms of anti-globalisation, articulated at national and global levels, again drawing on the notion of civil society. Lastly, the lion's share of David McNally's (2006) *Another World is Possible: Globalization and Anti-Capitalism* is concentrated around an analysis of the intersections of class, race and imperial warfare in contemporary capitalism, before a chapter which surveys a range of struggles – for example, conflicts over land in India, the mobilisation of landless workers in Brazil, and new forms of trade unionism in East Asia – then forms the basis for a reflection on the meaning of liberation and the postulation of guiding principles for anti-capitalist action.

Studies such as these are undoubtedly of value inasmuch as they constitute a revival in Marxist scholarship on the political economy of capitalism, and they have made substantial contributions to our understanding of how the current phase of neoliberal capitalism is structured and how this structuring in turn plays into the hands of economic and political elites across the world. Furthermore – as we have noted elsewhere (Cox and Nilsen 2007) – some strands of this scholarship have been important in unearthing the forms of elite agency that brought neoliberal capitalism into being (see, for example, R.W. Cox 1987, Overbeek 1990, Gill 1990, van der Pijl 1998). However, their usefulness and relevance in terms of developing a rigorous understanding of social movements are less obvious.

Very often, these studies offer synoptic and distanced accounts of various forms of resistance to neoliberal capitalism coupled with broad and sweeping interpretations of the potentials of such movements in the current conjuncture. As one of us has pointed out in a review of McNally, opting for an extensive bird's-eye view of global resistance often results in analyses that miss out on the complexities and dilemmas of actual mobilisation and the strategic lessons that flow from these (Nilsen 2008a). Furthermore, assessments of the progressiveness or otherwise of different strands of anti-capitalist politics, such as Kiely's, are often fundamentally divorced from a constructive engagement with the strategic and practical knowledge interests of movement participants. Much the same can be said for analyses that are content to establish that contemporary social movements represent a new phase in a contemporary counter-movement against the disembedding of capitalist production and accumulation (see, for example, Robinson 2004).

If such Marxist approaches enable a critical understanding of the political economy of contemporary capitalism, and may even at times identify what Bieler and Morton (2004: 103) call 'materially grounded opportunities for counter-hegemonic action' in the abstract, they do not engage with the reality of popular collective action: how people come to take action, how they make alliances and convince other people to take a broader perspective, how they resolve strategic dilemmas or assess their chances of winning. Movements from below are described, judged, or praised from on high, in what Gramsci called a 'contemplative' mode.

Furthermore, this mode positions movements as more or less interesting, sympathetic, or symbolic characters against a structural backdrop which is fundamentally given, and no reader can doubt that the real meat of the argument is in the relentless analysis of neoliberalism as structure. In this drama, movements can at best play doomed heroines. There is little scope for discussion of those crucial moments in which large numbers of people move from accepting the fundamentals of the current order as given to becoming active, conscious and collective agents on their own behalf. Small wonder that activists do not read such texts in order to think what to do – indeed, when structural theorists offer concrete prescriptions for action, they tend to be warmed-over versions of what activists are already doing (Cox 2010a).

Autonomist Marxism

Autonomist Marxism[7] suffers from much of this same contemplative difficulty. Saddled with an inherited vocabulary that is increasingly incomprehensible to outsiders,[8] its insertion within the academy has strengthened the tendency for this vocabulary to act as a form of cultural capital intended to signify political radicalism. As with many structural Marxists, autonomists are often excellent activists individually; again, however, the theory fails to adequately articulate their practical experience. At the core of present-day autonomist writing are valuable arguments about the limitations of state-centric forms of organising (Holloway 2002), coupled with a confidence-building emphasis on the power of popular creativity (Hardt and Negri 2000). What is fundamentally absent, however, is any serious discussion as to what movements should *do*, beyond 'more of the same' (Cox 2001b); and most autonomist commentary on movements consists of an elaborate theoretical celebration of movements which operate according to their preferred mode – without real discussion of how the movements they work with could go *beyond* their current mode of existence.[9]

Marxism as a Movement-Relevant Theory

Bevington and Dixon (2005) note that movement activists rarely read social movement theory; some do, however, read Marxist writing. Movements are not, of course, averse to seeing themselves celebrated in print, or to hard-hitting analyses of what is wrong with society; and these are not bad things, nor should we wish movements not to have sympathetic academics who are willing to lend their 'counter-expertise' to public debate. What such approaches do, however, is to remove Marxism from the field of movement theorising about *what we should do*. The academic mode of production within which such writing happens naturally encourages the contemplative mode (critical or celebratory) and discourages a praxis-oriented one; the net effect, once again, is to disengage theory from practice and construct a mystified relationship between the two. We are in search of a theory that can do more than simply pat activists on the back or agree that capitalism is bad. Below, we discuss briefly why canonical social movement studies does not constitute an adequate alternative, before moving to discuss the possible sources and shape of a Marxist theory of social movements.

The Poverty of Mainstream Movement Theory

If movement activists rarely read social movement writing, this is because it has often had little of substance to say about the struggles of the day (Cox and Nilsen 2007). There are a range of reasons for this, most notably the separation off of 'social movement studies' as a subdiscipline within the US academy – able to select in a thoroughly arbitrary and unrepresentative way from European research, which was historically more engaged with movements and less firewalled from social theory: indeed, much European social theory grew out of movement activism (Cox and Flesher Fominaya 2013) – one reason why activists tend to read radical social theory rather than social movements research.

US social movement studies developed within a context where revolution was not on the cards (as against the European experience of Resistance and 1989, the Asian and African experiences of decolonisation, or the Latin American conflicts between left and right), so that movements could be conceptualised as a particular institutional 'level' of an essentially fixed political order. Not only revolution, but political parties, trade unions, religious movements, nationalisms, subcultures and many other expressions of popular agency were written out of the founding equations of what was to count as 'movement' – a movement which, consequently, could hardly move (Cox 1999a). Hence the practical contribution of this literature is restricted to the difficulties facing a particular type of social movement organisation trying to motivate members, ally with elites, scrub up for the mainstream media, and so on. As we have written elsewhere:

> The risk in all this is of a great impoverishment of sociological and political imaginations, a falling back from the kind of vision that

> enabled, say, the English historian E.P. Thompson to detect and decode emerging and developing forms of popular struggle in phenomena as varied as eighteenth-century market riots, fence-breaking, poaching or 'rough music'; that enabled Charles Tilly – in an extended dialogue with Thompson's work – to locate a wholesale shift in the repertoires of struggle in the early nineteenth century; or that enabled Peter Linebaugh and Marcus Rediker to show how the everyday resistance of sailors and slaves could form the ingredients of strikes, rebellions and revolutions that shook the Atlantic world. (Barker et al. 2013: 6)

Thankfully, in recent years the dead weight of this particular orthodoxy has started to lift, at least in Europe (Cox and Szolucha 2013), and there is now much greater diversity in writing on social movements – a fact strongly influenced by the presence of numbers of participants and ex-participants from recent movement waves, themselves transporting various kinds of movement knowledge. However, the precarisation of academic labour, pressures for productivity and the massively increased role of project-related research funding all exercise very strong pressures in favour of the academic mode of intellectual production – pressures which are hard to resist without strong practical determination, structural relationships with movements and methodologies which build engagement in from the start (Fuster Morell 2009).

The net result is that while it is not impossible to carry out movement-relevant research under a rubric of social movement studies, it is far from the norm. Only in rare contexts such as Manchester's Alternative Futures and Popular Protest conference – one of the intellectual sources of this book – is it possible to encounter a majority of researchers whose primary orientation is to their movements rather than the logics of their discipline; this is in turn made possible not only by interdisciplinarity but by a situation which offers participants almost nothing by way of *academic* status in return for their participation. The consequence is a situation where there is much activist reflection on movements, *outside* the formal languages of particular disciplines and fields.

We do not consider it impossible to develop a practitioner-oriented, movement-relevant form of social movement research within the academy; however, to achieve this it would be necessary to build in an equal relationship to movements at the start rather than an add-on of 'dissemination', and to develop a power basis which enables some independence from purely disciplinary and academic logics. At present, the reverse seems to be the case: each new wave of movements brings not only movement-based researchers to the field but also researchers with no such relationship and little real interest other than in making a temporary splash in what they perceive as an undemanding field, used to secure funding and publications. All too often, such individuals are better at playing the academic game than movement-linked researchers, and exercise an unhealthy effect intellectually as well as politically.

Towards a Marxist Theory of Social Movements

If we are trying to recover Marxism as a theory from and for social movements, the place to start is in relation to agency, both the popular agency of the movements Marx and Engels were involved with as members, allies and opponents, and the elite agency which reshaped the world around them and against which they struggled to articulate a radical strategy. We agree with Thompson (1978) that the attempt to describe political economy as structure was in some ways a trap for the mature Marx; and with Lebowitz (2003) that the political economy of *capital*, described as system, misses out the opposing struggles of the political economy of *labour* to articulate itself against this system (see Chapter 4). In this sense, it is in the philosophical anthropology of the young Marx and Engels, in their political writings and their analysis of history, that we see them exploring agency most clearly, and with greatest concern to contribute to movement strategy.

The reason why Marxism remains a live force in social movements today is not because (say) the *concept* of neoliberalism carries an evidential force which sweeps all before it, but rather because certain kinds of activist 'good sense' transported by Marxism have taught later generations of activists how to make alliances between different groups, how to find common cause around radicalising the critique of broad social structures, how to name elite agency for what it is and how to construct struggles against it in a strategic key. It is this earlier 'good sense' that we seek to recover from Marxism: hence we are not proposing another Marxology grounded in recourse to textual authority but rather a reconstruction of what Marx and Engels themselves had to learn from the struggles of German peasants in the sixteenth and nineteenth centuries, from the Burns sisters and the streets of Manchester, from the networks of radical exiles in Paris, Brussels and London, from the Chartists and the development of union struggles, from the events of 1848 and 1871 and the development of working-class parties, and from watching the drama of colonisation and resistance in Ireland or in India.

To anticipate, this position was that agency was *situated* – shaped by class society, patriarchy, colonialism and so on, in immensely complex ways, which positioned actors in determinate material relationships with one another. It was also more or less *conscious* and *collective*: it was praxis, 'the unity of theory and action', and not simply practice – and these two went hand in hand. The more subaltern groups became conscious of their needs and experiences and reflected on their attempts to act, the more they developed their collective practice; and vice versa: alliance building, as in the classic passage from *The Communist Manifesto*, built broader awareness. Finally, this developmental process led to deeper and deeper challenges to the current structures of society, and ultimately to a struggle over what Touraine (1981) calls 'historicity', the way in which society produces and reproduces itself. All of this, of course, happened in conflict with the collective action of the wealthy and powerful – both their construction of new kinds of social relationships and their attempts to solidify those as a naturalised kind of structure.

In Chapter 2, we explore the notion of praxis more deeply, while in Chapter 3, we attempt a conceptualisation of the developmental processes of movements from above and below. In Chapters 4 and 5, we put this approach to social movements to work, first in an analysis of how the development of capitalism in general and neoliberalism in particular has been driven by the contentious dialectic of struggles between social movements from above and social movements from below, and then in an extended discussion of how the movement of movements can think strategically about winning the struggle against an economic and political system that is mired in a crisis of its own making.

2

'History Does Nothing': The Primacy of Praxis in Movement Theorising

> *History does nothing; it possesses 'no immense wealth', it 'wages no battles'. It is human beings, real living human beings who do all that, who possess and fight: history is not, as it were, a person apart, using human beings as means to achieve its own aims; history is nothing but the activity of human beings pursuing their own aims.*
>
> Marx and Engels, *The Holy Family*

The Narmada Valley in India looms large in the annals of the 'movement of movements'. Here, the *Narmada Bachao Andolan* (Save the Narmada Movement, NBA) has mobilised Adivasi (tribal) and caste Hindu peasant communities since the late 1980s against the construction of large dams on the Narmada River, which runs across central India to join the Arabian Sea off the coast of Gujarat. The mobilisation has targeted the distributional bias of the dam projects: while economically prosperous and politically powerful regions and groups stand to gain from increased access to irrigation and electricity, Adivasi subsistence producers and farming communities engaged in petty commodity production are at risk of acute impoverishment as a result of displacement.[1] Directing its energies against the Sardar Sarovar Project (SSP) – one of the largest dams on the Narmada – in particular, the movement has campaigned on many fronts, ranging from civil disobedience and non-cooperation with state authorities to transnational advocacy and judicial activism. Mobilising for more than a decade, the NBA registered some significant achievements: for example, the cancellation of World Bank funding of the SSP in the early 1990s and the issuing of an order to stop construction of the dam by India's Supreme Court in the middle of the 1990s. However, the NBA was dealt a severe blow in October 2000, when the Supreme Court finally ruled that work on the dam could be resumed and that the SSP should be completed as soon as possible.

In this context, the NBA organised a *dharna* – a sit-in demonstration – in front of the administrative headquarters in the market town of Alirajpur in western Madhya Pradesh, in late February 2003. Adivasis at risk of losing their land to displacement gathered to put pressure on local authorities to recognise their right to resettlement and rehabilitation. Alf joined the protestors in early March as part of his doctoral research, and spent a week observing the Andolan's intense activity: documents were gathered to prove claims to property; strategy and tactics were continually discussed in group meetings at the *dharna* site; direct actions targeting the local administration were organised and carried out. Ultimately, however, the *dharna* ended inconclusively as the local authorities refused to commit to a substantial review of the protestors' claims and demands.

During a lull in the *dharna*, Alf got talking to one of the NBA activists, who expressed her frustration over how, after the Supreme Court judgment, the Andolan had not been able to raise wider and more systemic issues about the dominant model of development in India. Rather, most of their time and energy was devoted to scrutinising the authorities' actions as they sought to push the construction of the dam forward, and to responding immediately through claims and demands that could secure at least a measure of compensation for the communities that had struggled against the SSP for more than a decade. 'So it's a bit like a game of chess', Alf suggested, 'where you have to constantly watch the opponent's moves and make your own counter-moves?' The activist nodded: 'Yes. It is a bit like that.'

This activist's frustration will be familiar to many movement participants. It is the frustration of being locked in a game where you are compelled to play by rules that you cannot question, that you had no role in designing, and that inevitably tend to bolster the status quo. The challenge for activists, then, revolves around how to question such games and the rules that structure them and to ultimately transcend their inherent constraints. As Chapter 1 suggested, this is a problem of theory: it involves activists locating their particular struggle in relation to a wider systemic context and developing strategies to link a specific struggle to anti-systemic movement projects. The question we grapple with in this chapter and the next is whether Marxism has something to offer here –

does it help us in our efforts to go beyond the games and rules that play into the hands of the powerful?

Theory and the Struggle to Change the Game

E.P. Thompson once remarked that the question is not whether we are on Marx's side, but whether he is on ours. The Marx of purely structural analysis is often a rather distant ally at best: naming and criticising capitalism within a fairly narrow field, but not suggesting what, if anything, we can *do* about it. If, however, we see Marxism as one of the most important languages in which social movements have spoken theory in the modern world, we can find other kinds of resources there. Marx did not fashion his theoretical apparatus for the battlefields of academia, but for the frontlines of the struggles shaping nineteenth-century society, which in turn shaped his thought. This awareness that the litmus test of theory is its relevance to activism was one of Marx's most original thoughts, stated as early as 1843 when he wrote the following in *Critique of Hegel's Philosophy of Right*:

> The weapon of criticism cannot, of course, replace criticism of the weapon, material force must be overthrown by material force; but theory also becomes a material force as soon as it has gripped the masses. Theory is capable of gripping the masses as soon as it demonstrates *ad hominem* [to the person], and it demonstrates *ad hominem* as soon as it becomes radical. To be radical is to grasp the root of the matter. But, for human beings, the root is human beings themselves. (Marx 1977: 137)

We take the radical 'this-worldliness' of Marx's theoretical practice as our starting-point for developing a distinctly Marxist theory of social movements. As the quote that opens this chapter suggests, Marx's work is characterised by a demystifying commitment to understanding social structure and historical process as nothing other than the product of human practice (see Larrain 1986: Chapter 4, Bensaïd 2002: Chapter 1). This commitment is in turn rooted in a particular philosophical anthropology – that is, a distinct way of thinking about *human species being*, what it means to be human (Geras 1983). The commitment to a view of society and history as constituted through collective human activity, and the rooting of this view in a conception of human species being as constituted around 'a combination of self-consciousness, material capacity, and collective organisation' (Dyer-Witheford 2004: 5) are not arbitrary. These dimensions of Marx's thinking come from the social, economic and political context he was embroiled in, both as a theorist and as an activist.

Why Think About Things This Way?

First, Marx's account of the importance of human needs grows out of a situation where those needs had become nakedly apparent. As capitalism and industrialism had 'proletarianised' labourers, small farmers, artisans and others – reduced them to a situation where they owned nothing but their children (*proles*) and their ability to work – so their poverty, unsheltered by any traditional forms of community or charity, exposed raw needs at their most basic. At the same time, nineteenth-century society also held out the vision of a 'wealth of needs', the possibility of human development as an ongoing lifetime project – at the time reserved for a tiny minority because of what Marx and Engels identified as the class nature of nineteenth-century European society. 'The social movement', in nineteenth-century language, was precisely this 'social question' in action, as powerful movements of the poor aimed *both* to overcome the exploitation at the root of their suffering *and* to open up these new human possibilities for everyone (Cox 2013a).

Second, Marx's account of human capacities, of what human beings can do, grows out of the developing capacities of the industrial working class which these proletarians became: constantly mobile, forever adjusting to new experiences and problems in the workplace and the city, constructing and sustaining liveable communities out of desperate slums and creating their own institutions to meet all manner of needs, from sheer survival to political change. The movements built on this self-organised basis valued skill and technical knowledge rather than custom or official pronouncements, and were increasingly confident of their own abilities to run the world without the intervention of rulers, bosses, or charitable institutions. These movements 'were indeed humanist – species being struggles to become human' (Dyer-Witheford 2004: 8).

Third, Marx and Engels' account of 'consciousness', of the nature of human thought, arises out of the development of distinctive working-class cultures and identities in this context: the creation of new ways of thinking and speaking, reflected not only in the theoretical traditions of their movements, but also in the forest of publications that grew up around these movements, from broadsheets and handbills to newspapers and pamphlets, in traditions of song and popular theatre, in traditions of reading and discussing, and in both individual and collective forms of self-education and debate constituting a 'Workers' University' (Cox 2010b).

Finally, their account of 'practice' certainly draws on an observation – common to their contemporaries – of the way in which nineteenth-century Europe had seen industrialists, engineers, governments and policy innovators transform both the natural world around them and their own societies. But it also rests fundamentally on their experience of how social movements from *below* had reshaped the world: overthrowing monarchs, undermining the structures of religious power, shaking the foundations of empires, struggling for universal rights and for equality.

In this chapter, we discuss 'Marx' in the textual and conceptual terms in which he and Engels attempted to articulate these experiences and the understandings they gave rise to, and talk about the radical shifts which this represented within the world of European philosophy, as well as some theoretical problems this understanding throws up. Although we have to write in these terms, it should be clear that underlying 'Marx the thinker' is this broader process of developing working-class thought: if Marx offers the most thorough-going articulation of this experience, it is this wider movement learning which is ultimately of most importance.

Rethinking Social Movements

Academic social movements theory today often sees capitalism and the state as a taken-for-granted framework within which movements represent a particular 'level' of political action – less structured than parties, unions, or churches but more organised than micro-level resistance and cultural agency – and where the main interest is in alliances with elites (political opportunities), acceptability to mainstream media (framing), and so on. This hardly works even for contemporary European movements (Flesher Fominaya and Cox 2013), still less for any broader picture of the world, in which most contemporary states have come into existence within living memory through movements *against* previous empires or dictatorships; where the separation of institutions such as parties or unions from movements, the institutionalisation or democratisation of forms of community struggle, or the crystallising out of overt campaigns from 'hidden transcripts' (Scott 1990) are not fixed facts but historically changing; and where the origins of institutions such as democracy, welfare states, party systems and the like cannot sensibly be understood in isolation from large-scale social movement struggles and revolutions.

With Touraine (1981) – but also with Marx – we propose a very different picture of social movement, one in which they do not obediently play a constructive role within a set of rules established from above, but in which they have been, for at least 300 years, part and parcel of struggles over 'historicity', the way in which human beings create their own societies and orient their priorities and development. This approach *relates* what in a compartmentalised analysis are the separate 'subfields' of the sociology of revolutions; the analysis of parties, unions or churches; conventional social movement studies; 'civil society' research; agency-oriented approaches to class, race and gender; micro-level analysis of resistance and cultural conflict in everyday life; analyses of changing phases of capitalist development, and the study of social change (Barker et al. 2013). Rather than proposing fixed positions for all of these, it is interested precisely in how these change: how, for example, an anti-colonial movement gives rise to an independent nation state and dominant nationalist parties, and how those in turn come to be challenged by movements which were once their subordinate allies. We make our own history; even if not under circumstances of our own choosing.

In this chapter, we place this philosophical anthropology at the centre of our attempt to theorise social movements from a Marxist perspective. We first define species being as the ability of human beings to satisfy needs through the conscious deployment of capacities in historically evolving social formations. We then move on to discuss the relationship between constancy and change in this conception of species being, and develop a distinct concept of *praxis* as the structured agency that animates social change. In the final section of the chapter, we engage with the inherently social and historical character of human species being and focus on how conflicts between what we call *dominant structures of entrenched needs and capacities* and *emergent structures of radical needs and capacities* are at the heart of how social movements animate the making and the unmaking of social formations across historical time.

This discussion is necessarily abstract, because the point is to find a space of freedom from the taken-for-granted contexts which our movements struggle against and from which we hope to free ourselves. We are looking not simply for a mythic space of freedom to serve as inspiration and alternative – important though both are – but for a clear understanding of how the kinds of situations which currently oppress, exploit and imprison us are constructed and what we really mean when we talk about movements transforming or overthrowing them. This starts from an image of what it means to be human.

Human Needs, Capacities and Praxis

Historical materialism 'rests squarely upon the idea of a human nature' (Geras 1983: 107). This human nature – our species being – is defined by *praxis*, which we define as the ability of human beings to satisfy our needs through the increasingly conscious deployment of capacities in historically evolving formations, terms we will explain below. This conception of species being runs as a guiding thread through Marx's work – originating in the *Economic and Philosophical Manuscripts* of 1844 and still animating his mature thinking in *Capital* – and in this section we explore the relationship between needs, capacities, and consciousness in human practice.

In *The German Ideology*, Marx and Engels presented a conception of *needs* which is fundamental to historical materialism as an ontological perspective:

> ... we must begin by stating the first premise of all human existence and, therefore, of all history, the premise, namely, that human beings must be in a position to live in order to be able to 'make history'. But life involves before everything else eating and drinking, a habitation, clothing and many other things. The first historical act is thus the production of the means to satisfy these needs, the production of material life itself. And indeed this is an historical act, a fundamental condition of all history, which today, as thousands of years ago, must daily and hourly be fulfilled merely in order to sustain human life. (Marx and Engels 1999: 48)

Our needs are constantly and fundamentally embodied: the satisfaction of our bodily needs 'is the absolute precondition of human existence and ... provides the impetus and telos of production' (Fracchia 2005: 49).[2] And, crucially, these needs impose 'corporeal constraints' (ibid.: 46) upon human activity. Our needs, in other words, constitute a foundational material reason why we cannot make history just as we please.

Human beings are also endowed with *capacities* that make it possible for us to satisfy our needs by transforming our environment through 'purposeful activity aimed at the production of use values', that is, of meeting needs (Marx 1990: 290). Marx referred to this activity as the 'labour process' and described it as follows:

> Labour is, first of all, a process between the human being and nature, a process by which human beings through their own actions mediate, regulate and control the metabolism between themselves and nature. The human being confronts the materials of nature as a force of nature. She sets in motion the natural forces which belong to her own body, her arms, legs, head and hands, in order to appropriate the materials of nature in a form adapted to her own needs. Through this movement she acts upon external nature and changes it, and in this way she simultaneously changes her own nature. She develops the potentialities slumbering within nature, and subjects the play of its forces to her own sovereign power. (Ibid.: 283)[3]

The labour process, Marx argued, is 'the universal condition for the metabolic interaction ... between human beings and nature ... and it is therefore independent of every form of that existence, or rather it is common to all forms of society in which human beings live' (ibid.: 290). Capacities, like needs, are also fundamentally corporeal – as Fracchia (2005: 47, 48) argues, our capacities are manifest in 'bodily instruments' and the 'bodily dexterities' that are developed when we use these instruments to produce use values to satisfy our needs. It is our corporeal capacities that make it possible for us to move beyond the relatively narrow parameters of our original ecological niche, to adapt to a wide range of natural and social environments, and to develop the tools and instruments that enable us to expand our capacity to create use values, however sophisticated (ibid.: 49).

Thus, if needs are corporeal constraints, capacities are corporeal enablements. These enablements and constraints are 'opposites in unity' in the sense that it is constraints in the form of needs which compel 'the organism to focus its energies and develop the capacities and dexterities that it does have' – that is, the existence of corporeal constraints that have to be addressed presents challenges that can only be met through 'the production of artefacts ranging from material goods to symbolic forms' (ibid.: 52). It is in and through human practice that the unity of these opposites is forged (see Heller 1976: 41–2).

The practical activities that we engage in to satisfy our needs are defined by what Marx (1990: 284) referred to as an 'exclusively human characteristic' – namely, *consciousness*. As human beings, we reflect on our needs and on how we deploy our capacities to satisfy these needs:

> The animal is immediately one with its life activity. It does not distinguish itself from it. It is *its life activity*. Human beings make their life activity itself the object of their will and their consciousness. They have conscious life activity. It is not a determination with which they directly merge. Conscious life activity distinguishes human beings immediately from animal life activity. It is just because of this that they are species beings. (Marx 1981a: 68)

It is this mediation of needs and capacities through conscious activity that we see as the core of praxis. This idea was first articulated through the concept of 'objectification':

> It is just in her work upon the objective world, therefore, that the human being really proves herself to be a *species-being*. Through this production, nature appears as her work and her reality. The object of labour, therefore, is the *objectification of the human being's species life:* for she duplicates herself not only, as in consciousness, intellectually, but also actively, in reality, and therefore she sees herself in the world she has created. (Ibid.: 69)

Objectification – the way in which our food production, bringing up children, toolmaking, writing or whatever simultaneously meets our needs, expresses ourselves and changes us – is a 'dialectical category' that seeks to illuminate 'the interaction of subjects with the world, both natural and social' (Fracchia 2005: 44). The same idea reappeared almost three decades later, in Marx's (1990: 287) exploration of the characteristic features of the labour process:

> In the labour process ... the human being's activity *via* the instruments of labour effects an alteration in the object of labour which was intended from the outset ... the product of the process is a use-value, a piece of natural material adapted to human needs by means of a change in

> its form. Labour has become bound up in its object: labour has been objectified, the object has been worked on.

In the emphasis on the interweaving of the material and the ideational in human activity, Marx's radical this-worldliness again comes into view. This constituted a fundamental rupture with the dualistic deep structure of western philosophy, which had seen the subject as apart-from-and-above the object, the mind as apart-from-and-above the body, and theory as apart-from-and-above practice – a move which mirrored relationships between the upper classes and the poor, Europeans and slaves, men and women.

Marx articulated 'a fundamental redefinition of the concepts of subject and object' (Fracchia 1991: 155) in which the separation between contemplative, knowing subjects and passive objects of knowledge were replaced by an emphasis on praxis as the conscious mediation of needs and capacities as both 'the fundamental ontological category' and 'the substance of history as development' (Rooke 2003: 177). Put another way, the subject of Marx's thought is people-in-history, trying to meet their needs in interaction with the natural world and learning from their attempts to do so: the notion of praxis implies a far broader picture of the changing nature of human economies and cultures than does the image of the isolated Thinker.

Constancy and Change in Human Species Being

That human beings have needs and capacities is a given fact across space and time. That these needs and capacities are mediated through conscious human activity – praxis – is always and everywhere the case. And this mediation is always already orchestrated through social relations – praxis, learning and action are not attributes of Robinson Crusoe, alone on a desert island, but of people with history, culture and relationships. All these are constant and universal features of human species being. But how do we then explain *change* in human species being – and does change in turn deny this constancy? Norman Geras captured the nature of this dilemma aptly:

> Today, we make and we watch movies, as before people did not. It is a new human potentiality and, for many, a need. But it is also a form of

> one of the oldest, most universal human activities there is: story-telling. Though they live as far away as can be, we may now communicate in an instant with people whom we care about. In *this* sense some of the potentialities and needs of the human species have developed. It remains, however, that there are people we care about strongly enough to want to maintain contact with them; and that we have a capacity for complex symbolic communication which enables us to do that. In *this* sense some of the potentialities and the needs are the same. (Geras 1995: 157–8)

As a way of resolving this dilemma, human species being can be conceived of as what McNally (2001: 7) calls 'an indeterminate constancy'. McNally uses this term to refer to how human bodies have 'a relatively fixed biological constitution' at the same time as 'the constants of bodily existence take shape through manifold and pliable forms of social life' (ibid.). Similarly, human species being can be thought of as an indeterminate constancy that takes and shifts shape through manifold and pliable forms of social life. So, on the one hand, human beings are defined by transhistorical needs and capacities that are fundamentally corporeal. These are the constants in this particular dialectical equation. On the other hand, these transhistorical needs and capacities simultaneously constitute that which renders possible 'an infinite though not unlimited range of … changing manifestations of human being – that is of socio-cultural forms' (Fracchia 2005: 40). It is praxis itself that makes these changing manifestations possible – praxis, in other words, constitutes the indeterminate element of the dialectical equation.[4] It is human thought and action which makes it possible to change how the social world works; any serious movement for change starts from some version of this realisation, but it remains a challenge to think and act from this broad perspective of possibility.

The Importance of Consciousness

To understand how praxis animates changes in species being, we have to consider the significance of consciousness. Marx had this to say about consciousness in the labour process:

> A spider constructs operations which resemble those of the weaver, and a bee would put many a human architect to shame by the construction of its honeycomb cells. But what distinguishes the worst architect from

> the best of bees is that the architect builds the cell in their mind before they construct it. At the end of the labour process, a result emerges which had already been conceived by the worker at the beginning, hence already existed ideally. (Marx, 1990: 284)

Having rejected the subject/mind–object/body dualism of western philosophy, Marx did not think of conscious reflection as elevated above the this-worldly realm of human practice. Rather than constituting a separate realm of ideas, consciousness is understood as one among many human faculties 'mired in the [material] realm of necessity' (Fracchia 2005: 155).[5] The essence of this view is presented in the following passage from *The German Ideology*:

> The production of ideas, of conceptions, of consciousness is at first directly interwoven with the material activity and human beings' material intercourse, the language of real life. Conceiving, thinking, human beings' mental intercourse, appear at this stage as the direct efflux of their material behaviour ... Human beings are the products of their conceptions, ideas etc. – real active human beings, as they are conditioned by a definite development of their productive forces. Consciousness cannot be anything other than conscious being, and the being of human beings is their actual life process. (1999: 47)

So, what is it about consciousness – a consciousness that is 'always afflicted with the curse of being burdened with matter' (ibid.: 50) – that makes it such a central animating dynamic in processes of social change?

We answer this question by a simplified account of how human beings deploy capacities to satisfy needs. First of all, we experience a determinate need. We then reflect on how that need is best satisfied within the given social and natural parameters in which we are embedded. And the way in which we ultimately use our capacities to satisfy our needs in turn becomes an object of reflection: we think about our experience of how we did things 'yesterday' in terms of how we could do things differently 'today' so that we may be in a better position to satisfy our needs 'tomorrow'.[6] In practice, of course, this logical sequence takes place within history, collectively and in situated ways: if we are baking a new type of bread or growing an unfamiliar plant, the existence or availability of that recipe or variety, our decision to attempt it, the kitchen or garden constraints within which we work, considerations of cost, time and physical abilities, and the people, books, or websites to which we turn when things do not work as expected are all part of this learning process – which is thus not ours alone but (in the widest perspective) humanity's.

Praxis is therefore a dynamo of change that perennially engenders new needs and new capacities for the satisfaction of those needs. Indeed, when Marx and Engels (1999: 48) note the existence of certain constant needs, the satisfaction of which constitutes 'the first premise of all human existence' and argue that the first challenge of 'any interpretation of history' is 'to observe this fundamental fact in all its significance and all its implications and to accord it its due importance', they are also emphasising the developmental character of the satisfaction of needs: 'the satisfaction of the first need (the action of satisfying and the instrument of satisfaction which has been acquired) leads to new needs; and this production of new needs is the first historical act' (ibid.: 49). Human needs, then, have to be located within and understood 'within a historical dialectic where the totality of needs unfold in a dynamic process fuelled by labour' which 'stimulates a dynamic of enriched needs' which in turn 'engage activities that generate capacities and a spiral of ever-new needs' (Grumley 1999: 56). And this historical dialectic is animated by the interrelationship between social being, experience and consciousness.

'Experience', in this sense, is best understood as the practical and tacit knowledge that human beings produce about the social and natural world in which they live as they engage and interact with this world. In other words, experience is constituted by practical-tacit knowledge *about* social being garnered *through* social being. This practical-tacit knowledge in turn constitutes 'an attribute of individuals by reason of their participation, active or passive, in relations with others within inherited structures' (Wainwright 1994: 107). Thompson described the relationship between social being, experience and consciousness thus:

> [Processes of change], if they are within 'social being', seem to impinge upon, thrust into, break against, existent social consciousness. They propose new problems, and, above all, they continually give rise to *experience* ... Experience arises spontaneously within social being, but it does not arise without thought; it arises because men and women ... are rational, and they think about what is happening to them and their world ... What we mean is that changes take place within social being, which gives rise to changed *experience*: and this experience is

> *determining* in the sense that it exerts pressures upon existent social consciousness. (Thompson 1995: 9–10)

Our experience of social being, then, is the stuff that consciousness is made from: we understand the world on the basis of our experience of being and acting in it, and this understanding in turn drives us to act – or not act – in specific ways. Experience thus becomes the unruly body of half-submerged knowledge mediating between objectively existing conditions and social consciousness of these conditions. Emergent new needs – and therefore also the need to develop practices to satisfy these needs – stem from processes of change in social being that we experience as a nebulous lack. This experience of lack in turn exerts pressures on our existing consciousness of how capacities are deployed to satisfy needs. This is what Gramsci (1998) means when he talks about 'good sense', rooted in our actual experience, as against the hegemonic 'common sense' which tells us how things are *supposed* to be and what we are *supposed* to think, feel and do. The resultant reflection might give rise to an explicit articulation of new needs and the capacities that constitute a necessary condition for their satisfaction.[7] Wainwright (1994) uses the experience of feminist consciousness-raising as a model for this process: how women who were *supposed* to be in near-ideal circumstances came together to articulate previously unspoken but increasingly powerful discontent, and in so doing created at one and the same time a movement and a theory which radically disrupted the gender relationships of previous generations.

Our conscious reflection on experience – and experience itself – are mediated through previously existing cultural systems of meaning and knowledge that we create in and through our situated engagements with otherness. These systems of meaning, as they cease to be visibly new creations and become taken-for-granted, seen as 'just how things are', give shape to our practical engagements with otherness, as 'culture does some of our thinking for us, providing answers to questions that we lack the time to examine ourselves' (Jasper 1997: 83). Marx put this as follows:

> It is always necessary to distinguish between the material transformation of the economic conditions of production, which can be determined with the precision of natural science, and the legal, political, religious, artistic or philosophic – in short, ideological forms in which human

> beings become conscious of this conflict and fight it out. (Marx 1981b: 21)

This might suggest a sharp distinction between the material transformation of the mode of production on the one hand and the ideological filters through which people perceive these transformations on the other – in other words, between objective and subjective. However, this would be a misreading of Marx's logic. Signs and meanings, as well as our ability to deploy signs and meanings through language, 'are not the result of arbitrary mappings of concepts onto the world' (McNally 2001: 97). Rather, this semiotic mediation emerges from 'corporeal representations that inform the activity of organisms in the world'. The 'image schemata' that are at the heart of articulated consciousness originate in 'recurring patterns in our lived experience of space, time, objects, and their relations' and meanings in turn 'emerge in the course of practical activity' (ibid.). Having emerged in the course of our practical activity, meanings in turn come to condition that practical activity.

The human development of signs runs parallel to the human development of tools:

> We fashion special artefacts, tools, solely for the purpose of manipulating the world and thereby, the behaviour the world elicits from us. And we create signs, a class of artificial stimuli that act as means to control behaviour ... Hence the relation between world and subject is never simply unidirectional, but is constantly mediated by tool and sign. (Bakhurst 1990: 207–8)

The creation of tools and signs is therefore vital to the social organisation of human needs and capacities: 'Just as the tool helps us to master nature, so the sign enables us to master our own psychological functioning' (ibid.: 208). And our relationship to the world is always mediated through semiotic filters – in and through our social being, we interact with 'an *interpreted* environment, an environment conceived of as being *of a certain kind* ... [T]he world is an environment endowed with significance, and the trajectory of the subject's behaviour is determined by the meaning he or she takes from the world' (ibid.: 208).

On this reading, culture is understood as being simultaneously 'socially constituted and socially constituting' (Roseberry 1989: 42). Culture is *socially constituted* in that it grows from the practical activities that revolve around the social organisation of the deployment of human capacities to satisfy human needs – culture, that is, is 'a product of past and present activity' (ibid.). And culture is *socially constituting* in that our practical activity is always saturated with and conditioned by 'the interpretative practices of the community' (Bakhurst 1990: 209).[8]

Thus within any specific social context, the ways in which we articulate our understanding of our needs and organise our attempts to meet them are determined – not fixed, but in a faster- or slower-moving process of (often internally unequal and contested) collective learning and praxis. These needs, and our capacities to meet them, are ultimately material, rooted in our corporeal nature. It is not simply that this nature provides a mooring post for the infinite variety of ways in which different self-enclosed 'cultures' can seek to meet our needs; rather, there are *histories* of these attempts, and conflicts within them. Thompson's *Making of the English Working Class* is a record precisely of such a large-scale, collective (and internally contested) learning process (Cox 2013a).

Learning can be lost or effectively resisted; what seems at one point like the only way forward can come at another to pose a major barrier to further development. This is particularly visible in social movements from below, as people struggle to find ways of articulating what the issue is and how to tackle it – against, perhaps, the background of a dominant 'common sense' (and attempts to import it into the movement), but also against understandable loyalty to the movement's own learning inheritance and reluctance to jettison ideas that have shown their worth in other circumstances. Movements' learning institutions can also be directly targeted, as in counter-revolutionary moments when movement organisations are destroyed, their participants killed, incarcerated, or driven into exile, their newspapers and books banned and the social networks which had supported particular understandings and perspectives are torn apart.

The Social and Historical Dimensions of Praxis

So far, we have discussed how the mediation of needs and capacities in and through praxis constitutes the kernel of human species being and how species being itself is *both* constant *and* changing. To understand why this understanding of praxis is significant for making sense of social movements, we need to consider the social and historical dimensions of species being in more detail.

The Sociality of Species Being

Marx's notion of human species being was based on the assumption of the inherently social character of praxis. In other words, our praxis is both constitutive of and constituted by forms of social organisation: when we act in the world to satisfy our needs, we do so in a cooperative manner, and this cooperation generates social formations that in turn condition our deployment of capacities to satisfy our needs. The idea of an unchanging human essence inherent in the individual was anathema to Marx, who criticised Adam Smith and David Ricardo for conceiving of the rational actor that inhabited their economic models 'not as an historical result, but as the starting point of history; not as something evolving in the course of history, but posited by nature, because for them this individual was in conformity with nature, in keeping with their idea of human nature' (Marx 1981b: 188).

Human nature, for Marx, was not 'an abstraction inherent in each single individual' but rather a quality that had to be understood in terms of 'the ensemble of social relations' (Marx 1999: 122). It is quite possible to read this as a rejection of the idea of species being (Althusser 1969). This, however, would be a mistake.[9] What Marx in effect does is to reject 'the ahistorical notion of any fixed or a priori essence of human beings' (Fracchia 1991: 159) and insist that our capacity to consciously deploy our capacities to satisfy our needs can only be realised in and through social relations. It is true that needs and capacities inhere in each and every one of us as individuals, but the actual satisfaction of needs and deployment of capacities is thoroughly social: it is through social relations that we develop our capacities to satisfy needs by learning skills; it is through social relations that we access the means that we use to satisfy our needs; it is through social relations that the results of our productive activity are distributed and consumed.[10]

Writing about the 'fundamental conditions' of history, Marx and Engels elaborated this idea in the following way:

> The production of life, both of one's own in labour and of fresh life in procreation, now appears as a double relationship: on the one hand as a natural, on the other as a social relationship. By social we understand the

> co-operation of several individuals, no matter under what conditions, in what manner and to what end ... Thus it is quite obvious that from the start there exists a materialistic connection of human beings with one another, which is determined by their needs and their mode of production, and which is as old as human beings themselves. (Marx and Engels 1999: 50)

This is not simply a question of social relations making praxis possible, because conversely praxis is constitutive of social relations: when we deploy our capacities to satisfy our needs in cooperation with other human beings, we create relatively stable and enduring lattice-works of social relations that shape praxis.

These lattice-works of social relations in which human beings are embedded can be considered as structures that are simultaneously 'enabling' and 'constraining' (Giddens 1979: 69–71). They are enabling in that they provide the means through which the deployment of capacities to satisfy needs can be initiated and enacted. Structures, in short, make praxis possible. But at the same time, structures constrain how we deploy our capacities to satisfy our needs as well as the direction in and extent to which we develop new capacities. Movements, for example, are possible *because of* the specific features of the social world as it is; it is those same structures that make it hard for movements to change things.

The ways in which structures constrain praxis can be understood using Raymond Williams's (1977) distinction between 'positive determination' as 'the exertion of pressures' and 'negative determination' as 'the setting of limits'. A particular structure will exert pressures on the ways in which needs are articulated. For example, in a capitalist context, the need for means of subsistence will be articulated as a demand for commodities on a market. Similarly, a given structure will exert pressures for our capacities to be deployed in a certain way. Again, in a capitalist context, our capacity to create use values is not put to use through direct production for subsistence, but through selling that capacity as labour power, in exchange for money that can then be used to purchase commodities on markets.

At the same time, a given structure will close off alternative articulations of needs and alternative deployments of our capacities: for instance, collectively organised production and distribution of use values according to a socially defined criterion of the need for means of subsistence is anathema to capitalism; it is therefore difficult to organise such activities in capitalist societies and there is a strong pressure to re-articulate them with capitalist relationships (as charity, as lifestyle, as youth project, and the like). Moreover, structures exert pressures and set limits to the development of needs and capacities – or rather, structures set limits to how far new needs and capacities are allowed to develop and pressures are exerted on whatever development takes place to assume a form and direction compatible with extant structures.

Setting limits to and exerting pressures on the articulation of our needs, the way we use our capacities to satisfy those needs, and the direction in and degree to which those needs and capacities develop within a given social formation ultimately produce a *dominant structure of entrenched needs and capacities*. This structure is 'consistently reproduced over extended periods of time' (Sewell 1996: 842) and in turn underpins the reproduction and relative stability of the social formation in which it is embedded.

However, if these lattice-works of social relations are enduring, they are also dynamic – they change over time, sometimes in a molecular manner that hardly causes a ripple on the seemingly pacific surface of society, and at other times seismically, striking along fault lines to the core of a social formation, causing it to burst asunder: society never actually stands still. This compels us to consider the historical dimensions of praxis.

The Historicity of Species Being

For Marx, historical processes of change in social formations were fundamentally related to the ways in which we deploy our capacities to satisfy our needs, and as such 'the whole of history is nothing but a continuous transformation of human nature' (Marx 1995: 60). Thus, when 'separate generations' make use of 'the productive forces handed down to it by all preceding generations' to satisfy their needs, they simultaneously carry on 'the traditional activity in completely changed circumstances' on the one hand, whereas, on the other hand, they modify 'the old circumstances with a completely changed activity' (Marx and Engels 1999: 57). It is from this dynamic that the historicity – the developmental character of human needs and capacities – of species being flows. In particular, the degree to and direction in which our needs and capacities develop may generate pressures for change – whether in the form of modifications that leave the deep structure of a given social formation intact, or in the form of transformations that give rise to new forms of social organisation.

A dominant structure of entrenched needs and capacities is not static. It is a dynamic entity that is subject to 'constant revision even in the course of reproduction' – and these revisions go on continually, even when 'the overall structural framework tends to be maintained' (Sewell 1996: 842–3). The modification of an entrenched structure of needs and capacities is related to 'the real development of conflictual relations' (Bensaïd 2002: 18) between dominant and subaltern social groups – that is, between groups that are differentially positioned in terms of their access to and control over power resources, which means that they are differentially endowed in terms of 'their control of social relations and … the scope of their transformative powers' (Sewell 1992: 20). The construction and reproduction of a social formation – and therefore also the kind of pressure exerted and limits set to the deployment, development and satisfaction of our capacities and needs, and the dominant structure of entrenched needs and capacities that emerges from this – occurs through a process of 'contention, struggle, and argument' (Roseberry 1995: 80) between dominant and subaltern groups.

This process is one in which the contending parties test their strength against each other, and draw what we call *truce lines* across the social landscape as struggles yield concessions, accommodation and compromise. These truce lines in turn become the object of contestation as new rounds of struggle unfold. Consequently, a dominant structure of entrenched needs and capacities is best conceived of as 'an internally contradictory totality in a constant process of change' (Rees 1998: 7).

Both dominant and subaltern groups seek to modify dominant structures of entrenched needs and practices. When dominant groups do so, they draw on their superior access to economic, political and cultural power resources to ensure that the ways in which needs and capacities are articulated and organised both reproduce and extend their hegemonic position in a social formation. Subaltern groups, on the other hand, will tend to seek to lessen the burden of domination and to carve out a space for the satisfaction of their needs within the parameters of a given social formation. When subaltern groups assert themselves in relation to dominant structures of entrenched needs and capacities, they most commonly start in one of two ways: (i) by resisting attempts by dominant groups to enhance their power by changing the social organisation of needs and capacities – for example, in the form of peasant revolts against increased taxes or workers' evasion of tighter discipline in the workplace, and (ii) by demanding modifications in the way a need is articulated within a given social formation so as to accommodate their own particular needs – for example, when racial and sexual minorities demand recognition or disenfranchised social groups demand civil and political rights. The outcome of such struggles is modification, not transformation – unless they develop further.

We have seen such struggles over praxis in recent years in the field of interactive media. Key to many of the movements of the late 1990s and early 2000s were attempts to translate the intensely communicative and democratic spirit of face-to-face organising into online forms. Developments such as Indymedia radically disrupted both the monolithic power of broadcast media, both state and commercial, at the same time as they undermined the internal control exercised by Leninist and nationalist groups over their own memberships. Early celebrations of this technological utopia as ushering in a bloodless revolution were exaggerated, as these models were in turn adapted for the purposes of commercial 'social media', safe 'invited spaces' of online comment 'below the line' in mainstream media and a newly vicious space for the right-wing politics of racist, misogynist and homophobic backlash. Yet these self-same new forms were re-purposed in turn by those who were young children when Indymedia was created, in European anti-austerity movements and the Arab uprisings of 2011. The cycle is not yet over, but it is clear that (like the truth), technology will not set us free, however important a space of struggle it remains (Gillan 2010, Gillan and Cox 2014).

Yet we know that structural transformations do occur – Bastilles are taken, empires are overthrown and whole forms of patriarchy vanish – and these things happen when subaltern groups organise to exert sustained pressure for change. So how do we account for those periods in history when a dominant structure of entrenched needs and capacities and the social formation in which it is enmeshed is fundamentally ruptured and replaced by something new and altogether different?

Radical Needs and Emergent Tendencies

A good starting-point for grappling with this question is Williams' (1977: 121, 125) insistence that within the context of a determinate cultural system there will be 'complex interrelations between movements and tendencies both within and beyond a specific and effective dominance' and thus that 'no mode of production and therefore no dominant social order and therefore no dominant culture ever in reality includes or exhausts all human practice, human energy, and human invention.' If we consider the relationship between needs and capacities in this way, within the context of a determinate social formation there will be complex interrelations between movements and tendencies both within and beyond a specific and effective dominant structure of entrenched needs and capacities. Consequently, no social formation or dominant structure of entrenched needs and capacities will ever exhaust the development of new needs and capacities through praxis. There will always be cracks.

Williams distinguishes between 'the residual' and 'the emergent' in his discussion of tendencies that move beyond 'the dominant' (ibid.: 122–3). The residual – which is not of direct concern here – refers to 'experiences, meanings and values' that are 'lived and practised on the basis of the residue ... of some previous social and cultural institution of formation'.[11] The emergent – which we will be concerned with – refers to 'new meanings and values, new practices, new relationships and new kinds of relationship [that] are currently being created' (ibid.: 123).

Emergent meanings, values, practices, relationships and kinds of relationships crystallise around new needs and capacities that are continually created through praxis. The emergence of new needs and capacities does not necessarily entail the rupture of a dominant structure or the social formation in which it is enmeshed. Through processes of modification, new needs and capacities can sometimes be incorporated as 'elements of some new phase of the dominant'. But new needs and capacities can also come to constitute 'elements which are substantially alternative or oppositional to the dominant structure of needs and capacities' (ibid.), and to the extent that they are, they push against this structure and contain the potential to transcend it.

In thinking more closely about such needs and capacities, Agnes Heller's (1976: Chapter 4) concept of 'radical needs' is very useful (see also Grumley 1999; Tormey 2001: Chapter 2). Heller developed the concept as part of her discussion of capitalism as a social formation with a 'structure of needs' that is characterised by the existence of 'certain needs' that are 'not satisfiable' within the parameters of that social formation. Capitalism ushers in a social system where 'needs are not allocated by birth but by status ascribed according to political and economic status' and where markets and exchange value give rise to 'a quantifiable structure of needs [which] has an emancipatory function insofar as it liberates individuals from naturally ascribed stations and provides them with the opportunity of more actively shaping their own needs and structures' (Grumley 1999:

55). Radical needs are spawned within and thus intrinsic to capitalism; they cannot 'be 'eliminated' from its functioning' (Heller 1976: 77).

What is it, then, that makes these needs radical in the sense of being substantially alternative or oppositional to capitalism? Radical needs are radical because of the transformative preconditions for and consequences of their satisfaction: '... it is not the *Being* of radical needs that transcends capitalism but their *satisfaction*' (ibid.: 77; original emphasis). Heller clarifies this by discussing the need for universality generated by capitalism. As capitalism erodes the boundaries between specialised forms of labour, a need for universality – a relationship to the whole and not simply a fragment of the social world – comes into being. However, the complete satisfaction of this need would require the transcendence of capitalism as a mode of production:

> The 'machine' that dominates in capitalist society makes the development of a universality of capacities indispensable. But while in capitalist society this tendency asserts itself as a natural law, the capitalist division of labour nevertheless 'serves as a barrier' to the development of universality. In order to realise this universality (no longer as a natural law asserting itself behind the backs of human beings), the working class must conquer political power and overcome the division of labour. (Ibid.: 92)

To satisfy the need for universality spawned by and within the capitalist mode of production, the capitalist division of labour has to be overcome so that 'the detail-worker of today, crippled by the life-long repetition of one and the same trivial operation' can be replaced by 'the fully developed individual ... to whom the different social functions he performs are but so many modes of giving free scope to his own natural and acquiring powers' (Marx, cited in Heller 1976: 92–3).

For us, radical needs should not be conceived of as something that is specific to capitalism, but more broadly, as needs that can be developed through praxis within the parameters of any given social formation and in relation to any given dominant structure of entrenched needs and capacities.[12] The defining feature of such needs is that their satisfaction requires the transformation of the social formation in which they originated. Furthermore, the conceptual vocabulary should be expanded to include radical *capacities* as well as radical needs. Sets of radical needs and radical capacities may then become 'the motives of the practice which transcends the given society' (Heller 1976: 90) when a social group develops new meanings, new values, new practices and new relationships around these needs and capacities. The outcome of such a process constitutes an *emergent structure of radical needs and capacities*. The practice which transcends the given society would then be mobilisation and collective action by the social groups from whose praxis this emergent structure of radical needs and capacities originally developed – in other words, oppositional collective action that consciously seeks to transform and transcend a dominant structure of entrenched needs and capacities and the social formation in which it is embedded, so as to enable the satisfaction of radical needs through the deployment of radical capacities.

The Agents of Stability and Change

Who historically articulates such projects that seek to realise an emergent structure of radical needs and capacities? The most immediate answer is, of course, subaltern groups – for the simple reason that these groups find themselves at a disadvantage within a dominant structure of entrenched needs and capacities and therefore also stand to gain from its dissolution. Moreover, it would not make sense for dominant groups to undermine their own hegemonic position in a social formation. Obviously, as the above discussion of modifications in dominant structures of entrenched needs and capacities makes clear, dominant groups *do* make concessions to the demands of subaltern groups, which in turn leads to modifications in extant ways of organising needs and capacities. But when concessions are made, they are nevertheless contained in a form that does not challenge or threaten the reproduction of the dominant structure of entrenched needs and capacities. In fact, dominant groups tend to pursue modifications in the dominant structure of entrenched needs and capacities that consolidate, maintain, or extend their hegemonic position.

Social groups are dominant or subaltern, most immediately, in terms of their power within a particular social formation, based on a combination of the consent of some groups to a particular form of leadership and the coercion of other groups. Dominant groups shape and direct social change to meet their own needs while making concessions to their allies and claiming to stand for the general interest; they thus hold particular forms of cultural prestige within an overall structure of legitimation. This is not simply a function of capitalism (or other forms of class society) or class relations, but holds equally for those relationships in which race or ethnicity are key to the division of labour and the satisfaction of material needs and those in which patriarchy shapes gender in material ways. Put another way, what is fundamental is the relationship to *material needs*, to *overall social power*, and to *culture*. In particular, the extent to which groups – including some which might 'objectively' seem to lose out – are in practice core members of a governing social coalition or take up a position of more or less resigned or energetic opposition, are key to understanding *what people actually do*.

Hence the positionality of dominant and subaltern groups is relative and processual, not something fixed or inherent. Anti-colonial struggles, for example, represent a struggle for radical needs and capacities – self-determination – by a subaltern group (the colonised) against a dominant group (the coloniser) the realisation of which will entail structural transformation (the end of the colonial order and the onset of national sovereignty). However, within the seemingly united subaltern group in such struggles there are usually internal differentiations between dominant and subaltern. We might, for example, find a colonial-period national elite whose aspirations to dominance were frustrated by their ultimate subjugation to the colonial power, but who possessed a political language – typically acquired through their schooling in the institutions of the colonial power – that could be used to challenge their overlords and mould a unified oppositional subject – typically 'the people' – in whose name the struggle is carried out. Peasants, industrial workers, women and ethnic minorities might all be drawn into the struggle in hopes of furthering their own agendas. The structural transformation that follows an anti-colonial struggle might in turn witness the disintegration of that homogenous oppositional subject and the manifestations of a new hierarchical structure where that same elite ascends to a dominant position within a newborn nation state, with a mixture of concessions and repression of its one-time allies. Present-day India and Ireland can both be described in this way.

Similar arguments can be made about, say, the decline of *anciens régimes* in the bourgeois revolutions of seventeenth- and eighteenth-century Europe where an emergent capitalist class, situated in a subaltern position *vis-à-vis* the traditional ruling groups (the monarchy and the clergy) but in a position of dominance *vis-à-vis* tenants and serfs, vindicated its own radical needs through the establishment of new constitutional powers and new forms of economic organisation, adding up to the constitution of a new social formation (see Gill 2003a: 44–7). This process also involved the mobilisation of other subaltern groups who then found themselves in conflict with the new élites (see Chapter 4).

Finding a Language for Change

The distinction between entrenched and radical needs and capacities – and therefore also between struggles that result in modifications and struggles that result in transformation – is not a distinction between watertight compartments. Radical needs do not appear fully formed. On the contrary – and given that 'whatever something is becoming … is in some important respects part of what it is along with what it once was' (Ollman 1993: 29) – radical needs emerge from the development of already existing needs and capacities through praxis, and their realisation as forces that might bring about transformation is by necessity a long, drawn-out and highly contingent process. When human beings develop new needs and capacities, within the parameters of dominant structures, they will commonly try to accommodate these within the existing social formation or to carve out a space where new needs and capacities can flourish without appearing as an anti-systemic threat to the prevailing social order.[13] These are, after all, outcomes which are easier to imagine from within a given social formation.

Similarly, when subaltern groups start to mobilise around emergent structures of radical needs and capacities, the oppositional projects they develop may well take the form of demands for modification of existing structures or be spoken in conventional, 'safe' languages, and only later develop into overtly transformative projects. This is part of what Marx communicates in *The Eighteenth Brumaire of Louis Bonaparte*:

> The tradition of all the dead generations weighs like a nightmare on the brain of the living. And just when they seem engaged in revolutionising themselves and things, in creating something that has never yet existed, precisely in such periods of revolutionary crisis they anxiously conjure up the spirits of the past to their service and borrow from them names, battle-cries and costumes in order to present the new scene of world history in this time-honoured disguise and this borrowed language … In like manner a beginner who has learnt a new language always translates it back into his mother tongue, but he has assimilated the spirit of the new language and can freely express himself in it only when

> he finds his way in it without recalling the old and forgets his native tongue in the use of the new. (1984: 10–11)

It takes time and struggle – within movements as well as in conflict with outside forces – to arrive at an open recognition of the need for a new social order. As Calhoun points out, the initial phases of workers' collective action in the early period of the Industrial Revolution were characterised by community as 'the crucial social bond' around which solidarity crystallised, and theirs was presented as a defence of 'past practices' and 'traditional values'.[14] It was only later that 'either formal or informal patterns of organisation extended to unify the class subjected to capitalist exploitation' and 'a new analysis of exploitation' came to be characteristic of workers' radicalism (Calhoun 1982: 7; see also Vester 1978).

Even if an alternative and oppositional project crystallises around a set of radical needs and capacities, its trajectory is still contingent. First among the reasons for contingency is repression and opposition by dominant groups in response to the challenge that has been made, and which might – or might not – prevent the realisation of an emergent structure of radical needs and capacities, for a time or permanently. Secondly, those periods in history when 'all that is solid melts into air' will tend to witness not just one but many articulations of radical needs and capacities – perhaps rooted in different subaltern groups, or groups defined by different degrees of subalternity – which are incompatible, and among which some will emerge as hegemonic and others will be marginalised. As Hill (1975) documents so compellingly in *The World Turned Upside Down*, the era that witnessed the decline of *anciens régimes* was not exclusively characterised by the designs of an emergent bourgeoisie, but also by the demotic, radical-democratic visions of a plebeian class, articulated by such groups as the Diggers, the Ranters and the Levellers. These visions, however, were marginalised as the bourgeoisie attained the upper hand in the era's struggles over hegemony (see Gill 2003a: 46–7).

Thus there is and can be no automatism to this process, of the kind sometimes ascribed to Marxism. *Because* needs and capacities are indeterminate; because what is at stake is the processes through which different groups of humans manage to articulate their needs, develop their capacities, reflect on their situation and organise collectively; because these processes depend on learning and discussion, and because they are internally and externally contested, there are multiple histories and trajectories, with many different outcomes. It is not that nothing can be said about the process: rather, what can be said, has to be said about the way in which human beings 'make their own history', or as Thompson (1977) put it, with biological rather than mechanical metaphors (or, we might suggest, creative and artistic metaphors).

This might seem like a weakness from the point of view of structural theory-building of a pre-Marxist kind, but it is what Marx's focus on praxis is *for:* to enable movements to stand on their own feet and view their situation and their opponents clearly, rather than seeking a magical resolution in technology, ideas, progress, or whatever. Realising that our societies represent the outcomes of long processes of learning and struggle, which meet (some of) our needs more or less well, within which we can perhaps extract concessions around others but where yet other needs will *never* be met without a radical change in how those societies are organised, we can try to identify clearly *who* is so closely tied to the dominant structures of entrenched needs and capacities that seeking to work with them will always be a mistake; *whose* needs are so badly served by existing arrangements that they are likely allies, worth trying to convince; and *who* may be capable of swinging either way, benefiting in some ways from the current arrangements but unable to satisfy other needs without a new kind of society.[15] From the abstract consideration of how societies are constituted through praxis, in other words, we return to the immediate and concrete terrain of struggle, mobilisation and alliance-building – but now on our own terms, not taking the given order for granted but seeing it as contingent and capable of being displaced.

Movement Praxis in Community Organising

We can illustrate the value of this temporary abstraction with a consideration of working-class community activism in the Republic of Ireland (Cox and Mullan 2001, Powell and Geoghegan 2004, Boyle 2005, Punch 2009, Cox 2010c, Zagato 2012). Pre-independence Ireland's relatively small and divided working class played a significant but subordinate role in the anti-colonial movement. Defeated by a Catholic, nationalist capitalist class in the 1913 Dublin Lockout, it played a supporting role in the 1916 Easter Rising and was substantially marginalised as a political player in the 1919–21 War of Independence and the following Civil War. The Free State established in southern Ireland proceeded to what has been called an Irish counter-revolution (Regan 1999), which saw the radical left – the labour struggles of 1919 onwards, independent socialist activism and the left of the republican movement alike – repressed, marginalised, or co-opted, a process which culminated in the ultra-conservative years of 'De Valera's Ireland' from the early 1930s to the late 1950s. A similar account could be written of the first-wave women's movement, as subordinate to both nationalist and unionist politics in the pre-independence period and suppressed or converted into conservatism subsequently.

One outcome of this history was the 'loyal opposition' character of the Labour Party (repeatedly junior partner in governments of the right), trade unions (keen not to be seen as threats to the national interest) and indeed most leftists within the republican movement. Hence until recently, the leading party for working-class voters has been the Peronist-like Fianna Fáil (Allen 1997), because of its clientelist distribution of benefits, while the main available language of class dissent for working-class people in the Republic has been support for republicanism because of its rejection of the existing state. It is not that more radical needs than the Irish status quo allows for have been absent; it is that it has been extremely difficult to express them practically in terms that have articulated any *emergent* structure of needs and capacities. Rather, working-class needs and struggles have tended to operate as the social conscience of nationalist groups, conservative or radical.

One of the few moments when alternative strategies have seemed possible developed from the 1970s onwards. In this period, the war in the north posed significant legitimacy problems for both Fianna Fáil and Labour in the south; the first flourishing of second-wave feminism, GLBTQ struggles and other counter-cultural movements undermined the once-unchallenged hegemony of the Catholic church; the complexities of the northern conflict created space for a number of working-class extra-parliamentary formations, north and south (Hanley and Millar 2009), and there were significant connections with international social movements, in particular Latin American struggles. In this context, too, the brief period of industrial development that preceded the oil crash, and processes of inner-city slum clearance with the creation of new purpose-built estates on urban peripheries, created space for less traditionalist modes of working-class self-organisation (Cox and Mullan 2001).

The outcome was the development of bottom-up organising processes in much of working-class Ireland using the language of community organising, community development and community education – its references to Alinsky, UN programmes and Freire indicating the extent to which language was borrowed to express an emergent praxis. Key to this praxis – which emphasised starting from locally felt needs, extensive processes of discussion and the exercising of local control – was the role of working-class women, outside the structures of the formal women's movement (Coulter 1993), and of local activists turning away from a primary loyalty to state-centred, nationally focused parties (socialist or republican) and towards on-the-ground organising around local needs. The conflict between this process and top-down statist approaches emerged around two areas: local organising against heroin dealers, constituting a direct challenge to an aggressively anti-working-class police force (Lyder 2005); and the struggle over housing in the massive new council estate of Ballymun in North Dublin.

If the state's repression of the anti-drugs movement led many participants to draw back from mass-based direct action, the housing strategy in Ballymun was organised with the goal of forcing the state to meet local needs, in bringing disparate and unaccountable state agencies around one table with local community organisers. The net effect, however, was that as forms of partnership with working-class communities and other social movements spread – paralleling a period in which Ireland moved *towards* corporatist decision making between the state, employers and unions – this process happened on the state's terms rather than those of working-class movements, and tended to demobilise self-organisation.

Social movements of this period – including the women's and environmental movements – sought an end to their previous exclusion from decision making and funding, and had no strategic perspective to enable an independent and more confident engagement with the state once (limited) funding and consultative opportunities were provided. The net effect – paralleling the US War on Poverty but with a two-decade time lag (Naples 1998) – was a gradual process of professionalisation and credentialisation for those activists who were able to engage with elite processes around service delivery, policy, legislation, research, funding, media, and so on, and demobilisation for those who could not or would not (INCITE! 2009).

By the end of the 'Celtic Tiger', the formal structures of community organisations, women's groups, trade unions, environmental NGOs, GLBTQ activism and a host of other social movements had become in effect subcontracted parts of the state, with little or none of the capacity for mass mobilisation, direct action, or even independent public expression which they had had when Irish community activism had been perhaps the most dramatic working-class self-organisation in western Europe outside Italy;

when Ireland had been one of the few countries anywhere in the world to thoroughly defeat nuclear power, and when women's groups, GLBTQ activists and their allies overturned what once seemed like an immovable Catholic hegemony on both private and public life (Cox 2010c).

When, from the mid-2000s on, the state embarked on a direct assault on their new subordinates, closing, absorbing and de-funding these once-independent groups (Harvey, 2014), it is no surprise that organisational leaderships – a mixture of an ageing founder generation with no intention of returning out into the cold and staff who were often not recruited as organisers but rather appointed as holders of state-approved credentials – have had no 'Plan B', but simply seek a return to their previous situation and their own expert territory of access to policy processes, service delivery, tendering for state funding and the like. Indeed, many are loyal allies of the Labour Party, now eagerly implementing austerity, so that a common response has been to develop pseudo-movements loudly calling for change while resisting any mass mobilisation or radicalisation of goals (Cox 2011a, 2012).

A new generation of activists across these different movements and communities, meanwhile, is developing *outside* these organisational husks, and will probably grow in strength as the latter demonstrate their inability to do anything more than provide cut-price services to the state as precarious subcontractors. An analysis of this forty-year process in terms of praxis – rather than the mystified account in which community development was the miraculous product of a UN programme, the women's movement responded to membership of the mysteriously progressive EEC, and social change in general results from enlightened elites handing down new policy initiatives and funding streams – makes it possible to think seriously and strategically about this situation. This does not require denying that *some* real needs were met in the process, at the same time as it acknowledges the dead end into which this process has canalised popular movements, demobilising the vast majority of their one-time participants.

In this process, we see the expression of needs in movements from below leading to the development of broader popular capacities – at the same time as the state has repeatedly found ways of co-opting, absorbing and ultimately decommissioning them. If social partnership has had the effect of demobilising movements and undermining their capacities for self-organisation, this was also enabled by the ways in which Irish working-class movements used statist and nationalist ideologies that channelled their capacities in particular ways and left them few alternatives when the state offered to get involved (on its own terms).

Irish activists can then think about the possibilities for struggle, mobilisation and alliance-building in the new, post-partnership period – without taking either nostalgia for partnership or resignation to the new, neoliberal onslaught on NGOs and community and voluntary groups as givens. Neither partnership (as co-optation) nor the state's current scorched-earth policy (as attack) can be understood *without* the broader presence both of the state and of social movements and mobilised working-class communities as strategic actors; and it is from a consideration of the ongoing conflict between the two that we can understand the social order as both contingent and capable of being displaced. A focus on the 'long revolution' of developing popular needs and capacities (Williams 1965) and the struggle over the direction of development (Tovey 1993) then offers a broader perspective within which we can analyse the specific institutional manifestations of particular moments of this century-long process – and explore new possibilities.

Concluding Remarks

In this chapter we have done some of the necessary groundwork for establishing the foundations of a Marxist theory of social movements. We defined species being as the ability of human beings to satisfy our needs through the conscious deployment of capacities in historically evolving social formations. We discussed these needs and capacities as a set of corporeally grounded predispositions that are mediated through conscious human activity and noted that Marx decisively broke with the subject–object dualism of western philosophy in this approach. As a result of this break, praxis becomes central to historical materialism as an ontological category and as the driver of historical change. Finally, we argued that the transhistorical predispositions of needs, capacities and conscious activity are realised through social relations; as a result of this realisation, a lattice-work of social relations emerges that constitutes the structural backbone of social formations that in turn persist as the simultaneously enabling and constraining conduits of praxis. These conduits in turn are subject to change as needs and capacities develop.

We then discussed the sociality and historicity of species being. Needs and capacities are inherent and fundamental attributes of species being, but their actual satisfaction, deployment and development occurs through social relations, which are thus enabling in relation to praxis. However, structures also constrain how we deploy our capacities to satisfy our needs, and the direction in and degree to which we develop new capacities and new needs, by exerting pressures and setting limits whose outcome is the formation of dominant structures of entrenched needs and capacities. Such structures – and the social formations in which they inhere – are internally contradictory totalities that undergo constant processes of change as dominant and subaltern groups contest over modifications of such structures.

Finally, we discussed developments in needs and capacities that engender structural transformations. Such transformations occur when subaltern groups develop new meanings and values, new practices and new kinds of relationship around emergent structures of radical needs and capacities – those whose satisfaction and deployment challenges the continued existence of a dominant structure of entrenched needs and capacities – and pursue the realisation of this emergent structure through mobilisation and collective action. Structural change as the outcome of such mobilisation, we argued, is not an inexorable law of history, but a deeply contingent affair whose exigencies are best elaborated through the study of concrete episodes of such mobilisation.

This marks a departure from the conceptual vocabulary generally associated with Marxist approaches to historical development – namely, forces, relations and modes of production.[16] This departure is intentional. It responds both to those who criticise Marxism for centring on an exclusive and deterministic focus on the production, consumption, distribution and exchange of material use-values and the matrix of social relations of class spun around these moments of the economic process (see, for example, Aronowitz 1983, Laclau and Mouffe 2001), and to those Marxists who, similarly, posit economic production as the hinge upon which everything turns, thus relegating other aspects of human practice to a secondary position and/or different logic (for example, Cohen 1978).

Putting praxis first in historical materialism entails the assertion that the basis of everything that exists is not 'the economy' as a reified subsystem but our capacity to create use-values through interaction with the social and natural environment in order to satisfy our needs – and the conscious manner in which we go about doing this. Thus, we are concerned with the generic features of situated, practical engagements with determinate otherness – other people and the natural world – which in turn yield 'worlds of artefacts – material, social and semiotic' (Fracchia 2005: 44). It is this – our species being – that enables us to engage in those activities that constitute the moments of the economic process and to create and change those social results that we conceptualise as forces, relations and modes of production.[17]

This conception of praxis enables a common frame of reference for understanding how human beings act and how human beings approach interactions with each other. For example, we could include socialist feminist discussions about 'reproductive labour' or childbirth, and world-systems accounts of the organisation of trade and finance, or the construction of a racialised division of labour globally, within this same general account of needs, capacities, consciousness and practice. Importantly for this book, political action geared towards changing such constructions can also be analysed in these terms. Our purpose, after all, is to 'reclaim, recycle and reuse' the movement thinking which made Marx and Engels's writing possible, for the purposes of present-day movements and in a shape which speaks to the problems of popular agency and human needs: to return it 'down to earth' from its current scholastic abodes.

From this historical materialism flows a sense of history which is moored in 'human beings practically constructing their lives', a sense of history 'given in the practical process whereby human beings realize themselves', and a sense of history which appreciates that 'this process of practical construction ... is not absolutely free but is conditioned by material circumstances and [social] relations which human beings have themselves produced ...' (Larrain 1986: 120). This must be the starting-point for a Marxist approach to the study of social movements. This means an approach in which social movements are conceived of ontologically as the animating forces in the making and unmaking of structures of needs and capacities, and thus of social formations as such. Moreover, it means situating these animating forces in a dynamic field where dominant and subaltern groups struggle over how the social organisation of human needs and capacities is to develop. This chapter is no more than a point of departure; much work remains to be done. Specifically, we still need a conceptual apparatus for analysing social movements once we have grounded them in this wider understanding. We turn to developing these concepts in Chapter 3.

3

'The Authors and the Actors of Their Own Drama': A Marxist Theory of Social Movements

To thoroughly examine all these questions, is it not to make real profane history of human beings in each century, to represent these people at the same time as the authors and the actors of their own drama? But from the moment that you represent human beings as the actors and authors of their own history you have, by detour, arrived at the actual point of departure since you have abandoned the eternal principles from which you at first set out.

Marx, *The Poverty of Philosophy*

'At the Heart of Society Burns the Fire of Social Movements'[1]

We argued in Chapter 1 that activists need theory to get beyond their movement's current situations. To be 'this-worldly' and 'movement-relevant', theory therefore has to offer activists a way of reaching insights about how to widen and deepen their own praxis as far as is possible at any given point, and to furnish grounded arguments for internal discussions on this. It also needs to reveal the collective agency behind the social structures they find themselves in conflict with, and hence a usable sense of their contingency. In Chapter 2, we laid the groundwork for such a theory by reading Marxism as a theory from and for social movements, which – by placing praxis in the centre – commits itself to a view of history as the product of collective human action, articulated in conflicts which encompass the totality of society and in turn define that totality.

This offers the basis for a theoretical perspective which posits social movements from above and below as the fire that burns at the heart of society. In this chapter, we articulate such a perspective in line with the arguments made in Chapters 1 and 2. Chapter 4 puts this perspective to work in analysing movements from above and below in the making and remaking of historical capitalism, while Chapter 5 uses it to offer a developmental analysis of contemporary movements against neoliberalism and their strategic potential.

We can situate this perspective more closely by contrasting it with the theories criticised in Chapter 1. Firstly, as a Marxist perspective it rejects the 'political reductionism' (Melucci 1989) of mainstream academic social movement theories, which position movements as a specific 'level' of a fundamentally given political order. Movements, we argue, are materially *situated* in the everyday reality of people's lives – needs, experience, relationships, praxis – and are better understood as extensions of this (for example, as class struggle: Barker 2013a) than as a subset of the political system.[2] We also argue for the need to understand movement at all levels: 'hidden transcripts', workplace and cultural resistance, churches and unions, parties and revolutions are not radically other than social movement unless we take the institutional structure of a very specific time and place as fixed. Any serious historical or comparative account will ask instead about what *kinds* of collective agency from below are present, and in what way, in a given context – rather than assuming that a particular kind of organisation always 'means' the same thing (that no anti-colonial party ever remakes the state in its own image, no insurgent church ever becomes a conservative sect, and no once-radical union movement ever becomes a co-opted part of the capitalist order) – or that movements never succeed in radically changing the system they oppose.

Secondly, we reject the dual ontology that animates structuralist Marxisms, which treat popular agency as a theoretical afterthought set against the much more significant role of political economy (many such Marxisms also struggle with a theoretically adequate account of the relationship between elite agency and the structures it engenders). We posit social movements – from above as well as from below – as the fundamental animating forces in the making and unmaking of the structures of needs and capacities that underpin social formations, and seek to treat the construction and maintenance of particular forms of hegemony or political economies as ontologically comparable to movements' (sometimes successful) attempts to displace, disrupt, or insert themselves within these.

Thirdly, however, autonomist writing tends to reproduce this dual ontology in reverse, celebrating popular agency rather than grimly mapping elite structure but still fundamentally unable to place them both on the same theoretical plane or offer strategic suggestions for what movements from below should do in order to change things. Instead, we consider movements as an animating force that emanates both from dominant and subaltern groups within a social formation.

Our fundamental critique of all three perspectives is their lack of history: they are written as though anti-colonial movements had never overthrown empires and themselves formed states in their own image; as though workers' movements had never threatened capitalism and found themselves selectively incorporated into new kinds of welfare state; as though the movements of 1968 had left no trace in the collapse of organised capitalism and the individualising practices of neoliberalism; as though religious struggles had never hardened into new conservative cultural hegemonies; as though the specific ways in which monarchies were replaced by democracies, fascisms were brought to an end, or Stalinisms collapsed did not in turn shape the power struggles of the new era. Instead, we are presented with a provincialism of the here-and-now as if it defined what movements might be capable of.

In the perspective we argue for, social movements 'are not a marginal rejection of order, they are the central forces fighting one against the other to control the production of society by itself and the action of classes for the shaping of historicity' (Touraine 1981: 29). More specifically, we define social movements as *a process in which a specific social group develops a collective project of skilled activities centred on a rationality – a particular way of making sense of and relating to the social world – that tries to change or maintain a dominant structure of entrenched needs and capacities, in part or whole.* Praxis and its social organisation are thus both the subject and object of social movements. Praxis is the subject of social movements in that movement activity consists of the conscious deployment of capacities to satisfy needs. Praxis is also the object of social movements in that movement activity seeks to change or maintain those structures through which human activity is socially organised, and give form and direction to the development of these structures.

We thus understand social movements as the way in which human practices are socially articulated through conflictual encounters between dominant and subaltern social groups. This leads to an analysis of social structures and social formations as the sediment of movement struggles – or as a kind of truce line which is continually probed for weaknesses by both sides and repudiated as soon as this seems worthwhile. Investigating social formations in this perspective means asking a processual and conflictual 'why'. Answering this question involves identifying the struggles from which a given truce line emerged, the power relations involved in it, and the tendencies towards forming new kinds of movement struggles that may lead to it being overrun, in one direction or the other.[3]

The meaning of 'social movement' proposed here is in a sense close to that common in the eighteenth and nineteenth centuries, when it was generally used as a 'metaphor for social change' (Raschke 1985: 23). In this period, the term 'social movement' was used in the singular, referring to change coming from subaltern groups directed at extant forms of domination and exploitation. It covered multiple forms and fields of activity, from spasmodic village upheavals to the creation of various types of counter-cultural institutions, and derived its force from the awareness of the distinct possibility that this activity could, and at times did, yield revolutionary outcomes. The term was closely related to the rise of 'the social question'– that is, elites' increasing awareness that there was a potentially powerful and thus also dangerous challenge emerging from the plebeian classes whose deference was no longer assured through the traditional methods of social control (Cox 2013a; see also Fischer 1966).

The proposition that social movements come from above as well as from below is closely related to Chapter 2's argument that modifications and transformations of dominant structures of entrenched needs and capacities flow from rounds of contestation, struggle and argument between dominant and subaltern groups. With superior access to economic, political and cultural resources of power – and thus possessing superior control of social relations and greater transformative powers – dominant groups typically seek to mould the shape that dominant structures of needs and capacities take, and to exert pressures and set limits on the development of new needs and capacities in ways that not only reproduce or maintain, but also extend that dominance. This typically revolves around the reversal of subaltern 'victories' from previous rounds of contention, struggle and argument in the form of concessions to and accommodations of subaltern demands and the dissolution of 'the moral economy' (Thompson 1993) that has emerged around these. The most recent example of this would of course be neoliberal restructuring, both in the welfare states of the North and the developmental states of the South (see Harvey 2005 and Walton and Seddon 1994).

Subaltern groups initially seek to lessen the burden of domination and to carve out a space for the greater accommodation of their specific needs within a given social organisation. Ranging from covert resistance to overt opposition, subaltern contestation can include: (a) resistance to attempts by dominant groups to alter the social organisation of needs and practices so as to extend their power – for example, peasant revolts against the landlord's attempt to increase taxes, commoners' bread riots in the face of rising prices, workers' evasions of shop-floor discipline, or women's resistance to right-wing movements aiming to restrict reproductive rights; (b) demands for modifications in the way a need is articulated and satisfied within a given social formation so as to incorporate to a greater extent their own particular needs – such as demands for recognition, inclusion and enfranchisement by ethnic, racial and sexual minorities deprived of political and civil rights, the politics of liberal feminism, or the conversion of counter-cultures into market niches; (c) projects for the revolutionary transformation of the social order with a fundamental reshaping of class relations, gender power, ethnic and racial structures, and so on, often manifested during revolutionary waves such as the late eighteenth-century Atlantic revolutions, the events of 1848, those of 1916–23, around 1968, and perhaps since the dawn of the new millennium (see Chapter 5).

Because 'normal periods' are, precisely, those in which movements from above hold the upper hand and can represent the world they have made as normal and natural – and are far more omnipresent than those from below, we start with a discussion of movements from above, the resources they draw on and the kinds of strategies they pursue, before turning to an analysis of movements from below, the developmental processes through which they sometimes unfold and how we can understand their praxis, and finally consider the nature of organic crises which see head-on conflicts between such movements, sometimes resulting in the formation of new social orders.

Social Movements From Above

'From castles and palaces and churches to prisons and workhouses and schools; from weapons of war to a controlled press', Williams (1977: 93) writes, 'any ruling class, in variable ways though always materially, produces a social and political order.' This productive activity constitutes the essence of what we call social movements from above.

A social movement from above can be defined as *the collective agency of dominant groups, which is centred on the organisation of multiple forms of skilled activity around a rationality that aims to maintain or modify a dominant structure of entrenched needs and capacities in ways that either reproduce or extend the power of these groups, and their hegemonic position within a given social formation.* The skilled activities that dominant groups organise around range from ways of structuring economic production, be that agricultural improvement in the age of enclosures or the globalisation of flexible accumulation in the neoliberal era; via political practices, whether counter-insurgency and policing strategies or models of crisis management espoused by international financial institutions; to cultural strategies such as the production of nationalist legitimating narratives or the construction of religious modes of structuring sexuality and reproduction. The rationalities at the core of mobilisation from above typically take the form of ideological offensives – for example, moral campaigns against popular customs during the era of primitive accumulation, or the propagation of an ethos of possessive individualism in the age of neoliberalism – for which dominant groups seek the consent of subaltern groups.

In promulgating these rationalities and organising these activities, movements from above take a bewildering range of institutional forms: social networks for the elite such as eighteenth-century Freemasonry, which in Britain brought together the aristocracy and the bourgeoisie; mass-participation organisations such as European Christian Democracy, which provided a popular basis for conservative politics in the post-fascist period; the think-tanks and policy networks which supported the rise of present-day neoliberalism, and transnational institutions such as the Trilateral Commission, the World Economic Forum, the World Bank and the International Monetary Fund, or the World Trade Organization.

Within routine sociology and mainstream social movements studies, the normal referent of the term 'social movement' is of course the collective action of non-elites (see Chapter 1). There are two reasons why we find it more useful to think of social movements as being articulated both from above and from below. First, collective agency is not something that is resorted to by subaltern groups alone; in normal times, it is the powerful, the wealthy and the culturally privileged who are most capable of producing collective agency in a sustained and effective manner. Secondly, it is this collective agency that in practical terms undergirds the construction and reproduction of the social structures, institutions and processes that serve the needs of these dominant groups.

But what is the intellectual and political value of this concept? Intellectually, it helps in demystifying social structures – it illuminates how structures that most of the time are experienced by most people as an inevitable part of the given order of things are in fact the historically specific results of the collective agency of dominant social groups. Furthermore, by allowing for an ontological comparability between the collective agency of dominant and subaltern groups, our understanding of collective agency itself expands. Rather than being simply a blip on the otherwise pacific surface of society, it becomes a common denominator for how both dominant and subaltern groups make and remake the social worlds that they inhabit.

Politically, the concept of social movements from above is useful in two distinct but interrelated ways. It relates directly to activists' experience of encountering conscious, determined and organised opponents rather than simply the inert resistance of a thing-like structure. Here, the concept is demystifying because it enables us to understand the current situation as a conjuncture emerging from previous conflicts between movements from above and movements from below – and our position in that situation: we are not simply faced with an anonymous and omnipotent 'system', an amorphous and pervasive culture of 'normality', or an impenetrable web of 'power'. The forces we confront certainly draw on these elements, but they are themselves the products of the past action of social movements from above. Crucially, this makes them subject to challenge from below.

Thus the concept of social movements from above enables us – both intellectually and politically – to grasp that 'the way things are' has been consciously produced, not only in the here-and-now, but also across historical time and across different spatial scales. In doing so, we can open greater theoretical space for the possibility that movements from below can construct their own world successfully – if they are capable of defeating movements from above. This entails thinking through the ways in which social movements from above craft strategies to produce, extend and reproduce the hegemony of dominant groups, by drawing on those groups' superior access to economic, political and cultural power resources.

The Power Resources of Social Movements from Above

Directive Role in Economic Organisation

Social movements from above draw upon and seek to maintain or expand the directive role of dominant groups in economic organisation. This directive role consists in the ability to determine what is to be produced, how it is produced and for what purposes, and, most importantly, the ability to appropriate the surplus that this production yields – that is, it consists in the ability to exploit the direct producers by 'compelling [them] to work longer than is necessary to produce the means of subsistence for themselves and their dependents' (Callinicos 1988: 50). This ability in turn derives from the defining feature of class societies as such, namely that 'one or more of the smaller classes, in virtue of their control over the conditions of production ... will be able to exploit – that is, to appropriate a surplus at the expense of – the larger classes ...' (Ste. Croix 1981: 44; see also Smith 1990: 39 and Sohn-Rethel 1978: 86–8).

Crucially, exploitation and thus also class relations as 'the collective social expression of the fact of exploitation' (Ste. Croix 1981: 43) are not self-perpetuating features of society; they have to be actively and consciously reproduced. This follows from the fact that exploitation 'will tend to evoke resistance, if only in such molecular forms as sabotage and ca'canny ...' (Callinicos 1988: 51). This resistance has to be actively curbed – through repression or accommodation – for accumulation to proceed as smoothly as possible and for extant power relations to be maintained or expanded.[4] Furthermore, a determinate economic organisation that enables a specific form of exploitation does not come about automatically, but has to be actively created through projects that seek to advance a new 'mode in which surplus labour [can be] extracted from the actual producer, the worker' (Marx, cited in Ste. Croix 1981: 51). The point, then, is to emphasise the agency that first produces and then buttresses what Marx (1990: 899) called '[t]he silent compulsion of economic relations' – both in terms of the conflictual origins of a particular pattern of economic relations and the equally conflictual internal transformations of that pattern, and of how that agency is motivated by the perceived need to establish, maintain, extend, or restore class power.[5]

Within capitalist relationships, exploitation occurs between 'two great hostile camps' (Marx and Engels 1888) – on the one hand, 'the class of modern capitalists, owners of the means of social production and employers of wage labour', and on the other hand, 'the class of modern wage labourers who, having no means of production of their own, are reduced to selling their labour power in order to live' (ibid.). The nexus between capital and labour represents 'the final and most complete expression of the system of producing and appropriating products that is based on class antagonisms, on the exploitation of the many by the few' (Marx and Engels, cited in Ste. Croix 1981: 50). Finally, the dynamic and form of capitalism as a system of surplus appropriation constantly changes. This is evident in the range of transitions between 'accumulation strategies' (Jessop 1990) in the historical development of the capitalist mode of production, such as that from organized to neoliberal capitalism (see Chapter 4).[6] These transitions are not simply determined by the objective laws of capitalism as a system. Rather, they have to be understood in relation to the conflictual encounter between capital and labour – between a capitalist class that seeks to extract surplus value in the most efficient way possible on the one hand, and a working class that attempts to assert its needs and interests in opposition to the imperatives of capital (see Lebowitz 2003, Cleaver 2000).

Class society, capitalism and neoliberalism – and the associated terms of class – are not the only dimensions of exploitation. Patriarchy – a concept whose historical and conceptual scale is closer to that of class society than that of capitalism, and which contains a wide range of historical forms – is another, with its associated terms of gender and sexuality. The same can be said for race and ethnicity, and the racialised global order we have inhabited since the rise of capitalism, with its multiple variations in recent centuries and the longer historical perspective in which ethnicity, statehood, slavery, and so on have structured relationships between class societies.

Were we to be writing a purely structural analysis, a discussion of these terms – class, gender, race, and so on as categories within present-day societies; how we conceive of the structuration of inequalities within those societies, and the wider theoretical and historical perspectives – would in itself prove a massive task, to say nothing of the challenge of understanding (say) the relationship between capitalism, patriarchy and the racialised global order as it has developed over these past five centuries, perhaps developing a conceptual apparatus which sees them as moments of a single process rather than separate structures, and the historical challenge of discussing both the changing forms this half-millennial order has taken and how we can understand the wider nature of post-hunter-gatherer societies. Much work has been done in this area in terms of the relationship between structural analyses and different theoretical traditions, in the forms (for example) of socialist feminism, Marxist analyses of race and imperialism, eco-feminism, and so on.[7]

Our interest here, however, is a rather different one: not to analyse the structures *produced by* the agency of dominant groups, but to understand how and why they produce these structures through their collective action. To rethink structure as collective agency in a non-conspiratorial key is a challenging task; in this book, we focus on the Marxist study of classed, particularly capitalist, agency from above in the production and maintenance of different accumulation strategies. Existing work on patriarchy and race/colonialism/ethnicity is also capable of being written in the mode of social movements from above, and of course in the final analysis we have to understand collective agency from above as a social movement which operates across all three dimensions simultaneously.[8]

Our focus on class relations in the sphere of production, then, is a key moment of this broader picture; but it is not the only one. Whether through attempting to reorganise power relations within the factory, restructuring the politics of childbirth and inheritance, or constructing new kinds of imperialism, social movements from above have always sought to use their directive position within the economic realm both to secure material benefits for themselves through the exploitation of others and to further strengthen their dominant role in this realm.

Privileged Access to State Power

Closely related to the power derived from the directive role of dominant groups in economic organisation is their privileged access to 'the political power that is pre-eminently ascribed to the state' (Poulantzas 1978: 147). The state, of course, 'makes its historical appearance as a means of political control' when a permanent surplus is being produced and class society crystallises (Smith 1990: 41). At this point, it comes to function as a modality in and through which the ability of dominant groups to control social relations is institutionalised and consolidated. This needs two caveats.

Firstly, it is not an argument that the state is a unified subject with agent-like capacities or 'a fixed sum of resources which can be appropriated by one social force to the exclusion of others' (Jessop 1982: 225). The state, rather, is best understood as an institutional ensemble that congeals from a wider matrix of power-laden social relations; its form and function reflect the balance of power that prevails between different social forces in a given conjuncture. Indeed, the form and functions of the state in a given context have to be understood 'in terms of their production in and through past political strategies and struggles' (Jessop 1990: 261).

Secondly, although the state is not simply an instrument of classed, gendered, or racial domination and while its power has to be grasped in terms of the power of the social forces that act in and through its institutional capacities, this does not mean that it is 'equally available to all forces and equally available for all purposes' (ibid.: 250). Precisely because of the superior position of dominant groups in the struggles that shape the institutional ensemble that constitutes the state, its structuring will provide 'unequal chances to different forces within and outside the system to act for different political purposes' (Jessop 2008: 37). It is this feature of state formation that makes it possible for dominant groups to draw on privileged access to state power as they act to reproduce and extend their hegemony.[9]

The structuring and workings of state power can be conceived of as capitalist 'to the extent that it creates, maintains or restores the conditions required for capital accumulation in a given context' (Jessop 1990: 354). This entails coercive intervention to secure private property rights – both in the means of production and in labour power – and the enforcement of contracts. Furthermore, states may actively seek, for example, to eliminate barriers to the mobility of capital and labour or to stabilise monetary systems. State intervention is also essential to regulate the accumulation process itself, particularly in times of crisis, when the imperative becomes that of ensuring the reproduction of basic mechanisms of accumulation. The state also plays a central role in providing the public goods and physical infrastructures that are essential to the smooth functioning of production and accumulation (see Harvey 2001: 274–5). Beyond this, the capitalist state is central to reproducing those social and cultural institutions that are important in shaping and sustaining accumulation – notably, gendered divisions of labour, the patriarchal family, and racial hierarchies (see Kotz, McDonagh and Reich 1994).

Most importantly, however, the state is the central strategic site in which the relations between factions of capital and relations between capital and labour are organised and mediated. This entails fusing together different groups of capitalists in a consensus around a specific accumulation strategy under the leadership of a specific fraction of capital (for example, industrial capital, commercial capital, or financial capital). Moreover, as we discuss further below and in Chapter 4, it entails deploying a mixture of consent and coercion in relation to the working class: as dominant groups act in and through the state, they typically strive to ensure that some sections of the working class accept the prevailing way of organising production while at the same time mobilising the coercive resources of the state to quell more intractable and radical forms of proletarian resistance (see Rupert 1990 and Silver 1995). The same is of course routinely true of the construction of racial hierarchies, co-opting some groups in order to subordinate others more drastically, and of the state's role in defining acceptable and unacceptable forms of gendered behaviour, family arrangements, sexuality, and so on.

Moulding Everyday Routines and Common Sense

Gramsci distinguished between two ways in which dominant groups establish and maintain their position in a given social formation. On the one hand, there is the coercive power that is exercised through the state to enforce 'discipline on those groups who do not "consent" either actively or passively' to the prevailing social order. On the other hand, however, there is '[t]he spontaneous consent given by the great masses of the population to the general direction imposed on social life by the dominant fundamental group ...' (Gramsci 1998: 12). This consent, Gramsci argued, ultimately rests on the ability of a dominant group to posit 'the development and expansion of the particular group ... as being the motor force of a universal expansion, of a development of all the national energies' (ibid.: 182).

Hegemony in this sense has two dimensions, which correspond to the 'theoretical' and 'directive' activities he attributes to intellectuals. If we consider that his key examples of 'traditional' intellectuals includes the role of the doctor, lawyer, or priest in the southern village, and that the intellectuals 'organic' to organized capitalism include the engineer, the time-and-motion man and the manager, fundamental to both sets of activities is the 'directive' organisation of daily life: defusing issues around (say) rent, domestic violence, or emigration in a way that reinforces relationships of clientelism rather than allowing for peasant self-organisation (Gramsci 1978), or reorganising daily activity within the factory and 'civilising' the workforce in ways ranging from time-discipline (Thompson 1993) to sexuality.

As Williams (1977: 110) observes, hegemony revolves around 'the relations of domination and subordination, in their forms as practical consciousness, as in effect a saturation of the whole process of living ... of the whole substance of lived identities and relationships ...': it is as much a matter of the practical organisation of everyday routines as it is one of the furnishing of bodies of knowledge (in the confessional or doctor's surgery, a production quota or new rules for workplace behaviour).

Thus social movements from above shape the common sense which gives meaning to everyday routines in a way that enables dominant groups to manage the task of providing effective directions and orientations to the life-activity of subaltern groups. On a wider scale, it is also about meeting some of their diverse needs selectively, in ways which reinforce existing power relations, and about providing a political language in which they can express their thoughts about the world they inhabit. In this complex process, the existing social order is variously represented and experienced as natural (unchangeable), as purposive (and beneficial to subaltern interests), and as legitimate (and offering a language through which subaltern grievances can be expressed).

Hegemony, however, 'can never be singular ... [and] it does not just passively exist as a form of dominance' (Williams 1977: 112). On the one hand, the consent of subaltern groups is achieved through more or less contentious negotiations:

> Undoubtedly, the fact of hegemony presupposes that account be taken of the interests and the tendencies of the groups over which hegemony is to be exercised, and that a certain compromise equilibrium should be formed – in other words, that the leading group should make sacrifices of an economic-corporate kind. (Gramsci 1998: 161)

Hegemony, then, is best conceived of as 'a continuous process of formation and superseding of unstable equilibria ... between the interests of the fundamental group and those of the subordinate groups ...' (ibid.: 182). While the interests of dominant groups ultimately prevail in the construction of a given compromise equilibrium, it remains a site in which 'power is always being contested, legitimated, and redefined' (Mallon 1995: 6).

On the other hand, the common sense that the social movements from above seek to mould is not exhausted by ideologies of dominance. Common sense, rather, is a form of 'contradictory consciousness' (Gramsci 1998: 333, Ytterstad 2012): ideologies of dominance which cast the status quo as purposive and legitimate, and, more generally, hegemonic ways of being in the world, are fused with the practical and often tacit subaltern experiences of an existing social order as problematic and with the subaltern skills and responses developed in response to these experiences (see also Thompson 1993: 86–7). Obviously, the mediation of social experience through ideologies of dominance is not inconsequential; as Gramsci argues, the tension with subaltern experience and needs can 'produce a condition of moral and political passivity' (ibid.: 333). However, this passivity is in turn regularly disrupted and destabilised by the workings of 'good sense' – a Gramscian concept we return to below, which encompasses the embryonic forms of a distinct subaltern consciousness

– as and when this becomes manifest in oppositional action from below (ibid.: 327–8). Thus, when we try to make sense of how social movements from above seek to mould everyday routines and common sense through the construction of hegemony, it is crucial to recognise that this is never 'a finished and monolithic ideological formation' but rather 'a problematic, contested, political *process* of struggle' (Roseberry 1995: 77).

If movements from above draw on, and seek to reinforce, their dominant position within economic relationships (of whatever kind), power structures, and everyday routines and common sense, they do so on a very wide range of scales. At one end of the scale is the manager successfully defusing a potential workplace conflict, the group shaming of a woman who breaches patriarchal rules, or the police officers brutalising minority youth – the routine, local, re-enactment and re-establishment of particular arrangements. At the other are vast processes of change such as the installation of neoliberalism as a global mode of economic organisation, the shift from private to public patriarchy in western societies, or the construction of national-developmentalist coalitions in newly independent states. Because their goal is to construct, maintain, or deepen a system, movements from above are faced with the challenge *both* of constructing and maintaining the particular skilled activities that express their rationality at a macro-level *and* of making this 'stick' in the recalcitrant complexities of multiple local contexts. Movements from above face a real challenge; and this is an important source of strength for movements from below. It also, of course, means that movements from above are forever *moving* in their responses to other social actors, and we now turn to this dynamic.

The Strategies of Social Movements from Above: Defensive/Offensive

When social movements from above mobilise economic, political and cultural resources in projects that seek to maintain or extend the hegemonic position of dominant groups, they do so in relation to how their activity is impacted by and impacts upon social movements from below. Acting within determinate fields of force, social movements from above craft strategies that we can broadly categorise as being defensive or offensive in character.

Defensive strategies tend to be deployed in the context of substantial challenges from below, and can involve either accommodation or repression. A defensive strategy focused on accommodation typically revolves around granting concessions to the claims and demands of movements from below with the aim of appeasing and defusing a force that might otherwise threaten the existing social formation. As we argue in Chapter 4, the coming of the Keynesian welfare state in the global North and decolonisation in the global South after 1945 are archetypical examples of an accommodative strategy from above. Raising wages in a specific workplace, or offering a successful union organiser a management position, are others, at a far smaller scale.

Defensive strategies centred on repression revolve around countering social movements from below through violent coercion and the suspension of civil and political liberties. A typical example of such a strategy would be the state terrorism that authoritarian regimes in Latin America unleashed upon democratic and other radical popular movements in the 1970s and 1980s (see Dávila 2013). Similarly, when the Chinese regime mobilised the army against protesters in Tiananmen Square in 1989, this was a strategic choice informed by the awareness that a movement which began as an uprising of students and intellectuals was attracting substantial support from the urban working class, and thus becoming a potential anti-systemic force (Selden 1993: Chapter 8, Meisner 1996: Chapter 14).

However, repressive strategies from above do not only revolve around the mobilisation of military force: social movement activists are used to authorities (courts, workplaces, school authorities, and so on) invoking sanctions, the use of physical coercion and low-level dirty tricks. The neoliberal decades in particular have witnessed the mobilisation of a range of molecular but by no means less significant forms of coercive power in the face of potential and actual discontent and opposition. To take just one example, in the mid-1990s, Britain witnessed the introduction of the Criminal Justice Act as an attempt to prevent counter-cultures ranging from new age travelling, squatting, and the rave scene from becoming loci of large-scale protest (McKay 1996) – a legislative signal which paralleled a much longer use of evictions, police harassment and exclusion from services directed against such groups.

More recently – and particularly in the context of the so-called War on Terror – legislation that purports to bolster national security has eroded fundamental civil and political liberties (Herman 2014, Chomsky 2007). These attacks on basic democratic precepts intertwine with the dramatic extension of powers of surveillance in everyday life (Matellart 2010), the intensified policing and incarceration of dispossessed and marginalised populations (Gilmore 2007, Wacquant 2009), and what is described as the militarisation of protest policing (Wood 2014, Scholl 2013) to constrain the spaces in which resistance to neoliberal capitalism is articulated and enacted, at both macro- and micro-scales.

Accommodative and repressive strategies are not mutually exclusive. Rather, social movements from above mobilise accommodative and repressive strategies in selective combination: while some movements might be met with partial inclusion or reforms from above, others may encounter systematic coercion – for example, in the way that the Italian *compromesso storico* brought together Christian Democrats and parliamentary Communists while the autonomous Left was suppressed, or in the way that the US civil rights movement was successful in bringing about significant national legislation, whereas the Black Power movement was met with coordinated campaigns of repression. Indeed, repressive strategies do not necessarily abandon all attempts at gaining the consent of subaltern groups; rather, they restrict the orbit of consent to a narrower set of groups whose participation is needed for the successful exercise of coercion (Cox 2014b). When faced with such projects, which seek to separate and exclude movements from below, it is crucial for activists not only to see civil and political rights as the gains of past movement struggles, vital to the future development of social movement projects, but also to seek to disaggregate the repressive coalitions potentially ranged against them (Cox 2014c).

When social movements from above resort to offensive strategies, these typically assume the form of attacks on the truce lines left by movement struggles of the past (for example, freedom of speech and assembly, workplace power, women's rights, or welfare gains). Such strategies seek to undermine and reverse victories won and concessions gained by movements from below in order to attain hegemony for newly dominant social groups, or to restore the power of already-dominant groups. The deployment of offensive strategies tends to occur in contexts and at conjunctures where an extant social formation – in whole or in part – enters into crisis and starts to show signs of breakdown. Although such systemic crises constitute a space in which movements from below can launch challenges, it is also a space where offensive movements from above can make a bid to consolidate or renew the hegemony of dominant groups.

Neoliberalism is, of course, the most recent example of an offensive movement from above seeking to restore and extend the hegemony of already-dominant social groups. As Chapter 4 argues, its prime achievement has been restoring the class power of capital by fundamentally undermining the social restrictions and regulations imposed on capitalist accumulation as a result of the struggles of working classes and colonised peoples in the first half of the twentieth century.

In yet other cases, social movements from above may show the dynamics of a 'passive revolution' where an alliance between existing and new dominant groups via the state enables the introduction of a new form of capitalism without directly dislodging existing dominant groups and the social relations on which their hegemony has been constructed (Gramsci 1998). Such dynamics were characteristic, for example, of the articulation of India's post-colonial development project, and of neoliberal restructuring in Mexico and Chile (Kaviraj 1997, Morton 2011, Motta 2008).

When confronted with offensive social movement projects from above, the difficulty for activists is often that of avoiding a purely defensive response, for example, by mobilising to protect institutions whose value can be ambiguous (indeed, it may be this very ambiguity which leads dominant groups to suspect that they can find popular allies when targeting them). Addressing this difficulty means moving beyond defensive responses to open up new spaces of conflict and to develop social movement projects that articulate alternatives both to existing institutions and the attacks of social movements from above. Movements from below in the global South have been capable of precisely this, in the sense that their resistance to neoliberalism has been gradually transformed from a defence of how some subaltern needs had been incorporated in post-colonial development projects to a championing of alternatives to both developmentalism and neoliberalism (Motta and Nilsen 2011, Nilsen 2015).

It should be clear from the complexity and scope of these examples that we are suggesting useful categories for empirical research and practical strategy rather than watertight conceptual compartments. Such categories help us, today, to see neoliberalism as process and project rather than eternal reality; to contrast the very different possibilities and limits of resistance in different places, and to think about how and where we can extend our alliances, raise the costs of the neoliberal assault and detach its allies. This is where mobilisation to transcend and construct something more valuable than 'the house that neoliberalism built' begins. This brings us to social movements from below.

Social Movements From Below: The Collective Agency of Subordinate Groups

The practical starting-point for social movements from below, and hence also for theorising them, is this: while social movements from above seek to create and consolidate economic and power structures which in turn give direction and meaning to the routines and lived experience of everyday life, social movements from below tend to reverse this order. Social movements from below, that is, grow out of people's experience of a concrete lifeworld that is somehow problematic relative to their needs and capacities, and from their attempts to combine, organise and mobilise in order to do something about this. A social movement from below can thus be defined as *the organisation of multiple forms of locally generated skilled activity around a rationality expressed and organised by subaltern social groups, which aims either to challenge the constraints that a dominant structure of needs and capacities impose upon the development of new needs and capacities or to defend aspects of an existing dominant structure which accommodate some of their specific needs and capacities.*

Movements from below are not static entities; they change and develop, and a crucial feature of these changes and developments is the possibility of moving beyond forms of collective action that are limited to specific and locally circumscribed grievances, demands and objectives. In the process of organising and mobilising, activists may come to 'join the dots' between their particular, situated experiences and the underlying structures that engender these experiences. In doing so, they may also come to 'join hands' with other groups engaged in oppositional projects elsewhere – an insurgent architecture which revolves around 'forging connections [and] finding conceptions that resonate across differences' (Cooper 2000: 218). This in turn can lead to alterations in the form and direction of collective action towards more encompassing movement projects seeking to achieve more radical forms of change.

This process – which we call the *movement process* – can be likened to a journey in which activists starts from 'the inside' – a lifeworld marked in all its aspects by the powerful workings of social movements from above – and work their way towards 'the outside' – an alternative social organisation of needs and capacities. In the following, we set out a theoretical framework that allows us to make sense of how activists proceed on this journey – that is, we propose a theory of how and why activists in movements from below can deepen, widen and radicalise the scope and direction of their praxis. The framework for this theorisation revolves around a series of ideal-typical categories that may allow us to grapple with the various phases of movement processes and the characteristic features of those mechanisms through which the praxis of subaltern groups 'shifts gear' towards more encompassing and radical projects. The idea of a movement process centred on the widening and deepening of the scope of collective action from below can sound suspiciously linear and teleological. With Lukács (1971), we want to stress that the notion of a movement process and the elements of this process outlined in the following sections are logical categories devised to grasp the possibilities and potentialities of development in the collective skilled activity of subaltern groups, not foregone conclusions or automatic trajectories.

Many movements do *not* develop in this way: people remain trapped in grumbling and resentment without taking political action, or come to act in purely local and particularist ways, or remain focused on a single issue. There are clearly also a range of conditions which make a difference as to whether movements develop, stay at a particular level of development, or fall back. Of particular importance here are the actions of movements from above – as opponents and addressees of movements from below, in their various interventions into movement processes, in the provision of intellectual leadership on their own terms, and so on.

Equally important, however, are movements from below: as we have noted above, this is where theory becomes crucial. Activist theory, not in any grand sense but in that of an 'ABC of activism', involves both learning from movements that fail to get off the ground or to get beyond a particular stage, and identifying the most strategic moves for movement development. For example, the kind of alliance building which tends towards generalising an issue and raising the stakes is clearly a fundamental step in movement development. Activists have to learn this – whether for themselves, painfully and slowly, via movement organisations and training, or through reading and reflection – in order to intervene effectively and to realise the potential for development inherent in movement struggles – and to support the fuller expression of the local rationalities underpinning the movement.

Local Rationalities and Militant Particularisms

In theorising a movement process, the starting-point is people's situated experience of a given lifeworld, the context of our daily lives and the multiplicity of practical routines and received wisdoms that give direction and meaning to everyday activity. In order to grapple with the experiential rationality that guides this activity, we draw on Gramsci's conception of common sense. This is essentially an amalgamation of two components: the established ways of doing things and their rationale, which constitute the molecular workings of the hegemonic projects of movements from above, and the practical and often tacit experience of those workings as somehow problematic and the various forms of practice developed as a response to and geared towards countering frustrations with the everyday status quo. These latter elements can be thought of in terms of Gramsci's notion of 'good sense', by which he referred to those more or less submerged aspects of subaltern consciousness that indicate 'that the social group in question may indeed have its own conception of the world'. For Gramsci, 'good sense' constitutes 'the healthy nucleus that exists in 'common sense' ... which deserves to be made more unitary and coherent' (1998: 327–8). Good sense, then, is that reservoir of practical consciousness that may serve as a basis for subaltern resistance.[10]

The nature and origins of good sense can be considered as a *local rationality*, which can in turn be defined as *a formal characteristic about the way people make sense of and engage with the world which is capable of being generalised and taking on a life of its own*. Such a local rationality is not a single monolithic 'thing' but rather those sets of ways of being, doing and thinking that people develop in attempting to oppose the routines and received wisdoms that define the hegemonic elements of common sense. The development of such ways of being, doing and thinking is in turn rooted in the experience of infringements upon subaltern needs and capacities that are accommodated in a dominant structure of entrenched needs and capacities, or constraints imposed upon the development of new needs and capacities. In the first case, local rationalities typically assume a defensive character in opposition to attempts from above to reorder extant structures so as to extend the power base of dominant groups. An example of such defensive local rationalities would be the 'moral economy' that informed the bread riots in the English countryside in the eighteenth century (Thompson 1993: Chapter 4). In the second case, local rationalities typically assume a more offensive character where subaltern groups seek to carve out greater space for the satisfaction, deployment and development of emergent radical needs and capacities. An example would be the Dublin-based counter-cultural movement milieux analysed by Laurence where projects of 'reflexive autonomy' or 'autonomous self-development' revolved around 'the creation of meanings and practices which not only defend the "free space" necessary for the project but directly enable this self-development ...' (Cox 1999b: 52).

To avoid accusations of romanticising resistance, we should say that we do not see local rationalities as hermetically sealed spaces of radical otherness and difference.[11] Again, Gramsci's discussion of good sense is instructive in that it emphasises the composite and often contradictory nature of subaltern consciousness and culture. Directly after the insistence that a subaltern social group 'may indeed have its own conception of the world', he proceeds to argue as follows:

> ... this same group has, for reasons of submission and intellectual subordination, adopted a conception which is not its own but is borrowed from another group ... [T]his is the conception that it follows in 'normal times' – that is when its conduct is not independent and autonomous, but submissive and subordinate. (Gramsci 1998: 327)

Local rationalities, then, are not a fixed essence of otherness inherent to subaltern social groups, but rather a repertoire of skills, practices and perceptions typically forged in conflictual dialogue with the hegemonic projects of social movements from above.[12]

This in turn means that local rationalities can be more or less developed and articulated in the collective skilled activity of subaltern groups as against those forms of rationality that characterise the hegemonic projects of movements from above. In highly repressive contexts, for example, they might exist as what Scott calls 'hidden transcripts' – as 'a critique of power spoken behind the back of the dominant' (1990: xii), and concealed under a veil of feigned compliance and deference. For example, mobilisation among Adivasis in the Narmada Valley started in a context where the relationship between oppressors – local representatives of the state – and the oppressed was one of total deference and submission which amounted to a state of 'everyday tyranny' (Nilsen 2010: Chapter 3). A catalytic intervention by urban, educated activists was necessary for a transition from deference to defiance to take place (see also Baviskar 1995: Chapter 8, Nilsen 2012). In other cases, they might exist much more openly and thoroughly as a cultural fabric that saturates the outlook and activity of subaltern groups. In contrast to the 'everyday tyranny' endured by Adivasis in the Narmada Valley, there are the 'cultures of resistance' that Peluso (1992) identifies among Javanese peasants who consistently defy and breach state forest laws as way of maintaining and controlling resource access and thus also their means of social reproduction.

Similarly, the 'pillarised subcultures' of the twentieth-century European working class, in countries such as interwar Germany or post-war Italy, represent situations where local rationalities had achieved a very large space for institutional articulation and whole generations could grow up within a taken-for-granted, partly oppositional culture (Cox 2009). In such contexts what is involved is not so much a 'whole way of life' as a 'whole way of struggle' (Hall 1989: 61). Lichterman's (1996) discussion of different forms of environmental protest captures this historical variability well. His middle-class,[13] mostly white, US Green participants found themselves largely isolated from the cultures they were born into and needed to construct new activist communities as a means of mutual support. By contrast, his black and Latina anti-toxics campaigners were thoroughly embedded in their own communities, where campaigning and political opposition were acceptable parts of everyday culture – and 'activists' were not seen as a separate kind of human being.

At times, a local rationality may give rise to or serve as the basis for overt acts of confrontation with and defiance of social movements from above. This might happen when subaltern groups come to act 'as an organic totality' (Gramsci 1998: 327) on the basis of the extraction and development of oppositional ways of being, doing and thinking in popular consciousness and culture:

> Critical understanding of self takes place therefore through a struggle of political 'hegemonies' and of opposing directions, first in the ethical field and then in the field of politics proper, in order to arrive at the working out of a higher level of one's own conception of reality. Consciousness of being part of a particular hegemonic force (that is to say, political consciousness) is the first stage towards a further progressive self-consciousness in which theory and practice will be one. (Ibid.: 333)

We propose the term 'militant particularism' for those forms of struggle that can emerge if such a process of extraction and development takes place: when local rationalities are transformed from tacit potentialities to explicitly oppositional practices deployed in conflictual encounters with dominant groups. An example can be found in Fantasia's analysis of wildcat strikes in an iron foundry in New Jersey (1988: Chapter 3), where intra-group affinities among workers crystallised as 'a locus of oppositional sentiment' in direct confrontations with plant management, and eventually manifested 'an incipient organizational form' through a network among those workers inclined towards radical activism (ibid.: 110). The wildcat strikes were specific conflicts over specific issues in a specific place that drew on 'cultures of solidarity' understood as 'a cultural expression that arises within the wider culture, yet which is emergent in its embodiment of oppositional practices and meanings' (ibid.: 17).

The concept 'militant particularism', coined by Williams (1989: 249), has been developed by David Harvey (1996, 2000) to refer to the particular origins of movement struggles. It refers to how 'politics is always embedded in "ways of life" and "structures of feeling" peculiar to places and communities' (Harvey 2000: 55, see also Harvey 1996: Chapter 1) and is hence characterised by this specificity and situatedness, both in terms of the issues that are struggled over and the practices, skills, idioms and imaginaries that are deployed in such confrontations. A militant particularism, then, can be defined as *those forms of struggle that emerge when a subaltern group deploys specific skills and knowledges in open confrontation with a dominant group in a particular place and at a particular time in a particular conflict over a particular issue.*

The extraction and development of local rationalities and concurrent eruption of militant particularist struggles can be a condensed and intense affair taking place over a short period – such as Fantasia's wildcat strikes – or a long and drawn-out process of confrontation, intervention, negotiation and persuasion between actors who see resistance as 'fertile' and those who see resistance as 'futile'. To continue our NBA example: its origins can be traced to a number of social action groups working with issues of tribal rights and welfare in Madhya Pradesh and Maharashtra (see Nilsen 2010). In the Adivasi villages of Alirajpur, Madhya Pradesh, the organisation Khedut Mazdoor Chetna Sangath (The Peasants and Workers Consciousness Union) or KMCS focused on securing the customary use rights of forest resources for tribal communities (Nilsen 2010: Chapter 3, Baviskar 1995: Chapter 8). This, however, meant confronting an 'everyday tyranny' enacted by low-level state officials – police officers, forest rangers, revenue officials – who regularly beat up villagers who were found using the forest or forest resources, and exacted heavy bribes from these communities to allow them access to the forest. This had become a regular feature of the relationship between villagers and state officials to the extent that overt resistance was unthinkable. This only changed when the villagers came into contact with a small group of urban, educated activists and together with them confronted the state officials with the unlawfulness of their actions, thus also asserting their own usufruct rights and civil rights.

These turning-points can be thought of as *catalytic events*, that is, as confrontational episodes in which the logic and legitimacy of dominant power relations are demonstrably reversed, thus constituting a tangible manifestation of the possibility and potentiality of resistance. Such catalytic events raise broader questions about 'official reality' and encourage people to think anew, to discover and articulate their own local rationalities. These particular events were of course underpinned by awareness-raising carried out by urban, educated activists among the Adivasi communities about the constitutional rights they possessed as citizens of the Indian nation, rights which would protect them against the wanton abuse of petty officials. In this sense, these activists played the role of *catalysts*, as someone who introduces new ideas or ways of thinking about extant social relations which has the potential of empowering subaltern social groups.[14] Catalytic events can then be understood as enactments of these ideas and ways of thinking – enactments which serve to validate both the ideas and the activists that introduced them. Furthermore, a constant theme in villagers' accounts was how, through this mobilisation process, they learned how to deal with their everyday tyrants. 'I learned how to speak to them' is a common statement among the activists in the villages of Alirajpur. Here we have, then, a militant particularism forged around the defence and extension of a particular local rationality, ripe with intersecting learning processes. The acquisition of an awareness of universal rights intersects with the more elusive breaking of fear and building of courage *vis-à-vis* former oppressors, which in turn intersects with the building of trust and solidarity with urban, educated activists, which in turn intersects with the acquisition of activist skills.

From Militant Particularism to Campaigns

In his discussion of the particularist origins of labour struggles, Williams emphasised the practical possibility of transcending those particularist origins and building towards a more encompassing form of mobilisation:

> Of course almost all labour struggles begin as particularist. People recognize some condition and problem they have in common and make the effort to work together to change or solve it ... The unique and

> extraordinary character of working-class self-organization has been that it has tried to connect particular struggles to a general struggle in one quite special way. It has set out, as a movement, to make real what is at first sight the extraordinary claim that the defence and advancement of certain particular interests, properly brought together, are in fact in the general interest. (Williams 1989: 249)

A fundamental aspect of militant particularisms is the fact that the practices, skills, idioms and imaginaries of which they are made up can be generalised, and that through such generalisation they can transcend the particular locale in which they emerged and potentially be applied across a spectrum of specific situations and singular struggles. This process takes place when activists involved in a particularist struggle in one given locale make connections with other activists engaged in similar struggles elsewhere, and start making those connections and finding those conceptions that resonate across differences. Through the making of such connections, activists typically discover and create common ground between them: 'common denominators' are discovered in the seemingly disparate conflicts in which they are engaged, common adversaries are named, and common strategies and collective identities are developed across social and spatial boundaries. These practical activities of mutual learning and development of self-understanding, communication, cooperation and organisation between militant particularisms bring about a widening and deepening of the scope of collective action. As such they constitute the first steps in a process through which movements from below may 'shift gears, transcend particularities, and arrive at some conception of a universal alternative to that social system which is the source of their difficulties' through 'a "translation" from the concrete to the abstract' (Harvey 2000: 241, 242). The organisation of militant particularisms across social and spatial boundaries thus entails something more than putting potatoes in a sack (Marx 1984); it entails the creation of a form of movement activity which we call *campaigns* and which can be defined as *the organisation of a range of local responses to specific situations in ways that connect people across these situations and around a generalised challenge to the construction of those situations.*

One obvious example is the development of opposition to toxic waste incinerators in Ireland in the late 1990s and early 2000s (Murray 2003, Leonard 2005). Rather than remain (as many politicians no doubt hoped they would) at the 'NIMBY' level of opposition to a specific incinerator site proposal – 'incinerators yes, just not here!' – or at the level of opposition to incinerators but acceptance of large-scale landfill 'superdumps', campaigners rapidly moved *both* to build national links with other anti-incinerator groups and to avoid being played off against anti-dump groups, developing networks arguing instead for alternative waste strategies. In this and similar processes (Allen and Jones 1990, Allen 2004), the local rationalities of poor rural communities proved thoroughly capable not only of generating their own militant particularisms but of creating large-scale campaigns connecting them with many other social actors.

The Narmada Bachao Andolan, as it eventually became, is another example of campaign-formation. Opposition to the dam project did not simply fall from the sky, but was the outcome of learning processes which in turn intersected with and underpinned organisation building (Nilsen 2010: Chapters 5 and 6, see also Baviskar 1995, Dwivedi 2006, Sangvai 2000). When the news of the impending dam project and the displacement of tribal villages that would follow in its wake dawned on existing social action groups in the states of Gujarat, Maharashtra and Madhya Pradesh, a two-pronged process was instigated. Firstly, an intense questioning of the authorities responsible for the project in order to attain proper information about the extent of displacement and the strategies for compensation and resettlement was implemented. Secondly, the organisations also conducted their own surveys of the extent of displacement, the claims of benefits that the dam would yield, and the resettlement strategies.

Two results followed: questioning the authorities was met with an unwillingness to provide answers, thus prompting a realisation that they could not be trusted; while the movement's surveying revealed that the extent of displacement was severely underestimated, the claimed benefits highly exaggerated, and the plans for resettlement dismally inadequate. Here we see a shedding of illusions about the character of the responsible authorities; but also a building of counter-expertise about the dam project itself – these changes representing a shift beyond the militant particularisms of the social action groups that had emerged in Gujarat, Maharashtra and Madhya Pradesh.

These processes in turn took place in the context of the emergence both nationally and internationally of a political space where anti-dam struggles throughout the world were establishing links between each other, and the emergence of a generalised critique of the social and ecological impact of big dams. In the Narmada Valley, this had political and organisational ramifications in that it became the basis for taking the mobilisation process towards the 'campaign level' through a declaration of wholesale opposition to the dam project and, moreover, the formation of the pan-state organisation the Narmada Bachao Andolan, from the various groups that had been working in the different states affected. Moreover, the Andolan's politics was not one of merely opposing the Sardar Sarovar Project, or the Narmada Valley Development Project of which it was a part, but a general critique of the destructiveness of dam projects as such (see Nilsen 2010: Chapter 8).

Campaigns typically cut across spatial scales. The NBA's pan-state campaign against the SSP was in turn nested in a network which spanned across spatial scales, from a national support network consisting of solidarity groups in urban centres to a transnational advocacy network linking the NBA with environmental and human rights activists in the North. This network was crucial in carrying out the successful campaign against World Bank funding of the Sardar Sarovar Project (see Khagram 2004, Sen 1999, Udall 1995).

Another example is opposition to genetically modified foods. The issues involved are clearly very different (as critics observe) for Indian farmers concerned about becoming more dependent on multinationals, for rural French activists hostile to the capitalist politics of food (Morena 2013), or for urban European consumers worried about the health risks involved – but the point is precisely that activists do not start out identical with each other.[15] The process of campaigning against GM foods was one of *connecting* these different militant particularisms in opposition to the hegemony of market logics.

The development of alternative waste management strategies in the case of Irish anti-incinerator campaigns and alternative technologies for the generation of electricity and hydropower in the Narmada Valley also testify to another potentiality inherent to the process of building campaigns. As Harvey (2000: 241) remarks, many militant particularist struggles start out as defensive projects – indeed, protesting incinerators and dams is initially an act of defence against their harmful and destructive effects upon people and environment. However, the widening and deepening of the scope of oppositional collective action may also entail a transformation towards something more proactive and offensive in that the focal point of activism may shift from a defence of that which was or is against the impositions of designs from above, towards an articulation of alternatives to extant practices and thus a widening of activists' perceptions of 'the limits of the possible'. Put slightly differently, a campaign can start off as a defence of entrenched subaltern needs and capacities and metamorphose into the articulation of emergent radical needs and capacities.

In Ireland, a powerful example has been the opposition to Shell's gas pipeline project in Erris, Co. Mayo. Here, a campaign which started with the health and safety concerns of local farmers about an experimental high-pressure pipeline set to run close to their homes developed through a set of alliances – with urban leftists, environmental activists and trade unionists – and the local experience of state and corporate repression into a much wider-reaching set of concerns: about the ownership of natural resources, the politics of energy, civil rights and the assertion of a different set of priorities geared around human needs. The campaign is now playing an important role in transferring this learning to communities in other areas facing fracking.

Towards Social Movement Projects

While the development of campaigns revolves around a process in which the boundaries of militant particularisms are transcended through translation between and abstraction from local struggles, the construction of collective identities that cut across socio-spatial divides, and the widening of activist perceptions of the limits of the possible, they are still a circumscribed form of praxis in that they do not take aim at the social totality as an object of transformation. Another way of saying this is that campaigns are typically constructed as field-specific forms of collective action: the organisation of local struggles against waste incinerators, for instance, may engender the articulation of a generalised challenge towards a certain kind of environmental policy and the positing of alternative approaches to environmental politics, but it does not necessarily or automatically – or for all participants – relate this challenge to those generative mechanisms inherent to a social totality which lead to the development and implementation of the specific policy-field the campaign is struggling in.

However, if activists pursue the insurgent architecture of connecting different localised struggles and indeed seemingly different struggles, if they engage in a critical interrogation of the structures that engender the problems they seek to address and that may frustrate their campaigns, they *may* also come to an understanding of the systemic dimensions of the specific field in which they operate, as well as their own place within this field. From this awareness, they *may* in turn start to move beyond the field-specificity of campaign politics and towards a form of movement activity which posits the social totality as the object of challenge and transformation. We propose the term *social movement project* for the conceptualisation of those forms of movement activity which involve making the connection between local situations as seen from below and the common features of their relationship to the social totality. Social movement projects can be defined as *(a) challenges to the social totality which (b) aim to control the self-production of society and (c) have or are developing the potential for the kind of hegemony – leading the skilled activity of different social groups – that would make (b) and hence (a) possible.*

Drawing on Touraine (1981), such a social movement project stands out from other forms of collective agency from below by virtue of its capacity to *identify* (I) its own actors socially; name its central *opponent* (O), and recognising that the social *totality* (T) is the product and object of such struggles. In other words, there is a return 'up' the sequence from opposing everyday routines to opposing the structures which generate them, and finally to directly confronting the movements from above which have constructed the whole. Touraine identified the worker's movement, and in his own period the anti-nuclear power movement, as movements capable of achieving this. We differ from his perspective in that we do not share the view that there is only one such potential movement in any given society; moreover, it is worth noting that the anti-nuclear movement in France and elsewhere drew strongly from the historic Left (Rivat 2013).

The alter-globalisation movement constitutes a case of such a development (see Chapter 5). The movement is the outcome of a long process of communication between campaigns and militant particularist struggles organised through these campaigns spanning much of the 1990s. Through this process, 'particular struggles came to be understood in terms of a more general set of interconnections between problems and movements worldwide' (Gill 2000: 138). Indeed, 'the spontaneity of Seattle was a long time coming' (Wilkin 2000: 42, see also Broad and Heckscher 2003). The movement was able to turn its hand to resistance to war on Iraq in 2003, to the struggle for power in Latin America and to resistance to austerity in Europe (Flesher Fominaya and Cox 2013), with shifts in emphasis and participation but sufficient capacity to relate one issue to another and to argue, against neoliberalism's TINA ('There is no alternative'), TATA ('There are thousands of alternatives').

The Narmada Bachao Andolan has, on its own and through national movement networks, embedded their campaign against dam building in an overarching critique of the dominant practices and discourses of development in post-colonial India. Concurrently, they have also articulated a vision of alternative development. The critique of dominant notions of development centres on the argument that the promises of national development articulated with the coming of Independence have been betrayed: subaltern groups have been marginalised both socially and politically, and natural resources are being depleted solely for the purposes of enriching elite groups. The conception of alternative development concurrently centres on social justice, environmental sustainability and participatory democracy (see Nilsen 2010: Chapter 8).

For instance, in conjunction with the monsoon *satyagraha*[16] of 2000, the NBA staged a celebration of India's Independence Day on 15 August. In the Adivasi village of Nimgavhan (Maharashtra), Independence Day began with the hoisting of both the Indian flag and the NBA's banner. Following this, a confrontational event erupted. Two teachers were present at the ceremony. They were employed at local state-run schools, but the reality was that these teachers hardly ever showed up to teach. The teachers were confronted by agitated villagers and activists who argued that their vocation amounted to little more than picking up their paycheques. This dismal state of affairs was then thrown into sharp relief with the following point on the programme: the congratulation of young Adivasis who had fared well in official schools after first having completed basic schooling in the Andolan's *Jeevan Shalas* – literally 'schools for life', built and run by the Andolan with a curriculum adapted to Adivasi realities. Following this, the celebrations continued in the nearby village of Domkhedi with the inauguration of a small hydroelectric project. A minor dam had been constructed on a small stream adjacent to Domkhedi, which, when combined with a pedal-powered generator, provided electricity to the village for the first time ever. Whereas the SSP threatened to displace the villagers from their lands and produce costly electricity that would only be available to affluent and predominantly urban consumers, here was a project controlled and executed at village level that actually had the potential of delivering a tangible improvement in people's lives.

Through the celebration of Independence Day, the NBA conveyed a narrative about its political project. It was a narrative which recognised the freedom struggle and the attainment of Independence as fundamental events and achievements. However, at the same time, it was a narrative of a national project profoundly out of kilter. The 'tryst with destiny', in this narrative, had gone awry; the promises of freedom and development have been hijacked by elite interests and thus betrayed – leaving large sections of the population by the wayside as outcasts. Simultaneously, the focus on the NBA's constructive activities expressed a political project of alternative development, which resonated far beyond the Narmada Valley. The vision of alternative development then centres on reclaiming the lost promises of the struggle for Independence – elements of past movement processes from below, harnessed by a now-dominant project from above – and devising strategies that will secure, say, social equality and participatory decision-making processes. Here we have something akin to a social movement project, whose most striking feature is that it has emerged through a long and drawn-out process of learning. This process has fundamentally revolved around the articulation of ever more encompassing and radical perspectives for understanding a very specific conflict (see also Nilsen 2008b, 2013).

At the heart of the challenges that social movement projects level at the social totality lie emergent structures of radical needs and capacities, and the transformative potentialities of a movement project resides in the objective of fully instantiating and realising such an emergent structure. Militant particularisms and the local rationalities from which they derive, as well as the campaigns through which militant particularisms are transformed into generic challenges to the construction of a specific kind of situation, may well express the development of new and radical needs and capacities. However, what sets social movement projects apart from militant particularisms and campaigns is this: to the extent that the latter are expressive of an emergent structure of radical needs and capacities, they are oriented towards its partial instantiation and realisation through the modification of extant structures, whereas the former consciously, actively and explicitly seek the transcendence of a dominant structure of entrenched needs and capacities and the constitution of altogether new forms of social organisation in which an emergent structure of radical needs and capacities can be fully instantiated and realised.

The alter-globalisation movement's slogan 'Another World Is Possible' provides a good example. It signals an insistence that alternative ways of socially organising the satisfaction, deployment and development of needs and capacities are within reach. In the words of de Sousa Santos (2003: 6–7), the slogan articulates a 'critical utopia' which revolves around a rejection of the 'conservative utopia' of neoliberalism and its 'radical denial of alternatives to present-day reality'. Alter-globalisation, in short, claims 'the existence of alternatives to neoliberal globalisation' (ibid.: 8). This marks a rupture *vis-à-vis* the early forms of protest against neoliberal restructuring, which were essentially defensive in character: strike waves in the North which sought to restore the Keynesian 'rights and entitlements threatened by neoliberal restructuring' (De Angelis 2000: 14) and the IMF riots in the South which sought to restore the social wage guaranteed in the developmentalist pact between the state and the popular classes (Walton and Seddon 1994: 48–50). It also marks a shift *vis-à-vis* many of the single-issue campaigns of the 1990s, which sought to curtail the scope of the project of neoliberal restructuring, for instance, the campaign against the Multilateral Agreement on Investments.

As we stressed earlier, the development of movement processes – be they in the Narmada Valley, in Mayo, or in and through the movement of movements – is open-ended. It depends upon the movement's capacity to extend its potential for hegemony through the forging of ever-more and ever-stronger connections with localised struggles as well as its capacity for resilience in the face of opposition from above. This is, of course, true for social movement projects in general – their fate is not written in the stars, but is worked out in their success or failure at connecting with local rationalities, militant particularisms and campaigns: for example, the relationship between the newer generations of anti-capitalist activists in Occupy and *indignados* movements, campaigns against austerity in various sectors of northern society, and wider social groups affected by neoliberalism.

This process can sound suspiciously linear, and of course as all activists know, it is easier to have a map of how movements *can* develop than to win the battles – both internal and external – which enable such a development. However, this analysis amounts to a kind of 'recipe' knowledge which experienced activists routinely draw on when engaging with local struggles. It is also, and importantly, a means by which newer activists can avoid having to constantly 'reinvent the wheel': not everyone (thankfully) starts in the situation of total domination by a movement from above. Thus the history of past movements can be drawn on for ideas, languages and repertoires of action (such as the constant referral to the past in Parisian revolutionary movements); contemporary movements in other countries or other sectors of society can form a valuable source of inspiration and support (such as the international links drawn on in the late 1960s by activists across northern countries), and 'traditionalised' social movements, which have become sedimented as everyday cultures, can be reactivated in response to new circumstances (such as the role of black churches in the US Civil Rights Movement). The sequence we suggest is thus a logical one, but not necessarily a chronological one in all cases (although as the NBA example suggests, individual movements can follow it more or less from one end to the other). In either case, it is praxis that drives this movement process and which can enable movements to develop, and to this we now turn.

Social Movements from Below as Praxis

So far we have presented a theory of social movements from below that emphasises the potential for change in the direction and form of the collective skilled activity of subaltern social groups. This section shifts the focus to a discussion of how praxis – the activity of reflecting 'today' on our experience of how we did things 'yesterday' so that we might do things differently 'tomorrow' – animates this process. We start with an elaboration of the making of critical consciousness and the production of knowledge through movement activity, and then move on to discuss struggles over meaning and the construction of discourses of resistance.

Consciousness and Learning in Social Movements from Below

In our discussion of the emergence of militant particularisms, we emphasised how such struggles tend to come about as the result of the abstraction and development of oppositional ways of being, doing and thinking in local rationalities. Here, we want to delve deeper into the character of this extraction and development by considering it as a learning process based on reflexive self-activity. As a starting-point, we propose the following two central processes in social movements: 'Firstly, movements *mobilize* people who were not necessarily previously active ... Secondly, social movements often *radicalize* people who were previously content with a view of the world designed for situations of relative quiescence' (Barker and Cox 2002: 21–2). The mobilisation and radicalisation that movements from below are based upon and entail involve a complex relation between experience, consciousness and knowledge.

To start with mobilisation: Barker and Cox (ibid.: 38) posit an admittedly simple but instructive model in which mobilisation results from a determinate experience of needs and capacities somehow being frustrated or constrained and people's equally frustrated or constrained attempts to do something about this through extant official channels:

> In the process they meet other people, and discover that this is a general situation, not just a reflection of their own inadequacies. They form an organization and try to lobby, but run up against increasingly systematic opposition. This experience brings home to them that the problem is not simply ill-will on the part of misguided individuals, but has deeper roots. (Ibid.: 38)

To become an activist, then, is in large part a question of learning that 'the system' does not work as it claims to, and that it will not simply stand aside and let people develop their needs and capacities freely, and thus also of learning that, in order to achieve change, people need to organize in order to build capacity to exert concerted and determined pressure against 'the system'. Movements can thus be understood as 'institutions' that people create 'that will enable them (indirectly, through a change in the social order) to meet needs that are currently not being met' (ibid.: 37).[17]

This model of mobilisation entails profound changes in consciousness; when people shed their illusions about extant structures and institutions, this is basically a process through which reflexive self-activity engenders a distancing from the hegemonic elements of common sense and simultaneously a process through which 'good sense' is rendered 'more unitary and coherent'. Gramsci attributed the capacity of subaltern groups for self-activity to a growing detachment from hegemonic conceptions of the world: 'If the ruling class has lost its consensus, i.e. is no longer 'leading' but only 'dominant', exercising coercive force alone, this means precisely that the great masses have become detached from their traditional ideologies, and no longer believe what they used to believe previously, etc.' (1998: 275–6).

In Freirean terms, what people develop through such reflexive self-activity is 'critical consciousness' in the form of the 'power to perceive critically *the way they exist* in the world *with which* and *in which* they find themselves …' (Freire 1972: 70–71). Hall's example of dominant, negotiated and oppositional understandings of strikes (see Chapter 1) is a good example of how critical consciousness develops: people move from accepting a dominant reading of the way they exist in the world where the current nature of this world and their place in it is accepted, to a negotiated reading in which aspects or parts of that existence and that world are viewed as unjust or unfit and in need of change, and ultimately towards an oppositional reading which involves a rejection of the extant social order as a whole.

The movement from dominant to oppositional readings constitutes a process of radicalisation, which takes place through and is nurtured by knowledge production in movement activity. It is a consequence of how activists within movements pose and seek answers to such questions as: 'What exactly are those needs and capacities that we feel frustrated about? What is it about the extant social order that leads to their frustration or imposes constraints upon them? How can we best achieve those changes necessary for their realisation?' These are questions that emanate from the practical concerns of taking movement activity 'forward':

> The starting point is often the practical critique of common sense … When budding activists start to think their way out of 'common sense' or to break what Blake described as 'mind-forg'd manacles', there is often an interest in forms of generalized understanding that might offer clarity, justification and a broader vision to underpin their activity. (Barker and Cox 2002: 10, 11)

Providing answers to such questions and developing such understandings are not contemplative affairs: answers are provided and understandings are developed through 'the two-way learning process involved in *movement*' (ibid.: 38–9). On the one hand, activists garner knowledge through their experience of encounters with opponents. This is first and foremost a result of the lessons drawn from the failures and successes of the strategies deployed in these encounters. Such successes and failures of course say something about the adequacy or otherwise of the means through which movements seek to realise their ends and thus enhance self-understanding within a movement. Furthermore, they reveal the inherent limits of the social order, both in terms of what dominant groups are prepared to or capable of accommodating in terms of challenges from below, and in terms of the cracks, fissures and weaknesses of this extant order which movements from below can exploit to develop momentum and leverage around the challenges they bring to bear on this order. Thus, an increasingly clearer self-understanding, a fuller grasp of social structure and historical process, and an increasingly adequate mode of organisation and struggle can be generated in the conflict with a movement's opponents.

On the other hand, activists garner knowledge through the sharing of experiences and discussions, dialogues and disputes over practical questions internally to the movement. Knowledge production in movements, especially as it is carried out by 'movement intellectuals', is characterised by two kinds of argument: firstly, 'the ideological and moral justification of the movement, the promotion and elaboration of its ideas and their defence against attack', and secondly 'the strategic and tactical proposal' as 'a complex proposition which links together a reading of the nature of the present situation ... with an action plan ... for the movement in the immediate future' (Barker and Cox 2002: 6). These arguments are in turn 'validated' internally in the movement itself, through their dismissal, acceptance, or modification by activists and finally and ultimately through the practical test of actual movement activity (see Barker 1996a).

So far we have mentioned concrete experience as a starting-point of the growth of awareness and knowledge production in movements from below and a clearer understanding of social structure and historical process as its result. To elaborate these points, we can turn to the following seminal passage from Piven and Cloward's *Poor People's Movements*:

> ... people experience deprivation and oppression within a concrete setting, not as the end product of large and abstract processes, and it is the concrete experience that moulds their discontent into specific grievances against specific targets. Workers experience the factory, the speeding rhythm of the assembly line, the foreman, the spies and the guards, the owner and the paycheck. They do not experience monopoly capitalism. People on relief experience the shabby waiting rooms, the overseer or the caseworker, and the dole. They do not experience American social welfare policy. Tenants experience the leaking ceilings and cold radiators, and they recognize the landlord. They do not recognize the banking, real estate, and construction systems. No small wonder, therefore, that when the poor rebel, they so often rebel against the overseer of the poor, or the slumlord, or the middling merchant, and not against the banks or the governing elites to whom the overseer, the slumlord, and the merchant also defer. In other words, it is the daily experience of people that shapes their grievances, establishes the measure of their demands, and point out the targets of their anger. (Piven and Cloward 1977: 20–21)

It is this determinate experiential basis – interpreted through cultural idioms unique to its time-space location – which gives militant particularisms the specific and circumscribed character of their grievances, demands and targets, and modes of representation. However, we argue that if activist knowledge production *starts* from specific experiences garnered in a concrete, particular and local lifeworld, it can *develop* towards an understanding of the dominant structure of entrenched needs and capacities that ultimately engender these experiences. Put differently, activists in a workers' movement may come to understand how monopoly capitalism generates the speeding rhythm of the assembly line, activists in movements of the unemployed may come to understand the workings of US social welfare policy behind the experience of the caseworker and the dole, and activists in a housing rights movement may come to understand the banking, real estate and construction systems that lie behind the leaking ceilings and the cold radiators.

Thus concrete experience – and our struggles to meet our needs – point towards underlying, abstract relationships and structures that explain why 'face-value' organising meets particular kinds of limits. Another way of putting this is that movements from below have an interest in gaining a broader understanding by organising, connecting different partial perspectives and extending their struggles (see Chapter 1). Indeed, it is the development of such understanding that underpins the construction of social movement projects as the logic implicit in participants' skilled activity is extended to a more comprehensive standpoint (Cox 1998: 7). As we stressed in Chapter 2, praxis is always already semiotic and cultural. So too with the praxis that animates social movements from below: it is characterised by struggles over the meaning of idioms and the interpretation of experiences of exploitation and oppression through such idioms.

Struggles over Meaning and Discourses of Resistance

The starting-point for a discussion of 'the ideological forms in which men become conscious of [a] conflict and fight it out' (Marx 1981b: 21) is the *relational* character of subaltern consciousness and culture. The sociolinguistics of Vološinov (1986; see also McNally 1995, 2001, Collins 2013) provide an apt lens through which to grasp the distinctively semiotic and cultural dimension of this argument. Vološinov's basic point is that in any given social formation there is, on the one hand, a common body of language with relatively stable meanings and, on the other hand, different social groups with different experiences of their positionality in that social formation who deploy that body of language to express and make claims for recognition of these experiences: 'Sign', Vološinov argues, 'becomes an arena of class struggle' (1986: 23).

All signs, that is, are 'refracted' by the 'intersection of differently oriented social interests within one and the same sign community' and are thus characterised by a range of inflections that reflect these differential interests and experiences – what Vološinov calls 'social multiaccentuality' (ibid.). This refraction and multiaccentuality stems from the active approaches of dominant and subaltern groups to the use of those words, idioms and symbols that the sign community is made up of: 'Conflicts between groups and classes ... interpolate every sign' (McNally 2001: 114). Dominant groups, Vološinov argues, will seek 'to impart a supraclass, eternal character to the ideological sign, to extinguish or drive inward the struggle between social value judgements which occur in it, to make the sign uniaccentual' (1986: 23). Subaltern groups on the other hand will tend to 'develop genres of their own which accent aspects of social experience, oppositional attitudes and the like, that official discourses attempt to deny' (McNally 1995: 18).

This affects how we understand the engagement of social movements from below in struggles over meaning. Following Steinberg's (1999: 741–2) call for a dialogical approach to such struggles, the point of departure becomes 'seeing culture itself as a terrain of struggle' and 'social movement culture more as an appropriation from a dominant culture' than a radical expression of otherness:

> Rather than engaging in the wholesale process of pitting one discursive construction of social life against a completely different alternative, challengers generally engage in a piecemeal process of questioning certain meanings contained within a genre as the opportunity to problemize words and other representations represents itself. (Ibid.: 747)

The goal of movements from below in struggles over meaning thus becomes to 'delegitimate hegemonic genres within a field while appropriating pieces to inflect it with their own subversive meanings' (ibid.: 751). The signs and meanings within certain hegemonic genres – ideologies of dominance – that are singled out for contestation can be thought of as 'loci of consciousness formation' (Harvey 1985: 252), which are subjected to oppositional interpretative practices, and from which struggles over 'who shall have "tenure" of significant terms, that is, whose wider referential system and whose "evaluative accent" shall predominate' (Barker 2002: 6) flow and unfold.

Barker's 2002 analysis of community opposition to the closure of a children's hospital in North Manchester provides a good example of such a struggle over meaning. In a series of consultation meetings between the Manchester Health Authority and local people, the Authority sought to justify their initiative with reference to an ambition to focus on community-based health services. This, however, opened up for virulent protests from the floor. Rather than buying into the notion of 'care in the community' as a more humane approach to the provision of health services, local people argued that it was a thinly veiled attempt 'to justify what turned out to be cuts in public welfare spending' (ibid.: 6). In making these arguments they drew on their previous experiences in which '"community" was becoming associated with privatising and closing public services, in both the mental health and geriatric fields' (ibid.) and thus also invoked 'opposed associations and meanings and … differently perceived realities of working-class life' (ibid.: 7). As Barker puts it: 'The protestors claimed "tenure" of the word "community"' (ibid.).[18]

While struggles over meaning might start out as a piecemeal process of questioning certain meanings within an ideology of dominance, they may eventually – typically as part of the development of a sustained radical campaign or a social movement project – throw up more comprehensive political imaginaries which function as a kind of semiotic 'matrix through which this resistance [defines] itself' (Sundar 1997: 6) which we refer to as a *discourse of resistance*. This typically constitutes a more or less coherent challenge to the ways in which signs, symbols and idioms are rendered 'uniaccentual' in ideologies of dominance, and thus also to dominant groups' attempts to represent an existing social order as natural, purposive and legitimate in the form of a more or less systematic exposition of and claiming of tenure for the subaltern meanings or evaluative accents of these signs, symbols and idioms. A discourse of resistance will thus contain an argument to the effect that social life *can* be organised differently – an argument for the *possibility* of change – and that it *should* be organised differently – an argument for the *necessity* of change, which typically challenges an extant social order with reference to a set of normative principles that it violates through infringing upon or constraining subaltern needs and capacities. This indictment of the social order thus also provides justification to the efforts of a given group to bring about such change. Furthermore and crucially, a discourse of resistance will indicate the direction that such processes of change should assume in order for progressive alternatives to be realised.

Such discourses of resistance will tend to be woven of both particular and universal strands; that is, the claim that social life can and should be organised differently, the moral indictment of the extant order, the justification of resistance, and the claims made about the direction of change will be carried out partially through idioms and symbols drawn from cultural traditions and repertoires specific to a given place and time – what Peet and Watts (1993: 16) call 'regional discursive formations' – and partly through idioms and symbols that have come to transcend determinate locales and thus have attained a more universal status. This dialectic of universality and particularity in discourses of resistance is evidenced, for example, in the way that the slave rebellion that broke out in Saint Domingue in 1791 and which culminated in the creation of Haiti after a twelve-year struggle was informed by the notions of universal rights which imbued the French Revolution (see James 2001, Dubouis 2004, Fischer 2004).[19]

The dialectic of universality and particularity is also present in the way that in seeking the assistance and recognition of Shona peasant communities in their war for the liberation of Zimbabwe, ZANLA guerrilla soldiers steeped in socialist ideology and headed by a leadership 'who professed a commitment to leading Zimbabwe into the modern world' (Lan 1985: xvi), had to recognise and relate to Shona traditions of ancestral spirits and their mediums: 'If the guerrillas were to be helped by others, they had to recognise others ... The young fighters therefore had to enter into dialogue with these ancestors, to justify and explain their actions and to seek help' (ibid.: xiii). This interweaving of universal and particular idioms and symbols in discourses of resistance testifies to yet another aspect of the cultural interpretation of exploitation and oppression that goes on in social movements from below: 'As challengers develop discursive repertoires ... they also peer into the actions and histories of other challenging groups and their struggles to see what is available within their discursive repertoires' (Steinberg 1999: 752).

The question arises as to what we can and cannot attribute to discourses of resistance. Scott (1990: 78) argues that 'the subordinate classes to be found at the base of what we historically call revolutionary movements are typically seeking goals well within their understanding of the ruling ideology.' As with Piven and Cloward, this expresses a half-truth. Obviously, if discourses of resistance are to be taken seriously as expressions and statements of a movement's self-understanding, we should not assume that they represent a kind of 'blueprint' or 'carbon copy' of a uniform consciousness or rationality or outlook that saturates a movement and its participants (see Barker and Cox 2002: 41, Steinberg 1999: 741, Cox 1999a: 169–70). Indeed, within a movement, different activists are, as Steinberg (1999: 741) puts it, 'capable of reading different, divergent, and potentially contradictory meanings' into discourses of resistance.

However, the Kautskyian assumption that subordinate groups are typically caught within their local experience (Piven and Cloward) and hegemonic ideologies (Scott) is problematic. Of course, this does represent 'business as usual' to some extent: were it not so, a social order would not be hegemonic. But the extent to which it is true *within social movements* is one of the key issues which movements from above and below struggle over. Scott's Malaysian peasants, survivors of a brutal counter-insurgency campaign, and Piven and Cloward's American workers, caught in the US anomaly of a particularly weak left, do not represent a universal situation, any more than radical ideology always comes from 'outside intellectuals', as both analyses imply.

It is true that radical intellectuals can sometimes create contexts where they do not have to fight dominant ideologies in their own lifeworlds to the same extent as less privileged groups. Another way of reading the same situation, drawing on Lichterman's observations (1996), is that privileged radicals often come from backgrounds which are so hostile to their politics that they have to form discrete subcultures. Subaltern radicals may not have the capacity to cut themselves off from their communities of origin in the same way, and so have to argue differently – but at the same time they can often find *more* support for their basic hostility to wealth and power among their friends, family and neighbours.

Furthermore, *politics* plays a large role in relation to how a particular discourse works within a movement. Gramsci observes that while the Catholic church tends to try to prevent its intellectuals from challenging the 'simple' too much – the same kind of politics of knowledge which Scott or Piven and Cloward assume – the role of a communist party is rather to engage in a process of popular education in order to develop the understanding of *all* participants. Laurence would add, from his own experience of working-class community activists, that it is by no means the case that the university-educated radical is 'above' and the subordinate organiser 'below' in such relationships. Community activists understand power, exploitation and culture in ways which are simply not available from within a university seminar – or, for that matter, in many radical organisations. The commitment embedded within popular education processes of 'starting where people are' may mislead those who set their political standard in university terms, as the adoption by an elite of a particular vocabulary.[20]

When we look at the slow democratic development of popular movement praxis (Gillan 2010), what Williams described as the 'long revolution' (1965), things may look different. This is what urban activists found when they started attempting to 'radicalise' the indigenous peasants of Chiapas, only to discover that – as they put it – they had been resisting for 500 years. An effective movement politics in our terms is precisely one in which the situated good sense – the local rationalities – of *subordinate* groups in struggle comes to the fore, and where a movement's structures and practice enable those rationalities to shape the further development of militant particularisms, campaigns and ultimately movement projects.

Conclusion: Movements From Above and Below – Organic Crisis and Social Movement Struggles

To return to the actual politics of movements: social movements from above and below engage in struggles over historicity, that is, they engage and encounter each other in struggles over the direction and form of the development of the social organisation of human needs and capacities. Such struggles occur when movements from below have returned 'up' the sequence from opposing routines in localised struggles to opposing the structures from which these routines emerge and – ultimately – the social movements from above which have sought to install these structures.

If and when movement projects from below have developed a capacity for hegemony that allows the articulation of a challenge to the social totality and take aim at the control of the self-production of society, they can usefully be referred to as 'world-historical movements' (Katsiaficas 1987: Chapter 1). The term refers to those movements that throw up and animate '[p]eriods of crises and turmoil *on a global scale*' that are 'relatively rare in history' (ibid.: 6). Katsiaficas discerns 'a handful of such periods of global eruptions' and associates them to the years 1776–89, 1848, 1905, 1917 and 1968 (ibid.: 6, 18; see also Arrighi, Hopkins and Wallerstein 1989):[21]

> In each of these periods, global upheavals were spontaneously generated. In a chain reaction of insurrections and revolts, new forms

> of power emerged in opposition to the established order, and new visions of the meaning of freedom were formulated in the actions of millions of people. Even when these movements were unsuccessful in seizing power, immense adjustments were necessitated both within and between nation states, and the defeated movements offered revealing glimpses of the newly developed nature of society and the new kinds of class struggles which were to follow. (Ibid.: 6)

During these periods, new political subjects inspired and guided by new imaginaries have deployed new skills and practices to push for radical social change. At each conjuncture, such movements from below achieved substantial alterations in extant social orders. World-historical movements and the processes of change that they give rise to can usefully be related to Gramsci's conception of 'organic crisis' (see Chapter 1).

This could, of course, entail a situation where revolutionary movements from below launch a 'war of manoeuvre' against a beleaguered, passive, decaying order – an order which is at best, perhaps, capable of mustering a defensive response to the challenge. However, as Hall notes in his discussion of organic crises – and as elites have learned – defensive responses will generally be insufficient in the context of an organic crisis:

> If the crisis is deep – 'organic' – these efforts cannot be merely defensive. They will be *formative*: aiming at a new balance of forces, the emergence of new elements, the attempt to put together a new 'historic bloc', new political configurations and 'philosophies', a profound restructuring of the state and the ideological discourses which construct the crisis and represent it as 'lived' as a practical reality: new programmes and policies, pointing to a new result, a new sort of 'settlement' – 'within certain limits'. (Hall 1983: 23)

Organic crises and their trajectory, then, are also shaped by offensive movements from above, that is, movements that typically take aim at social structures which bear the imprint of the past victories of movements from below and the constraints that these impose upon the power of dominant groups. And such offensive movements from above may in turn spur defensive responses from below. Thus, an organic crisis should be conceived of as a complex field of force animated by 'a dialectic between reactionary and progressive forces in search of a solution, a new order' (Gill 2003b: 33). At the heart of such a scenario lies the breakdown of those 'truce lines' handed down from past rounds of movement struggles, and thus also the eruption of those antagonisms and contradictions which they held in check. New terrains of struggle open up where movements from above and below vie for command over the direction of imminent systemic changes, or seek to prevent these changes from taking place in the first place.

Gramsci's (1998: 177–8) distinction between 'conjunctural' and 'organic' movements on the historical terrain goes some way towards capturing the patterning of the field of force between defensive and offensive movements from below in times of crisis, where the 'conjunctural' consists of those forces that seek to defend the status quo, whereas the 'organic' consists of those forces that 'give rise to socio-historical criticism'. Conjunctural movements are those defensive responses – from above and below – and, conversely, organic movements are those offensive responses – from above and below – that emerge in times of crisis. We do not propose these categories as sets of diametrical opposites, but rather as broad general categories that may help us find our bearings as we approach the empirical study of those periods in history that qualify as organic crisis.

Organic crises are by definition radically contingent. But as particular movements gradually develop hegemony, through partial or total victories, the space under contention is narrowed down. There is a degree of 'path dependency' – emergent social changes close off or crowd out alternative possibilities. As a provisional guideline, we might posit the following general scenarios: a successful movement project from below will tend to result in some kind of revolutionary transformation; a social movement project from below that is 'disarmed' through an accommodative response from below will tend to lead to significant reformist modifications, while the basic structures of the social formation stay the same. A successful repressive response from above will lead to a 'return to normalcy', at least for a time; and a successful offensive social movement from above will lead to significant modifications but this time in favour of dominant social groups in the form of the reversal of restraints upon their power.

In Chapter 4, we first discuss the organic crisis which gave rise to neoliberalism. Following a discussion of neoliberalism as the key movement from above of our era, we explore the ways in which it in turn has entered its own period of organic crisis. In Chapter 5, we discuss the movement of movements, and contemporary anti-austerity movements, as responses from below which both respond to this weakness of neoliberalism and accentuate it, before asking how the crisis might conclude – and what we can do.

4

'The Bourgeoisie, Historically, Has Played a Most Revolutionary Part': Social Movements from Above and Below in Historical Capitalism

> *The bourgeoisie, historically, has played a most revolutionary part.*
>
> *The bourgeoisie, wherever it has got the upper hand, has put an end to all feudal, patriarchal, idyllic relations. It has pitilessly torn asunder the motley feudal ties that bound human beings to their 'natural superiors', and has left remaining no other nexus between one human being and another than naked self-interest, than callous 'cash payment'.*
>
> Marx and Engels, *The Communist Manifesto*

'The economists', Marx quipped in *The Poverty of Philosophy*, 'explain to us how production is carried out in the relation given, but what they do not explain is how these relations are produced, that is to say the historical movement which has created them' (Marx 1995: 113). This brief statement expresses one of the core concerns that informed Marx's analysis of the capitalist mode of production, namely the need to lay bare its historicity: capitalism is not a timeless mode of production rooted in the species being of 'the small and big Robinsonades' who constituted 'the starting point of history' (Marx 1981a: 188) for Smith and Ricardo, but a specific way of organising the dialectic of human needs and capacities that originated at a particular point in historical time, as a result of definite political projects that were able to give a certain form and direction to societal transformations. In making this point, Marx does much more than simply raise an epistemological critique of classical political economy. He also makes a fundamental political point: in reminding us that capitalism has a historical origin in collective human practice, he also underlines the possibility that its historical end can be brought about through collective human practice.

Drawing on this key insight, this chapter analyses how the *longue durée* of historical capitalism has been constructed and moulded in conflictual encounters between social movements from above and below. Our point of departure is a critical discussion of how capitalism was made possible through 'primitive accumulation' and 'bourgeois revolution' – two intertwined processes which were energised by the pursuit of political projects by *both* dominant *and* subaltern groups. We then move on to present a conceptual framework that allows us to distinguish between different phases of capitalist development from the eighteenth century to the present. Drawing on Karl Polanyi's (2001) notion of a 'double movement', we argue that the *longue durée* of historical capitalism can be understood in terms of a series of shifts from a 'disembedded' (market-centred) form of *liberal capitalism* that prevailed from the late eighteenth century to the early twentieth century, to a 're-embedded' (state-centred) form of *organised capitalism* that was dominant from the post-war years to the late 1970s, and ultimately towards a 'disembedded' form of *neoliberal capitalism* from the 1980s to the present. We will argue that this was not an automatic process but one structured by collective agency of movements from above as well as substantial resistance by movements from below in each transition.

This analysis has three purposes. Firstly, understanding that capitalism – and its various forms – are the contested and contingent product of human agency places the Marxist emphasis on human beings 'making their own history' squarely at the centre of analysis. Of course we do not make history under circumstances of our own choosing; some outcomes are very likely and some battles are uneven, but neither are the outcomes given in advance, to be known by access to some secret key of history. The struggles *matter*, and even in defeat the nature of the conflict often shapes what follows.

Secondly, just as the simple celebration of movements from below (or proselytising for particular strategies) without attention to the nature of the forces they confront is one-sided, so too is a 'Marxist' account which simply presents an elaborate account of the products of these historical struggles as the inevitable outcome of the interplay of particular theoretical categories. It is in the nature of movements from above that human beings come to experience the world they create as, precisely, *structure*: as economic system, state institutions, the shape of culture. It is important for social analysis and political practice to understand movements from above and below within a single set of ontological categories and types of explanation, rather than to reproduce the apparent separation of fixed structure and sporadic resistance. Our account represents a de-mythologised account of the social world as a collective if not fully intended human creation.

Thirdly, to understand the nature of present-day movement struggles and systemic crises, it is crucial to see what is at stake not only in the surface terms of 'issues', opinions and arguments but in the encounter between movements (above and below) struggling for control of historicity, that is, society's capacity for self-creation (see Chapter 2) – a capacity which consists not only of the transformative encounter with nature but also of the transformative encounter with each other, in the workplace, or in the streets. If neoliberal capitalism strives to create certain kinds of subjects, so too do movements from below – in the same moment as they strive to unmake or remake the meaning of property, work, self-expression, identity, power and the rest of the social world.

Primitive Accumulation: The Making of Capitalist Social Relations

The making of the capitalist mode of production was predicated upon the coming into being of a foundational social relationship: the capital–labour relation. This relation is between the capitalist class – or as Marx (1990: 874) put it, 'the owners of money, means of production, means of subsistence, who are eager to valorise the sum of values they have appropriated by buying the labour power of others' – and, on the other hand, the working class – that is, 'free workers, the sellers of their own labour power, and therefore the sellers of labour'.[1] The bedrock of the capital–labour relation is 'the complete separation between the workers and the ownership of the conditions for the realization of their labour' and the process through which this separation is brought about – *primitive accumulation* – 'is a process which operates two transformations, whereby the social means of subsistence and production are turned into capital, and the immediate producers are turned into wage labourers' (ibid.).

So why was primitive accumulation a necessary precondition for the genesis of the capitalist mode of production? Eric Wolf provides a clear answer to this question:

> Labour power is not in itself a commodity created in order to be offered for sale in a market. It is an attribute of human beings, a capability of *homo sapiens*. As long as people can lay their hands on the means of production (tools, resources, land) and use these to supply their own sustenance – under whatever social arrangements – there is no compelling reason for them to sell their capacity to work to someone else. For labour power to be offered for sale, the tie between producers and the means of production has to be severed for good. (Wolf 1982: 77)

Once this tie has been severed, the ground is prepared for a fundamental restructuring of the social organisation of human needs and capacities in the sphere of production as 'people who are denied access to the means of production must come to those who now control the means and bargain for permission to operate them' in return for a wage 'that will allow them to pay for what they need to sustain themselves' (ibid.). With primitive accumulation, then, the buying and selling of commodities – including labour power – on markets becomes 'the principal determinant and regulator of social reproduction' (Wood 2002: 97) and integral to the ways in which the satisfaction of human needs and the exercise of human capacities is organised and structured.

In seventeenth-century England, the separation of direct producers from their access to the means of production was achieved, above all, through the 'expropriation of the agricultural producer, of the peasant, from the soil ...' (Marx 1990: 876). This process of expropriation was rooted in the increasing market orientation of the landed classes: successful participation in commercial agriculture had become particularly important to the landowning classes from the sixteenth century onwards; they therefore started using their property in new and more productive ways: 'The result was a highly productive agrarian sector, in which landlords and tenants alike became preoccupied with what they called "improvement", the enhancement of the land's productivity for profit' (Wood 2002: 106). Improvement in turn necessitated 'the elimination of old customs and practices that interfered with the most productive use of land' (ibid.: 107) and this elimination was carried out through the enclosure of the commons.

Enclosure basically entailed '[t]he conversion of commonable lands, whether on wastes, commons, or village fields, into exclusively owned parcels, and the concomitant extinction of common rights, of which the most important one was that of pasture' (Blomley 2007: 2). Whereas the earliest enclosures in England date back to the period from 1220 to 1349, the practice picked up serious momentum in the sixteenth and seventeenth centuries as 'modern notions of private property as individually owned and spatially exclusive first began to solidify in the legal, administrative and popular imaginations' (McDonagh 2013: 1). By the onset of the eighteenth century, three-fourths of England's agricultural land had been enclosed (see McNally 1988: 7–9).

The enclosures were truly 'a revolution by the rich against the poor' (Polanyi 2001: 37), in which a social movement from above rooted in the landed classes 'conquered the field for capitalist agriculture, incorporated the soil into capital, and created for the urban industries the necessary supplies of free and rightless proletarians' (Marx 1990: 895). In a process that reflects how social movements from above act in and through the state to consolidate hegemonic power structures, enclosures came to be pursued actively by the state, as Parliament began to pass Enclosure Acts. Between 1700 and 1815 'more than 65 million acres of common fields and commons were enclosed by acts of Parliament – an area equal to nearly 20 percent of the total land of England' (McNally 1988: 11; see also McNally 1993: Chapter 1, Neeson 1993).

The Globalisation of Primitive Accumulation

Primitive accumulation, however, was not confined simply to changes in the agrarian structure of the English countryside. It was a global process which was instrumental in giving rise to the capitalist world-system as a globe-spanning division of labour in which territories, populations and resources were inserted into global circuits of production and exchange and global hierarchies of economic and political power (see Wallerstein 2011).[2] It was colonial expansion that globalised primitive accumulation, and Marx catalogued its 'idyllic methods' as follows:

> The discovery of gold and silver in America, the extirpation, the enslavement and entombment in mines of the aboriginal population, the beginning of the conquest and the looting of the East Indies, the turning of Africa into a warren for the commercial hunting of

> blackskins, signalled the rosey dawn of the era of capitalist production. (Marx 1990: 915)

Marx's catalogue is an apt description of the various systems of labour control and resource extraction that European states developed and imposed as they subjected ever-larger parts of humanity to colonial tutelage (see Wolf 1982: Part 2). Key among these systems was transatlantic slavery, which first emerged in response to labour shortages in the silver mines of Spanish America and the sugar plantations that had been established in Brazil and the Caribbean (ibid.: 157).

By the middle of the seventeenth century, the British were the dominant force in the slave trade, and by 1807 British factors, merchants and traders had brought more than 3.6 million African slaves to the New World (Blackburn 1988, Robinson 2000). 'Slave labour', writes Blackburn, 'supplied the most coveted and important items in Atlantic and European commerce: the sugar, coffee, cotton and cacao of the Caribbean; the tobacco, rice and indigo of North America; the gold and sugar of Portuguese and Spanish South America' (1988: 3). Slavery and the slave trade were in turn part of a wider process in which European states developed commercial networks on a global scale, which ultimately enabled substantial merchant groups to control 'a variety of enterprises from putting-out networks and peasant agriculture to slave plantations and factories in the modern sense' (Banaji 2010a: 274). Colonial expansion, then, was a process through which 'a new and international division of labour springs up, one suited to the requirements of the main industrial countries, and it converts one part of the globe into a chiefly agricultural field of production for supplying the other part, which remains a pre-eminently industrial field' (Marx 1990: 579–80).

Processes of primitive accumulation were thus coeval and mutually constitutive in the core and periphery of an emergent capitalist world-system: colonial modes of appropriation came to interlock with 'the wealth-creating potential of the new capitalist relations in the capitalist core' (Heller 2010: 103). At the heart of this transformation – a transformation that according to Marx constituted 'the revolution that laid the foundation of the capitalist mode of production' (Marx 1990: 878) – we find the structured agency of dominant and subaltern groups, situated in determinate historical conjunctures and responding to the emergence of opportunities for and compulsions towards changing the way in which human needs and capacities are socially organised.

Primitive accumulation, and the creation of capitalism, do not just happen by some automatic logic. They have to be made: against the double resistance both of the dispossessed, who defend their access to the means of production, seek to reverse their dispossession, and enter into new struggles within the nascent wage labour relations, and of residual elites, both those who see no place for themselves in the new dispensation and those for whom the costs of change seem greater than the potential benefits. They are thus processes of struggle, of the formation of new hegemonies and alliances and the coercion of opponents.

The role of the structured agency of social movements from above and from below in the production of capitalism becomes particularly evident when we consider how the initial making of capitalism's fundamental social relations was paralleled by the making of a new form of state in which 'the "wealth of the nation" (i.e. the formation of capital and the relentless exploitation and impoverishment of the mass of the people) figures as the *ultima Thule* of all statecraft' (ibid.: 879).

Bourgeois Revolution: The Making of the Early Capitalist State[3]

The enclosure movement, Barrington Moore writes, constituted a 'massive violence exercised by the upper classes against the lower' (1991: 29). This violence was in large part mediated through and exercised by the state. The enactment of parliamentary enclosures – a practice which made the law 'the instrument by which the people's land is stolen' (Marx 1990: 885) – is a key example of how primitive accumulation was predicated upon the use of 'the power of the State, the concentrated and organised force of society, to hasten, hot-house fashion, the process of transformation of the feudal mode of production into the capitalist mode, and to shorten the transition' (ibid.: 915–16). The enactment and use of law – or what Marx called 'bloody legislation against the expropriated' (ibid.: 896) – to control the floating population of landless paupers created as a result of the enclosure movement is one example. The fact that the state came to play such a central role in mediating the trajectory of capitalist development in the seventeenth and eighteenth centuries was itself the result of a profound transformation – namely, the *bourgeois revolution* that redefined the balance of power between social forces in English society and inscribed this new balance of power in the capacities and functioning of the state (Hill 1980, Mooers 2001).

The bourgeois revolution in England – the conflictual period stretching from the eruption of open conflict between Charles I and Parliament in 1640 to the Hanoverian succession of 1688 – was rooted in social convulsions that had unsettled established hierarchies of class power during the sixteenth century. At the outbreak of the conflict, the English ruling class consisted of an aristocracy of peers and greater gentry – in other words, big landowners who lived off the rents they charged from their tenants. Beneath this ruling class were the middling and lesser gentry, whose landholdings were comparatively smaller and their political power much less salient. It was the small producers – the 'middle sort' – that constituted the largest social class in England at this time: in agriculture, this class was comprised by peasant farmers, and in the nascent industries by the artisans (Manning 1996).

During the second half of the sixteenth century, the ranks of the landowning classes had grown significantly, and as a result the gentry had also expanded its political power at the expense of the aristocracy: 'Participation of landed gentlemen in the exercise of political power was increasingly seen as a right which flowed directly from ownership of property' (McNally 1988: 39; see also Hill 1980: 112–13). The Stuart monarchy installed in 1603 reacted to this development through 'an attempt to reconstruct centralized monarchical power' (McNally 1988: 9). This reaction in turn prompted the landed classes to rebel against the king and the political order of which he was the apex. The English Civil War, stretching from 1642 to 1649, can thus be understood as arising out of 'a rebellion by landed gentlemen against this tendency towards absolutism and in defence of rights that had been won during the previous one hundred and fifty years' (ibid.). In pursuing this rebellion and defending Parliament against monarchical encroachments, the middling and lesser gentry made headway by constructing a set of vertical alliances with 'the middle sort' – a class 'that was steadily becoming more and more alienated from the monarchy as a result of the imposition of non-parliamentary taxation and what was regarded as Popish religious policies' (Heller 2010: 124).

With the end of the Civil War, a period of intense contention began over the character of the emerging English polity. However, with the restoration of monarchy in 1660, it was evident that it was the more powerful and wealthy segments among those who had rebelled who were in a position to determine the form of the state that was crystallising. The number of county seats in the House of Commons was expanded to reflect the rise of new centres of wealth. Property qualifications were introduced that 'disenfranchised smaller freeholders' and gave 'the vote to solid men of property among copyholders, leaseholders, clothiers, merchants etc.' (Manning 1996: 136). At the same time, the restored monarchy was stripped of its former powers. The aristocratic classes thus found themselves in a situation where their political power had been curtailed, but – on the basis of the wealth and property they had retained – they could benefit from the new spaces of accumulation that had emerged during the seventeenth century (ibid.: 111). This helped to 'reconcile the aristocracy to the victory of the new social order in which they had a secure position' (Hill 1980: 121). With the Hanoverian succession of 1688, a new historical bloc had been consolidated: 'after 1688 no further attempt to reform the electorate was made ... The monied men stepped in to control this system made safe against democracy' (Hill 1967: 112).

As Brewer notes, the English revolution can in many ways be understood as 'a struggle over the British state – about how it should be structured and what it should be allowed to do' (1989: x). Like movements from below, movements from above also struggle to find an adequate form. Along with the long-running, often molecular processes of legislation (Enclosure Acts, for example, were typically extremely local in their application), we can add the various state forms which were explored following the fall of Charles I – Parliament, Protectorate, Restoration, Glorious Revolution, the development of new forms of corporation, the role of the army as incipient political forum and even more importantly the argument over different forms of church.[4] It was not a foregone conclusion that the capitalist movement from above would take the specific forms that it did, and the eventual settlement had many peculiarities.

The state that was eventually constructed, on the basis of the new historical bloc of social forces which emerged through the revolutionary process, was endowed with significantly increased powers in the military and fiscal domains:

> Britain was able to shoulder an ever-more ponderous burden of military commitments thanks to a radical increase in taxation, the development of public deficit finance (a national debt) on an unprecedented scale, and the growth of a sizeable public administration devoted to organizing the fiscal and military activities of the state. (Ibid.: xiii)

Fiscal and military strength was in turn important in terms of enabling Britain to advance so decisively in the world-system and to eventually constitute itself as a hegemonic power in the eighteenth and nineteenth centuries (see Arrighi 1994: Chapter 3). Internally, the main preoccupation of the state was that of facilitating the spread of market forces – for example, through active encouragement of agricultural improvement, the coordination of colonial trade, and the relaxation and abandonment of guild regulations, town oligarchies and other restrictions on industrial activity: 'The economy of the market-place was extended into regions where hitherto more feudal, patriarchal relations had prevailed' (Hill 1961: 201).

At the same time, the early capitalist state 'had a generally recognized internal function of preserving the subordination of the lower classes' (Hill 1967: 128) and this it did through the use of law and punishment. Christopher Hill notes that between 1688 and 1780 'the number of offences which carried the death penalty rose from about fifty to nearly five times that number. The vast majority of these were offences against property, and most offenders, in London at least, were under twenty years of age' (ibid.: 181). Laws against popular infringements on private property were coupled with restrictions imposed upon the poor – that is, the emergent proletariat – such as the Act of Settlement of 1662, which sought 'to immobilize the working population, in order to deprive political opposition of the chance of organizing itself, to protect London and corporate towns from a surplus of labour, and to keep labour cheap in the countryside' (ibid.: 192; see also Thompson 1975, Linebaugh 2006). In other words, the early capitalist state was simultaneously moulded by, and enabling of, the offensive strategies of a social movement from above that sought to entrench the hegemony of propertied classes in seventeenth-century England.

Resistance in the Era of Primitive Accumulation and Bourgeois Revolution

So far, we have seen how the seventeenth and eighteenth centuries was an era in which dominant groups acted collectively in ways that made effective use of their economic and political power to craft social relations and political forms that were conducive to the advance of capitalist accumulation. In other words, we have seen how capitalism had to be *made* by and through the collective agency of social movements from above. However, dominant groups were not unconstrained in their exercise of agency from above. Quite the opposite: the dispossession wrought by primitive accumulation and the forms of political domination put in place through bourgeois revolution were intensely contested from below as subaltern groups resisted dispossession and mobilised around alternative visions of future social orders.

In the English countryside, '[t]he late sixteenth and early seventeenth centuries in particular were marked by popular and sometimes violent opposition to the extension of private property rights' (McDonagh 2009: 193). Commoners defended their customary rights against enclosure in a number of ways, including hedge-breaking, impounding and rescuing animals, collecting resources previously held in common, mass trespasses and mass ploughings: '... communities sometimes asserted their rights simply by taking them.' (McDonagh 2013: 15) Direct action was paralleled by more legalistic forms of resistance, which ranged from refusals to sign bills of enclosure via individual suits to the Star Chamber, to parliamentary counter-petitions to contest enclosure-initiatives from above (Neeson 1984, 1993, McDonagh 2009, Blomley 2007, Wood 2007b).

Resistance to enclosure often took the form of militant particularist struggles, erupting as a 'reaction to a specific threat to existing agricultural practice in the form of conversion to pasture' (McDonagh 2013: 19; see also Neeson 1984). However, the grievances generated by dispossession of customary rights could at times come together in more radical social movement projects centred on a 'plebeian politics' that 'was capable of mounting fundamental attacks on social inequality' and calling for 'a radical *reconstruction* of society from the bottom up' (Wood 2007b: 4). This happened as early as during the Pilgrimage of Grace in 1536 and again during the uprising of 1549.

Even more significantly, agrarian discontent was an integral element in the egalitarian radicalism that challenged the political projects of the propertied classes during the English revolution. Movements such as the Levellers and the Diggers expressed this most clearly. The Levellers effectively wove together the various grievances of the 'middle sort'– that is, independent small producers like artisans and small farmers – into a more comprehensive programme for political change (Manning 1991, Hill 1976). Above all, they sought to end the oppression of the poor by the rich through decentring political power: 'The aim of the Levellers was to reduce the political power, and end the political monopoly of the rich'

(Manning 1991: 412). Importantly, the Leveller-linked mutinies of 1649 were largely structured around refusal to participate in Cromwell's war in Ireland, framed in terms of solidarity with anti-colonial struggles: 'the cause of the Irish natives in seeking their just freedoms ... was the very same with our cause here in endeavouring our own rescue and freedom from the power of oppressors' (cited in Moody, Martin and Byrne 1991: lxii–lxiii).

While the Levellers 'accepted the sanctity of private property, and their desire to extend democracy was within the limits of a capitalist society', a more radical vision was articulated by the Diggers (Hill 1976: 123). The Diggers 'called on the poor to organize themselves for practical action', which took the form of the establishment of collective communities where land was held and tilled in common, and decision-making powers were vested in the community itself (ibid.: 131; see also Kennedy 2008, Gurney 2012). Ultimately, it was only repression by the state that was capable of extinguishing these radical social movement projects and the challenge they posed to the propertied classes and to the kind of economy and polity they sought to construct (see Manning 1991).

It was not just the English peasantry who rebelled against primitive accumulation: the enslaved and the colonised were equally virulent in their opposition to dispossession and subjugation. The seventeenth and eighteenth centuries witnessed the emergence of slavery as 'the very foundation of New World enterprise' (Robinson 2000: 110) but the same era saw enslaved populations time and again come together to contest their unfreedom and exploitation. For example, the British Caribbean witnessed one significant slave revolt every two years on average between the Barbice rising of 1731 and the Demerara rebellion of 1823. Jamaica was shaken by revolts in 1669, 1672, 1673, 1678, 1682, 1685, 1690, 1733, 1734, 1760, 1765 and 1772. In North America, revolts erupted several times across the eighteenth century (Genovese 1979, Blackburn 1988).

Like resistance to enclosure, the grievances that motivated slave revolts were tangible and circumscribed, and gave rise to militant particularist struggles: 'The liberty the slave aspired to would be that of freedom from unremitting toil, from daily abuse and from being at the continual command of another' (Blackburn 1988: 55). In challenging the oppressive tyranny of the plantation labour regime, slave resistance deployed a wide repertoire of practices, ranging from everyday strategies that sought to lessen the slaveholders' exactions of labour to open confrontations that tended to be marked by violence against people and property (Genovese

1979). However, like resistance to enclosure, revolts against slavery could also become the source of much more radical movement projects. Above all, this is evident in the struggle for national liberation in Saint-Domingue, which eventually yielded 'the first black national state' in the Americas (ibid.: 85). The rebels in Saint-Domingue appropriated the bourgeois-democratic idiom of the French Revolution and put it to effective use in their assaults on slavery and colonial subjugation:

> [The slaves] had heard of the revolution and had constructed it in their own image: the white slaves in France had risen, and killed their masters, and were enjoying the fruits of the earth. It was gravely inaccurate, in fact, but they had caught the spirit of the thing. Liberty, Equality, Fraternity. (James 2001: 66)

Culminating in the double defeat of colonialism and slavery as Haiti was formed in 1804, this 13-year struggle entailed 'an incipient "politicization" of slave resistance as it achieved forms which aimed at, and could guarantee, general emancipation. In the conditions of the Atlantic world of the early nineteenth century, this had to take the form of legislation backed by an effective territorial state' (Blackburn, 1988: 527).

Crucially, resistance to enclosure in the Old World and revolt against slavery in the New World were woven together in the Atlantic axis that was so integral to the growth of commercial capitalism in the eighteenth century. The upshot of Atlantic trade could not have been possible without 'the toil of a motley, mobile and cosmopolitan proletariat of seafarers, port and construction yard workers ...' (ibid.: 59). This 'multi-ethnic class' actively resisted the many forms of dispossession that were integral to the rise of the capitalist world-system (Linebaugh and Rediker 2000: 7).

Popular anti-capitalist traditions also found their manifestations in the conspiracies of indentured servants – many of whom were dispossessed peasants from England and Ireland – and slaves in the Caribbean and in the newly founded colonies in North America; in the self-organisation and concerted opposition of sailors to the naval labour regimes of the maritime state; in piracy; and in the riots of workers in the port cities on both sides of the Atlantic (ibid.). Thus, if the Atlantic axis of early capitalist development was a cauldron of accumulation, it was also a furnace in which the levelling traditions of the English revolution merged with the oppositional imaginaries of other dispossessed groups – chief among them African slaves – to constitute a genuinely transatlantic form of subaltern radicalism, which from the early seventeenth century to the early nineteenth century haunted 'English Atlantic capitalism' (ibid.: 5).

At the end of the day – or rather the end of the eighteenth century – it was evident that the world that was coming into being would be moulded by the collective agency of social movements from above rooted in propertied classes. However, the fact that this point could only be reached through the mobilisation of force against social movements from below underlines our fundamental argument, that capitalism was not simply the predestined result of the churning of productive forces and relations of production, but the contingent product of a 'historical movement' (Marx, 1995: 113) animated through structured collective agency. The rest of this chapter maps out how capitalism has continued to be moulded through a contentious dialectic of movements from above and below, from the late eighteenth century until the present. First, however, we outline the conceptual apparatus that we will use for this exercise.

Capitalism and Its Changing Historical Forms

The Essence of Capitalism

In its barest essence, capitalism is a mode of production which is founded upon the capital–labour relation and in which economic activity is overwhelmingly geared towards the production of commodities that are exchanged on markets – that is, generalised commodity production.[5]

Furthermore, accumulation under capitalism is characterised by a particular dynamic, namely that of expanded reproduction. The beginning and the end of the 'circuit of capital'[6] – 'the transformation of money into commodities, and the reconversion of commodities into money' (Marx 1990: 248) – do not exhibit 'any qualitative differences between its extremes' (ibid.: 251). What does occur, however, is a quantitative change: 'More money is finally withdrawn from circulation than what was thrown in at the beginning'. This 'increment excess over the original value' (ibid.) constitutes 'surplus value', which is then funnelled back into the process of production as investments, thus reproducing the circuit of capital at an expanded scale. This has implications, for example, in terms of the continual attempts at expansion of capitalism into previously un- or decommodified areas of social life (including the individual psyche), the constant battering at the 'Chinese walls' of non-capitalist cultures, and the ever growing contradiction between increasing physical production and a finite planetary ecology.

Surplus value is basically constituted through 'the difference between the value labour congeals in commodities in a working day and the value the labourer gets for surrendering labour-power as a commodity to the capitalist' (ibid.: 124). The extraction of surplus value in capitalist accumulation is based on the power of capital over labour constituted in and through the capital–labour relation.[7] Workers are paid a wage whose long-term minimum is set by the cost of the wage goods that are necessary for labour to reproduce itself in a given historical context. However, by virtue of having purchased the right to dispose of their labour power, capital ensures that workers perform 'surplus labour' – that is, labour over and above the value of the wages paid in the exchange between capitalist and worker (ibid.: 300–302).

If we stopped our account of the essence of capitalism here, we would be lapsing into what Lebowitz (2003) calls 'one-sided Marxism' – one that conceptualises capitalism and its workings solely in terms of the logic of the ways in which capital seeks to perpetuate expanded reproduction, and which assumes its permanent success in doing so (Thompson 1977). What such a perspective elides is the fact that the capitalist mode of production is animated by the conflictual encounter between capital's need to extract surplus value to ensure growth and expansion and 'the worker's own need for development' (Marx 1990: 772).

Lebowitz (2003: 80–84) therefore proposes that we consider the circuit of capital – the purchase of labour power, the production of commodities and the exchange of commodities on markets – in terms of two distinct political economies: the political economy of *capital*, centred on the extraction of surplus value to underpin expanded reproduction, and the political economy of *labour*, in which working-class people seek to secure their social reproduction by combining in struggle against the imperatives of capital accumulation. In the final analysis, this is a struggle over how human needs are to be satisfied and how human capacities are to be deployed.

This struggle plays out in the labour market, where workers combine and mobilise to force up the price of their labour power. It also operates in the process of production, where workers combine and mobilise to contest 'the capitalist character of direction and supervision within the labour process' (ibid.: 91). Ultimately, workers may struggle against 'the rule of capital' by challenging 'its ownership of the products of labour which underlies its power as mediator in the labour market and the sphere of production' (ibid.: 171). The political economy of capitalism as a social form, then, has to be understood in terms of 'the complex resultant of the changing balance of class forces in a struggle as they interact within a framework determined by the value form' (Jessop 1990: 197).

We can add to these accounts other kinds of struggles equally inherent to capitalism as a social form: ethnic and racial conflicts generated both by the ever-moving boundary of capitalist relationships (for example, indigenous, anti-slavery, or anti-colonial struggles) and by the inequalities internal to capitalism (for example, conflicts around race and work, around the political participation of different populations, or competition and warfare between nation states); struggles around gender and sexuality shaped by the relationship between the domestic economy and wage labour (such as Walby's (1991) distinction between private and public patriarchy), conflicts around the gendering, commodification, or externalising of caring labour (Lynch and McLaughlin 1995), issues around the relationship of the family to property and inheritance (and hence reproduction and sexuality), or the role of different (ethnic) family forms as relative protection from a dominant culture or the reproduction of that culture, in situations of labour migration, post-slavery, or post-colonial relationships.

This is not to say that every movement is 'really about capitalism' or class; it is rather that the way in which we inhabit specific forms of capitalism which also involve specific racial and global divisions of labour and particular forms of patriarchy means that the agents in struggle and the terrain of their conflict are deeply shaped by the *material* production of life in all its many complexities.

Historical Capitalism

When we move from the terrain of the abstract – capitalism in its barest essence – to historical capitalism – as it is actually organised in a specific period of time and in specific regional locales – we are immediately confronted with the fact that 'there is real scope for variation in the rhythm and course of capitalist development' (Jessop 1990: 198). This is evident in the existence of differently patterned political economies across space and time. In the following, we put forward a periodisation of capitalism which highlights how different phases of capitalist development derive their distinct political economy as a result of cycles of struggle between social movements from above and social movements from below. More specifically, we want to highlight how these cycles of struggle are enmeshed in moments of organic crisis, and how they animate processes of transition from one phase of capitalist development to another.[8] To do this, we need to have a set of basic conceptual tools.

The political economy of a given phase of capitalist development will find its manifestation in a stable constellation of three key elements: (i) accumulation strategies that organise the circuit of capital around a particular model of economic growth capable of sustaining the expanded reproduction of capitalist accumulation (ibid.: 129); (ii) forms of state defined by a particular way of organising the state's functions, activities and capabilities, based on the emergence of a historical bloc of social forces (Cox 1987: 129), and (iii) particular ways of organising accumulation and governance in the capitalist world-system based on the ability of a specific state to exercise 'functions of leadership and governance over a system of sovereign states' – what Arrighi (1994: 27) calls 'world hegemony'.

In bringing these elements together, social movements from above will draw on their directive role in economic activity, their privileged ability to act in and through the state, and their capacity for binding together dominant and subaltern groups in hegemonic formations. The creation of a hegemonic formation moves along two axes – horizontally, in that it is necessary to create unity between different dominant groups around a specific set of overarching objectives; vertically, in that the consent of (some) subaltern groups has to be elicited, normally by granting concessions to (some) demands of social movements from below (see Silver and Slater 1999). As Chapter 3 noted, movements from above express themselves through a variety of institutional forms: corporations, states, political parties, armed forces, religion, the law, public opinion, and so on. These forms in turn are often arenas of contestation and cooptation: apparently fixed, on closer examination they are often key locations of struggle.

A period of crisis in capitalism as a whole, in turn, revolves around the unravelling of a given political economy: accumulation strategies fail to enable growth; forms of state no longer facilitate governance; a world hegemon is no longer able to give direction and leadership to the world-system. In a crisis, hegemony unravels along two axes: horizontally, the unity between different dominant groups evaporates and gives way to intra-elite rivalry; vertically, the consent of subaltern groups – and the resignation of coerced ones – erodes, and gives way to social movement projects that seek to give an alternative direction to nascent processes of social change. A period of crisis, therefore, is also a terrain of resistance structured between social movements from above searching for and pursuing projects that can regain lost hegemonic ground and social movements from below attempting to advance counter-hegemonic projects (see Chapter 3).

In the mapping that follows, we are concerned with how this dialectic of struggle has produced distinctive political economies from the late eighteenth century until the present. We distinguish between three periods of capitalist development – liberal capitalism, stretching from the late eighteenth century until the mid-twentieth century; organised capitalism, from the post-war era until the end of the 1970s, and neoliberal capitalism, which came into being in the 1980s and which we are still living under. When we investigate how these three periods of capitalist development have been moulded through cycles of struggle between movements from above and below, we focus on how the outcomes of these cycles of struggle have given rise to political economies in which capitalist accumulation is disembedded from, or re-embedded in, social regulations.

We draw on the heuristic that Polanyi (2001) devised in his seminal study *The Great Transformation*, where he suggested that the rise of capitalism was driven by a 'double movement' – firstly, a movement to disembed markets from various pre-capitalist regulations, and secondly, a counter-movement to re-embed markets in social regulations that constrained the logic of commodification. For Polanyi, it was this double movement that explained the transition from a market-centred form of capitalism in the nineteenth century to a state-centred form of capitalism in the twentieth century (see Dale 2010). Given the recent flourishing of scholarship that deploys Polanyi's heuristic to make sense of the rise of neoliberalism, we are not claiming any originality here. What we hope to do, however, is to link the heuristic of disembedding/re-embedding to the contentious dialectic of social movements from above and below in times of organic crisis and thus to move beyond Polanyi's functionalist argument that the re-embedding of capitalism was the outcome of society's need for self-protection (see Halperin 2004).

The Era of Liberal Capitalism

The era of liberal capitalism crystallised in the late eighteenth century on the basis of the profound reorganisation of the economy and polity that had been brought about by the collective agency of propertied classes around the North Atlantic space in the two preceding centuries. This reorganisation had created new spaces of accumulation and rid the state of 'the administrative organs that most impeded capitalist development' (Hill 1980: 134). The nineteenth century was an age in which these achievements were consolidated as markets – and hence the logic of commodification – and were thoroughly disembedded from social regulations; the power of capitalist classes were entrenched in forms of state that drove this process of disembedding, and the capitalist world-system came to be structured according to British free trade imperialism.

Accumulation in the Era of Liberal Capitalism

The first half-decade of the era of liberal capitalism – typically associated with Britain's Industrial Revolution – was characterised by the emergence of forms of industrial activity that were

> ... organized almost entirely on the lines of the family business enterprise, using methods of accounting and business practices which were entirely traditional ... Ownership and management were one and the same; the size of the firm was such that the whole industrial structure could reasonably be characterized as highly decentralized. (Harvey, 1999: 143)

This would gradually change during the second half of the nineteenth century. Cotton gave way to coal and industry was increasingly penetrated by science. The British economy witnessed exponential growth on the basis of a 'great global boom' in which 'the combination of cheap capital and a rapid rise in prices' offered the propertied classes bountiful investment opportunities (Hobsbawm 2004: 44, 45).[9] This was also the era when economic liberalism finally prevailed: 'The remaining institutional barriers to the free movement of the factors of production, to free enterprise and to anything which could conceivably hamper its profitable operation, fell before a worldwide onslaught' (ibid.: 50).

Ultimately, accumulation in the era of liberal capitalism was predicated upon two key power relations – the power that capital wielded over labour, and Britain's position as the hegemonic power in the world capitalist system. The subordination of labour to the power of capital in this period was not only evident in rampant exploitation in the process of production;

it was also manifest in the fact that the working class was not a significant entity in terms of consumption: 'The domestic market of the poor ... was not considered a major foundation for really spectacular advance' (ibid.: 48). The majority of workers thus 'remained solely a factor of production rather than of consumption', notes Halperin (2004: 99).[10]

To realise profits, capitalist classes relied on that other pillar of power constituted during the sixteenth and seventeenth centuries – the colonial division of labour, and Britain's position at the apex of this hierarchy. This was not only in the sense that cheap raw materials were appropriated through slave-based labour systems in the Americas. Britain's colonial possessions also furnished the key export markets for the commodities produced by Britain's budding industries:

> In terms of sales, the Industrial Revolution can be described except for a few initial years in the 1780s as the triumph of the export market over the home ... And within this expanding market, in turn, the semi-colonial and colonial markets, long the main outlets for British goods abroad, triumphed. (Hobsbawm 2005: 20)

As Halperin argues, this constellation served a key purpose for the social movement from above that moulded this era of capitalism:

> The development of exogenous demand and consumption through the export of capital and goods, together with the continued use of methods of increasing absolute surplus value at home, ensured that the benefits of expanding production would be retained solely by the property-owning classes. (Halperin 2003: 107)

It also, of course, placed the extension and deepening of colonial relationships at the centre of capitalism's continued productivity, leading to the 'scramble for Africa', the deepening of internal colonisation in Russia and North America, the building of land empires in Asia and the inter-imperial competition which found its expression in 1914.

Liberal Capitalism and the State

The disembedding of capitalist accumulation was fundamentally driven by the workings of 'the liberal state' (Cox 1987: 129) that emerged from the bourgeois revolution of the seventeenth century and was consolidated in western Europe and North America in the 150-year period leading up to 1848. The drive towards disembedding was inscribed in the interventions that defined the functioning of the state during this period. Key among these were the removal of any remaining vestiges of feudalism and mercantilism in economic life, establishing the necessary conditions for the consolidation of commodity and labour markets, ensuring the soundness of finance (above all, through the application of the gold standard), and finally the mobilisation of capital through direct state investment and the installation of legal frameworks that facilitated private capital formation (ibid.: 130–33).

The ability of the liberal state to drive disembedding has to be understood in relation to the consolidation, during the first half of the nineteenth century, of a historical bloc of dominant groups unified around a singular imperative: 'Keeping the poor away from political power came to be seen as a fundamental pre-condition for the functioning of laissez-faire and the protection of private property' (Silver and Slater 1999: 174; see also Cox 1987: 137–8).

The form of state that was brought into being in the capitalist heartlands rested on a horizontal alliance between emergent capitalist groups and aristocratic landowners (Saville 1994: Chapter 4). This constellation of social forces excluded the labouring poor, who were subjected to persistent processes of dispossession and marginalisation in the countryside and to fierce exploitation in the emerging industrial cities. Alongside the working classes, substantial segments of the middle classes also found themselves at a disadvantage in the new economic regime and partly excluded from political power: 'Labour and the disgruntled petty-bourgeois on the verge of toppling over into the unpropertied abyss, therefore shared common discontents' (Hobsbawm 2005: 55).

During the first three decades of the nineteenth century, this discontent fuelled a new wave of contention in which labour and parts of the middle classes rallied around democratic demands inspired by the legacies of the French Revolution (ibid.: 141–2). These stirrings in turn provoked a response from above aimed at eroding the incipient unity between labouring and middle classes around democratic claims. In Britain, a series of reforms were passed – for example, the Reform Act of 1832, the Municipal Corporations Act of 1835, and the repeal of the Corn Laws in 1846 – that defused middle-class discontent (Cox 1987: 136–7, Hobsbawm 2005: 364). Together with these laws, there occurred 'a qualitative improvement in the organisation of the coercive powers of the British state against those of its working people who were themselves combining into effective mass movements' (Saville 1994: 66).

These responses enabled the absorption of the middle classes into the historical bloc of dominant social forces, which was ultimately consolidated in response to the subaltern upsurge of 1848 (Hobsbawm 2005: 359–71). In Britain, the Chartist movement was defeated as 'the enhanced power of the state confronted the mass movements of working people on a scale never experienced during the previous century' (Saville 1994: 66). And in continental Europe, revolution turned to counter-revolution and restoration as 'symbiotic alliances between old landed wealth and new industrial elites were established' (Silver and Slater 1999: 175) as the foundation for 'passive revolutions' – that is, transitions towards capitalism and bourgeois rule that unfold 'without dramatic upheavals ... The old feudal classes are demoted from their dominant position to a "governing" one, but are not eliminated, nor is there any attempt to liquidate them as a social whole' (Gramsci 1998: 115).[11]

This process went hand-in-hand with the introduction of 'moderate middle class constitutions' across much of continental Europe (Hobsbawm,2005: 364) in the period *following* the repression of the movements of 1848. Popular agency could no longer be put back in its box, as the post-1815 reaction had sought to do; rather, elites needed to find ways of working with it through appropriate political forms: liberal nationalism and Bonapartism both enabled the incorporation of middle-class groups and sought to stave off the challenge raised by the 'social question' (Cox 2013a).

As growth resurged across the capitalist world-system in the second half of the nineteenth century, the politics of revolution from below were consigned to the fringes until the turn of the century.

The Capitalist World-system in the Era of Liberal Capitalism

From the late seventeenth century onwards, the British state proceeded to conquer 'a world-encompassing commercial and territorial empire' (Arrighi 1994: 218). Consequently, the country's dominant social groups gained 'an unprecedented command over the world's human and natural resources' (ibid.: 218). This position of power was then put to use in organising the global economy according to a system of 'free trade imperialism' based on 'the United Kingdom's *unilateral* adoption of a free trade practice and ideology' (ibid.: 55; see also Kiely 2010: 42–51). Britain was thus in a position 'to govern the inter-state system as effectively as a world-system' (ibid.: 55).

The era of British hegemony in the world-system was also an era in which a colonial division of labour and a concomitant 'racially hierarchical organization of global space' (McIntyre and Nast 2011: 1466) were consolidated (see also Wallerstein 2011: Chapter 3). At the onset of the nineteenth century, western states controlled 35 per cent of the earth's land surface; by 1914, this had increased to 85 per cent (Arrighi 1994: 53). This process was a crucial element in the process of disembedding that moulded the political economy of liberal capitalism.

'The central historical fact of the colonial era', McMichael and Raynolds write, 'was the violent incorporation of colonial lands and peoples into an expanding world capitalist economy driven by the process of commodification' (1994: 317–18). Of course, this did not entail that the colonial periphery came to witness the emergence of a form of capitalism characterised by 'technology-driven mass production', but rather that a '*structural logic*' was brought into being in which 'a division of labour crystallized, binding together agricultural suppliers of food and raw materials and the industrialized regions' (Callinicos 2008: 145). The natural and human resources of colonial territories were appropriated and used according to the exigencies of accumulation in the northern core of the capitalist world-system. In particular, agricultural production came to be geared towards expanding the supply of tropical products to serve as raw materials for metropolitan industry and articles for mass consumption for the working classes in the northern core of the world-system (see Friedmann 2005, Wolf 1982: 312–53), at times, as in India and Ireland, at the cost of the decommissioning of peripheral industries. And, as we have seen, colonial markets came to constitute a central moment in a circuit of capital that was decisively shaped by the economic and political power of dominant social groups in the nineteenth century.

The capitalist world-system of the nineteenth century was, as a whole, shaped by the collective agency of dominant groups, acting in and through states whose functions were increasingly honed to advancing commodification and mobilising force to ward off challenges to the fundamental structures of power within this system. Within the parameters of this system, subaltern groups in the colonised world were subject to forms of exploitation that eventually generated large-scale crises of reproduction. As Davis (2002) has documented, the famine crises that swept across Asia, Africa and Latin America in the late nineteenth century left as many as 60 million people dead. Those who perished were overwhelmingly peasants whose livelihoods had been eroded due to the unequal terms on which they had been integrated into the circuits of global commodity exchange: 'Millions died not outside "the modern world-system", but in the very process of being incorporated into its economic and political structures' (ibid.: 9).

The Transition to Organised Capitalism

So far, we have seen how the era of liberal capitalism was structured by social movements from above pursuing collective projects that sought to disembed spaces of accumulation – both nationally and globally – from the constraints of previous eras. These projects were fundamentally mediated by a developing state form that facilitated the exercise of power by propertied classes, and rested on pillars of power that subjugated working classes and colonised people – both economically and politically – to an expansive process of commodification.

The brave new world of liberal capitalism, however, would not last. The first half of the twentieth century was a period in which economic and geopolitical crisis combined to destabilise the hegemony of capitalist classes and colonial rulers. And – most importantly – it was a period in which movements from below mobilised to challenge and rupture the pillars of power upon which liberal capitalism had been founded. Ultimately, this cycle of struggle – which spanned the capitalist world-system as a whole – would give rise to a new phase of capitalist development, in which accumulation came to be embedded in institutional forms that accommodated key aspects of the social movement projects developed and pursued by working classes and colonised peoples.

The first signs that liberal capitalism was running out of economic steam were manifest in the global economic depression that stretched from 1873 to the middle of the 1890s (Hobsbawm 1987: Chapter 2, Wolf 1982: Chapter 11). This worldwide downturn 'ended the long era of economic liberalism' as free trade imperialism gave way to protectionism, centralisation and concentration gathered momentum in industry and finance, and business organisations became increasingly centred on scientific management (Hobsbawm 1987: 38–9, 44). The objective of these strategies was to recover profits, which was successfully achieved: 'From the middle of the 1890s until the Great War, the global economic orchestra played in the major key of prosperity rather than, as hitherto, the minor key of depression' (ibid.: 48; see also Arrighi and Silver 2003). During the 1920s, economic liberalism made an unabashed but short-lived return, as the crash of 1929 and the ensuing global depression left 'the political credibility of high finance and liberal governments' in smithereens (Silver 2003: 143).

During the same period, the hegemonic order of *Pax Britannica* entered a phase of terminal systemic chaos. Imperial expansion from the late nineteenth century onwards was fuelled by inter-state rivalry that gradually intensified in the opening decade of the 1900s. This process culminated in the eruption of the First World War – 'a catastrophe from which nineteenth century capitalism would never recover' (Arrighi 1994: 173) and which ended with an upsurge in popular struggles both in the northern core and the southern periphery of the world-system. When war broke out once more – this time on an industrial scale – in 1937–41, it was evident that the imperial world order of the nineteenth century could not be restored (Halperin 2003: 283).

Mobilisation from Below

However, liberal capitalism did not simply wither from the top down. Its demise was ultimately brought about by a period of sustained mobilisation from below that stretched from the 1880s to the end of the Second World War. During these six decades, working classes and colonised peoples developed social movement projects that were capable of forcing dominant social groups onto the defensive.

In the northern core of the capitalist world-system, two developments were at the core of this process. First of all, a new generation of trade unions came into being in which skilled and unskilled labour joined ranks against capital in forms of mobilisation that were 'more aggressive and political, and less sectional' than that which had prevailed in the second half of the nineteenth century (Silver 2003: 134). Secondly, mass-based working-class parties became a normal presence in the political landscape (ibid.: 135). As Hobsbawm (1987: 87) has noted, this development was an integral part of a more general democratisation of the politics of bourgeois society. The new state forms explored in much of Europe in the second half of the nineteenth century – a shift from dynastic to nation states, the development of constitutional monarchies with limited suffrage based on property rights, and the domination of nationalist and republican forms of politics – proved unable to deflect the increasing significance of the 'social question'.[12] In various tempos, British, French and German workers emancipated themselves from reliance on the ideologies and parties of middle-class politics (Thompson 1963) and developed their own forms of mass participation.

These changes occurred at a time when the working classes had expanded in size and had become concentrated in proletarian neighbourhoods in urban centres – a development which 'facilitated both the rapid spread of protest across categories of workers and plants, and a growing common class consciousness' (Silver 2003: 135). The tangible outcome of these processes was a steadily increasing wave of labour protest from the late nineteenth century until 1945. Despite two world wars, labour insurgency was still of such strength and scale that the long-term response from above could not simply come in the form of repression alone: '... the emergence of politically organized working classes was a profound transformation and required more than a modification of tactics: a fundamental change in ruling class strategies were required' (ibid.: 136). Thus, dominant groups resorted to a strategy centred on defensive concessions to the demands of organised labour, and these concessions would in turn come to undergird the class compromise between capital and labour in the post-war era. At the same time, structured popular participation in politics became a necessary starting-point for stable *right*-wing politics as well, and this period saw the development of fascism as well as that of Catholic parties, aiming to adopt the lessons of the SPD (Cox 2014b).

Colonised peoples faced the twin subjugation of an economic order that appropriated natural and human resources according to the imperatives of accumulation in the core of the world-system, and colonial states that denied them even the most fundamental democratic rights: 'Under British hegemony, non-Western peoples did not qualify as national communities in the eyes of the hegemonic power and of its allies, clients, and followers' (Arrighi 1994: 63). In the closing decades of the nineteenth century, opposition to western colonial rule was articulated by native elites who 'made little or no attempt to mobilize the mass of the population into the nationalist struggle' (Silver 2003: 147). This changed, however, in the aftermath of the First World War, as anti-colonialism was transformed into a popular social movement project.

Inspired by the revolutions in Ireland, Mexico and Russia, nationalist leaders became increasingly preoccupied with the expansion of the mobilising orbit of anti-colonialism. As anti-colonial movements increasingly turned to more militant forms of mass-based struggle (Silver and Slater 1999: 202–3), the elite leadership of these movements built vertical alliances with the struggles of the peasantry – still the most numerous subaltern group in the colonial periphery – and nascent working-class movements. This also entailed a widening of the anti-colonial agenda: moderate demands for constitutional reforms gave way to agendas that fused demands for national sovereignty with demands for social justice (Wallerstein 1990: 23–4, Silver and Slater 1999: 203, Ramnath 2011). In a parallel development, anti-colonialism also came to be increasingly integrated across the peripheral regions of the world-system: '[the] anti-colonial struggles that had adopted the broad approach of mass nonviolence had begun to converse with each other from as early as the 1927 League Against Imperialism conference in Brussels' (Prashad 2007: 27; see Ramnath 2011). Similarly, dialogue developed between the insurrectionary forms of Irish and Asian anti-imperialism (O'Malley 2008). Eventually, these conversations 'elaborated a set of principles that both skewered the hypocrisy of imperial liberalism and promoted social change' (Prashad 2007: 29).

Mexico and China had shown that large-scale popular mobilisation around nationalist demands in colonial and semi-colonial countries could morph into more radical revolutionary movements (Silver and Slater 1999: 208). The response from above – from the colonial powers – bore the imprint of this realisation as a large-scale process of decolonisation, first in Asia and then in Africa, was set in train in an attempt to pre-empt radicalisation (ibid.: 209). In much of Asia, this was done in the face of popular anti-colonial movements hardened by the collapse of imperial rule and subsequent resistance to Japanese occupation. With the emergence of a new generation of independent states, militant nationalism would give way to national projects of development in a post-colonial world.[13]

The Political Economy of Organised Capitalism

The era of organised capitalism – stretching from the end of the Second World War to the end of the 1970s – has to be understood in the context of how social movements from below had altered the balance of power between dominant and subaltern groups across the North-South axis of the world-system. This transformation, in turn, was manifest in the way in which capitalist accumulation came to be re-embedded in institutionalised social regulations that circumscribed the process of commodification that had been the central animating impulse of liberal capitalism.

The Accumulation Strategies of Organised Capitalism

Across the North-South axis, the re-embedding of market forces in the era of organised capitalism gave rise to new accumulation strategies that in important ways reoriented growth away from a sole focus on the enrichment of propertied classes and colonial powers.

In the global North, capital and labour had reached a historical compromise in which the former accepted regulations that improved wages and working conditions and secured full employment, and the latter accepted 'managerial controls within, and a depoliticization of demands beyond, the workplace' (Kiely 2007: 53). This constellation became the foundation for the functioning of 'high Fordism' (Harvey 1990) as an accumulation strategy centred on mass production for mass consumption. The production process was characterised by 'highly capital-intensive machinery, rigid divisions of labour within the workplace, and massive production runs on specific products' (Kiely 2005: 52). In contrast to the era of liberal capitalism, in which export markets were more important than domestic markets, it was, above all, domestic consumption that fuelled market demand: 'Growth was mainly centred on the domestic market' (Glyn et al. 1991: 48).[14]

Fordist accumulation strategies came to be at the heart of a period that is often referred to as the golden age of capitalism – that is, the period from 1950 to 1973, when the 'macroeconomic pattern' in the global North was characterised by '(i) rapid and parallel growth of productivity and capital stock per worker; and (ii) parallel growth of real wages and productivity' (ibid.: 47–8). Profit rates were consistently high while consumption and production grew at roughly equal rates, and this combination in turn secured the reproduction of the initial rate of accumulation (ibid.: 48).

However, the golden age of capitalism did not embrace all sections of the working classes. As Harvey (1990: 138) has pointed out, collective wage bargaining 'was confined to certain sectors of the economy and certain nation states where stable demand growth could be matched by large-scale investments in mass production technology'. Furthermore, there were sectors of the economy in which 'high-risk production still depended on low wages and weak job security. And even Fordist sectors could rest upon a non-Fordist base of subcontracting' (ibid.: 138). The result of these exclusions was a labour market that was deeply segmented as 'race, gender and ethnicity often determined who had access to privileged employment and who did not' (ibid.: 138).

In the global South, the post-war era brought about a radically new conjuncture in which the erstwhile leaders of anti-colonial movements were faced with the challenge of modernising stagnant economies and breaking free from the structures of dependency that locked the newly independent states of the Third World into a subordinate position in the world-system, while simultaneously offering selective rewards to some of the most active movement constituencies. The accumulation strategy that came to prevail across the post-colonial world is often referred to as developmentalism, and it centred on two key elements: agricultural modernisation and import-substituting industrialisation.

During the era of liberal capitalism, agriculture in the colonial periphery had been geared towards providing raw materials and foodstuffs for the economies of the northern core. Consequently, the agrarian sector was poorly attuned to contributing to domestic economic growth (McMichael and Raynolds 1994). Most states in the global South therefore pursued programmes of agricultural modernisation centred on land reforms that were intended to give rise to a class of independent capitalist farmers and the introduction of technological innovations that would boost productivity. The ambition was to create an agricultural sector that could contribute to the growth of domestic industry and supply urban consumer markets (see Araghi 1995, McMichael 1997).

Import-substituting industrialisation was focused on promoting and protecting the expansion of domestic industry in order to 'reduce the dependence on expensive manufactured imports, and relatively cheap primary product exports' (Kiely 2007: 51). Drawing on a combination of subsidies, tariffs and public investment, the state was supposed to funnel 'the flow of domestic private investment into sectors with high social returns and away from those in which returns on investment may have brought enormous private profits but were of less developmental significance' (Chibber 2004: 229). Peasant and worker movements expected to see benefits for at least some of their members, thus also defusing or co-opting the continuing political potential of these movements.

At one level, developmentalism was successful as an accumulation strategy:

> Between 1950 and 1975 income per person in the developing countries increased on an average by 3 per cent p.a., accelerating from 2 per

> cent in the 1950s to 3.4 per cent in the 1960s. This rate of growth was historically unprecedented for these countries and in excess of that achieved by the developed countries. (Glyn et al. 1991: 41)

This rate of growth, however, conceals highly uneven developmental trajectories. In agriculture, some progress was made in terms of promoting land reform and boosting food production, but as Friedmann (1982) and McMichael and Raynolds (1994) have pointed out, countries in the global South remained dependent on importing food from the global North.[15] And the period between 1960 and 1980 was one of de-peasantisation as 'both the rural population as a percentage of total population and the agricultural labour force as a percentage of total labour force declined in all regions of the Third World' (Araghi 1995: 350). Similarly, import-substituting industrialisation yielded mixed results: East Asian countries like Taiwan and South Korea witnessed the emergence of potent industrial sectors, while other regions – for example, Latin America and South Asia – witnessed an economic trajectory in which domestic capitalists could socialise their risks and losses and privately appropriate the gains of growth. 'The end result', Chibber summarises, 'was that there was development and growth – but at enormous cost to the public' (2004: 239; see also Chibber 2003, Evans 1995, Kohli 2004, Kiely 2007).

Forms of the State in Organised Capitalism

The re-embedding of accumulation could not have occurred without the emergence of forms of state characterised by modes of intervention and regulatory capacities that were shaped in important ways by the new equations of power that had been engendered by movement struggles from below in the first half of the twentieth century.

In the West, the liberal state gave way to the Keynesian welfare state – a form of state that worked along both an economic and a social axis to re-embed the dynamics of the market. In the economic realm, the Keynesian welfare state was characterised by a mode of intervention that sought to regulate business cycles by securing relatively stable 'demand conditions' through 'an appropriate mix of fiscal and monetary policies' (Harvey 1990: 135). The outcome of this was to secure *both* high profit rates for capital *and* full employment for labour. Furthermore, the state became a central arbiter between capital and labour through its mediation of wage bargaining and by reconciling income policies with other aspects of macroeconomic policy to ensure the maximisation of 'output, welfare, and employment' (Cox 1987: 222). In addition, the state took a more active role in the economy through public investment in sectors 'vital to the growth of both mass production and mass consumption' (Harvey 1990: 135), such as transport and public utilities (see also Glyn et al. 1991: 61).[16]

In the social realm, the Keynesian welfare state was characterised by the institutionalisation of access to social protection through the public provision of health care, housing, education, unemployment benefits and other transfers, and the introduction of public pension systems (ibid.: 59–61). Moreover, post-war welfare regimes were characterised by progressive taxation systems that redistributed income from capital to labour, which in turn reduced inequalities in market incomes and wealth holdings in western societies (Mann 2012: 281). The coming of the welfare state thus entailed an expansion of the rights and entitlements of citizens in the social domain – what Mann describes as 'the development of social citizenship in capitalist democracies' (ibid.: Chapter 9). At the heart of the institutionalisation of social citizenship lies a process of decommodification – that is, an expansion of 'the degree to which individuals, or families, can uphold a socially acceptable standard of living independently of market participation' (Esping-Andersen 1990: 37).[17]

The kernel of the historical bloc of social forces that buttressed the Keynesian welfare state was the historical class compromise between capital and labour. As we pointed out above, this was a compromise in which capital conceded to labour the imposition of regulations, both in the labour market and in the production process, as well as through new forms of social protection administered by the state, while labour accepted the rule of capital and channelled claims and demands through depoliticised, corporatist channels. In entering into this compromise, capital essentially resorted to a defensive strategy, aimed at defusing worker radicalism and securing the consent of subaltern groups in a vertical alliance to ensure the reproduction of capitalism as an economic regime.

Smith (2011: 17) has referred to this constellation as a form of 'expansive hegemony' constituted in relation to 'the bounded national state within which claims and rights were made in the language of "citizenship"'. Expansive hegemony was in turn made possible by the compromise between capital and labour noted above – a compromise in which '[g]overnments and big business accepted the permanence of unionism, while unions accepted the right of management to make ongoing changes in the organisation of production to increase productivity' (Silver 2003: 152). However, it is important that this compromise did not encompass the working classes in their entirety. The construction of a compromise between capital and labour emerged through a two-pronged strategy in which 'cooptation of the "responsible" elements of the labor movement through institutional reforms and mass consumption was supplemented by fierce repression of the "irresponsible" elements – both in the USA and western Europe' (Silver and Slater 1999: 207).

In the global South, post-colonial nation building came to be centred on the imperative of economic modernisation. This process of modernisation was orchestrated by a particular form of interventionist state – commonly referred to as the 'developmental' state (see Wade 1990, Chibber 2004). As Chibber notes, the economic interventions of the developmental state were characterised by a shift from '*managing the effects* of accumulation to *accelerating its pace*' (2003: 14; emphasis in original). States in the global South would promote land reforms, substitute for private capital by establishing public enterprises in the infrastructure and capital sectors, provide affordable credit to domestic business groups, and protect national industry from international competition (ibid.: 15). These interventions were coordinated through the modality of development planning: 'National planning separated national and global market priorities, enclosing national economies and instituting state redistributive systems to make national markets serve national citizens' (Ludden 2005: 4046). These 'national planning regimes' were not anti-market. Rather, the orientation was towards enhancing and supplementing private investment and constituting 'a combined public-private apparatus for monitoring and managing national economies' (ibid.: 4046).

National planning was also instrumental in depoliticising development in the global South. Postcolonial development was portrayed as a technical exercise in which experts would select policy solutions according to objective criteria rather than a form of social change that had to be brought about through mobilisation and struggle. The outcome would be a form of economic progress that would serve a national common good (Chatterjee 1993: 201–5).

The depoliticisation of development cannot be understood in isolation from the political conjuncture that emerged as a result of decolonisation. As we argued above, the making of anti-colonialism as a social movement project was predicated on the forging of an alliance between nationalist elites and popular classes. With the advent of decolonisation, nationalist elites had achieved their foremost goal, and as they emerged at the political helm of the newly independent states 'the cross-class alliance of the nationalist movements tended to dissolve' (Silver 2003: 158). What emerged in its place was a reconfiguration of social forces into what has been referred to as a 'developmentalist alliance' (Cardoso and Faletto 1979: 131). Typically, these developmental alliances would consist of a horizontal axis that brought together pre-existing dominant groups – above all, industrial capital and landed elites – around development strategies developed and administered by state managers (themselves often tied to middle-class nationalism), and a vertical axis that incorporated subaltern groups – both the urban working class and vast masses of rural producers and labourers – into the post-colonial historical bloc (Walton and Seddon 1994: 46–8).

Movements and revolutions were reconfigured as states, parties and distributive mechanisms. The incorporation of subaltern groups was underpinned by the extension of a 'social wage guarantee' by the developmental state in the form of price subsidies, public services and employment in the public sector (ibid.: 45–6). Ultimately, these concessions underpinned the demobilisation of the popular classes and their consent to an elite-led postcolonial development project. However, as in the case of the compromises that underpinned the political economy of organised capitalism in the global North, the developmentalist alliance had its exclusionary dimensions: it privileged formal sector workers over informal sector workers, the urban poor took precedence over the rural poor, the domestic sphere and women's reproductive labour were devalued relative to the public sphere and men's productive labour, and ethnic minorities were often excluded from the nationalist division of spoils (see Motta and Nilsen 2011: 7).

World Hegemony in Organised Capitalism

By the early twentieth century, Britain's capacity to govern the world-system had been eroded. Inter-state and inter-imperialist rivalry generated a period of intense systemic chaos between 1914 and 1945, and by the end of the Second World War the US had arisen as the new hegemonic power in the capitalist world-system (Arrighi 1994: 61).

In contrast to the imperial world order governed by Britain, American hegemony in the post-war era was shaped in fundamental ways by social movements from below and the defensive response from above that sought to remake 'the inter-state system to accommodate the demands of non-western peoples and the propertyless' (ibid.: 66). The key reforms won through the advance of social movement projects across the North-South axis came to be bolstered by the emergence of a world order in which free trade imperialism gave way to what Ruggie (1982) has referred to as 'embedded liberalism'.

Following the negotiations at Bretton Woods in 1944, a system was put in place to regulate the flows of trade and finance in the world economy (see Kiely 2007: 42–7, Helleiner 1994: Chapter 2). Under the aegis of the Bretton Woods system, trade came to be organised through 'a strategy of bilateral and multilateral intergovernmental negotiations of trade liberalization, aimed primarily at opening up other states to US commodities and enterprise' (Arrighi 1994: 71). Although the dominant position of the US in the world economy was reflected in its influence in such negotiations, the new structure that was put in place – institutionalized through the General Agreement on Trade and Tariffs – 'left the pace of trade liberalization in the hands of national governments' (ibid.: 277).

An equally significant change took place in the realm of finance. Liberal capitalism had been characterised by a scenario in which 'the circuits and networks of high finance had been firmly in the hands of private bankers and financiers who organised and managed them with a view to making a profit' (ibid.: 278). The new international financial architecture that was put in place at Bretton Woods was fundamentally different: by establishing the dollar-gold system of fixed exchange rates, the fluxes and flows of world money came to be regulated by a network of government institutions – central banks such as the US Federal Reserve, as well as the International Monetary Fund and the World Bank – whose policy imperatives were shaped by 'considerations of welfare, security, and power' rather than simply the private maximization of profit: 'World money thus became a product of state-making activities' (ibid.).

The era of organised capitalism, then, was characterised by the intertwined embedding of commodification at both national and global scales. The embedded liberalism of the post-war world order underpinned 'an international trade and payments system that facilitated an unprecedented boom in the growth of trade and of national output and productivity' (Glyn et al. 1991: 70). This in turn reinforced and entrenched the social compact between capital and labour in the global North as integral to sustaining the equation of mass production for mass consumption that was at the heart of capitalism's golden age.

Furthermore, embedded liberalism at a global scale was also significant in that it opened up a certain space for the articulation and implementation of national projects of development in the global South – perhaps most significantly by enabling newly independent states to shield domestic markets through protective tariffs and to give direction to the trajectory of industrialisation by means of 'credit allocation, state planning, capital controls, and some public sector investment' (Kiely 2005: 54). However, this space remained circumscribed by the reproduction of hierarchical relations of dependence in the world economy and – as the bloody arc of military coups such as Iran (1953), Guatemala (1954), Indonesia (1965), and Chile (1973) testify – the readiness of the US to resort to force in the face of Third World regimes that sought to push beyond the narrow parameters of 'national capitalist development' (Desai 2004: 171).

The Unravelling of Organised Capitalism

This 'golden age' of organised capitalism started to founder in the late 1960s. In the global North, the high rates of growth, productivity and profits that had been the hallmark of this era since the early 1950s were reversed (Glyn et al. 1991: 72–88, Brenner, 2006: Chapters 8 and 9, Armstrong, Glyn and Harrison 1991). Fordism, as Kiely (2005: 62) has noted, had reached a point of exhaustion in which further productivity increases would be dependent upon 'the intensification of management pressure on labour and the speeding up of already established work practices' – but attempts to do so were foiled by militant trade unions. With the hike in oil prices in 1973–74, the economies of the global North entered into a major recession in 1974–75 (see Armstrong, Glyn and Harrison 1991).

Recession in the core states of the global North in turn had significant consequences for the world economy. The US found that its hegemonic position in the world-system was eroding: the country ran a constant trade deficit with its main competitors – Japan and West Germany – and these states consequently needed fewer dollars to buy US goods. As the value of the dollar started to fall, the Nixon administration resorted to a series of measures that ultimately undermined the dollar-gold system of fixed exchange rates. As the financial architecture of Bretton Woods gave way to 'a new system of floating rates and freer capital movement' (Kiely 2005: 60) a key feature of embedded liberalism – the embedding of global finance in a regulatory framework – had been effectively abandoned (see Glyn et al. 1991: 98–110, Helleiner 1994: Chapters 4 and 5).

The collapse of the Bretton Woods system was an integral element in a process that ultimately undermined the postcolonial development project in the global South. While the economies of southern developmental states had registered high growth rates in the first half of the 1970s, this growth was highly unevenly distributed: it was above all the newly industrialising countries in East Asia that witnessed high growth rates, while Latin American and African countries increasingly stagnated (McMichael 2004, Kiely 2007). To cover payment deficits and to sustain savings and investments in their national economies, states in the global South turned to international banks that were flooded with excess dollars and operating within the parameters of a liberalised financial system. Consequently, between 1973 and 1979, the total outstanding public long-term debt – a debt increasingly made up of private-sector bank loans – of countries in the global South tripled (Glyn et al. 1991: 112, McMichael 2004: 126). This created structural vulnerabilities that would be decisive in enabling the advance of neoliberalism in the global South (see below).

Ultimately, however, the unravelling of organised capitalism involved something much more fundamental than simply the stagnation of accumulation strategies. The reforms that were introduced from above to counter the advance of the social movement projects of working classes and colonised peoples in the first half of the twentieth century were in crucial ways centred on depoliticisation – that is, economic and political concessions were granted from above in exchange for demobilisation and consent from below, including high levels of popular involvement in mass parties and other organisations representing their interests within this framework. The late 1960s, however, witnessed the sundering of this equation across the North-South axis as acquiescence gave way to a new cycle of global revolt (Katsiaficas 1987, Wallerstein 1989, Harman 1998b).

In the global North, the revolt of 1968 was predicated both on a repoliticisation of the Fordist structuring of the capital–labour relation and the emergence of new social movements from below that challenged the wider edifice of organised capitalism. Militant labour struggles from Italy to Detroit accelerated the growth of wages and dug into corporate profits, while successful campaigns for the expansion of welfare rights increased the indirect costs of capitalist exploitation (Holloway 1995; see also Armstrong, Glyn and Harrison 1991). However, it was not just capital's right to command in the context of the production process that came under attack in the revolt of 1968 in the global North.

With the rise of new radical movements, the wider edifice of organised capitalism was challenged: 'A new politics of recognition ... provided a central plank from which these anti-authoritarian movements were pitted against the professional politics of a stale social democratic consensus and of a crass consumer culture' (Watts 2001: 172). The gendered underpinnings of organised capitalism – a sharp division between paid employment and housework, the exclusion of women from professional employment, a sexual order geared to the married, heterosexual family – were challenged and fundamentally disrupted by women's and GLTBQ movements.

The ethnocentric definitions of national welfare states and core employment regimes were challenged by a new assertiveness on the part of immigrant communities and ethnic and regional minorities. Counter-cultural movements challenged the definition of interests – a privatised existence, lifelong and intensive employment, consumption for its own sake – which was central to organised capitalism. Most fundamentally, perhaps, top-down solutions in which more or less representative elites distributed gains in return for passive support were challenged by an extra-institutional left and grass-roots movements which stressed direct participation and control (Wainwright 1994). The result was – in essence – the emergence of 'a fundamental crisis of "normality" affecting all aspects of the post-war order' in the global North (Overbeek and van der Pijl 1993: 14).

In the global South, the revolt of 1968 took the form of an attack on 'the nationalism and institutionalized elite politics ... of the first generation of independent Third World states' (Watts 2001: 172) as well as in the upsurge of a radicalised Third Worldism (Berger 2004). Ranging from democratic grass-roots movements to guerrilla insurgencies, the revolts against the 'first-generation Bandung regimes' (ibid.: 11) saw subaltern groups that had been at the margins of the equations of compromise that held together the developmentalist alliance – for example, the urban poor, the informal working class, small and marginal peasants and landless labourers, women and indigenous groups – coming together in social movements from below that challenged the exclusionary and dispossessory ramifications of the postcolonial development project (see Nilsen 2015).

Asia and Africa also witnessed the outcome of armed struggles for national liberation that eventually gave rise to what Berger (2004: 19) has called 'second generation Bandung regimes' – that is, states that espoused 'a more radical, a more unambiguously socialist Third Worldism than the first generation Bandung regimes'. Parallel with the emergence of these new struggles in the global South, the transnational Third World project was radicalised by the Non-Aligned Movement's call for a New International Economic Order – that is, a radical restructuring of the international economy in order to enable the countries of the global South to break free from their subordinate and dependent position in the world-system (see Prashad 2012: 24–34).

The conjuncture in which the global revolt of 1968 crystallised was one of organic crisis. The hegemony of dominant groups – carefully constructed through a strategy in which defensive concessions combined with selective repression to demobilise the upsurge of working classes and colonised peoples – fractured as new movements from below threatened to rupture fundamental structures of power in the capitalist world-system. In the global North, the persistent failures, throughout the 1970s, to restore accumulation through Keynesian policy interventions, combined with the inability of governments across the political spectrum to re-establish consensus and stability to give rise to a situation in which it was evident that the reproduction of hegemony depended on an offensive response from above – that is, a response that was capable of disarticulating 'old formations' and reworking 'their elements into new configurations' (Hall 1979: 15). Ultimately, this response took the form of 'a *political* project to restore the power of economic elites' (Harvey 2005: 14) – namely neoliberalism.

It is important to stress that this outcome was neither predictable (at the time) nor inevitable (with hindsight). The long-running crisis which saw 'liberated zones' more or less briefly in Prague, Paris and Derry, American humiliation in Vietnam and the rise of guerrilla movements across Latin America and Asia was one in which most participants expected a resolution either from the new Left or the older, fascist Right. Neoliberalism did not simply 'rise like the sun at the appointed time': it gained support from one-time members of the ruling bloc as a resolution to an ongoing crisis which would meet their interests in an aggressive way.

Neoliberalism as a Social Movement From Above

Neoliberalism, in our analysis, is best understood as a social movement from above that pursued an offensive strategy that sought to restore the power of capital over labour by reversing the victories that had been won by movements from below in the first half of the twentieth century. In doing so, neoliberalism effectively disembedded capitalist accumulation from the institutionalised regulations that had circumscribed the dynamic of commodification in the era of organised capitalism and crafted a political economy in which the market has become the fulcrum of the organization of human needs and capacities.

In the following, we first describe the construction of neoliberalism as a transnational political project before discussing how the restoration of the power of capital over labour is inscribed in the political economy of neoliberal capitalism. We do not want to argue that the neoliberal project is a behemoth that is everywhere and always capable of creating a world in its own image. Jamie Peck (2010a: 30) is entirely correct in arguing that if neoliberalism 'has become omnipresent ... it is a complex, mediated, and heterogeneous kind of omnipresence, not a state of blanket conformity'. However, by conceiving of neoliberalism as a distinct era of historical capitalism, we hope to contribute a politically enabling analysis that can illuminate 'how struggles in different socio-spatial arenas and across spatial scales might link with one another' (Hart 2002: 820).

Constructing the Neoliberal Project

The construction of neoliberalism as a political project has unfolded in a series of discernible phases from the inter-war years until the present. Its origins – a phase that Peck (2010a: xi) refers to as 'its inauspicious beginnings as a reactionary cult' – can be dated to the decades between 1920 and 1950, a period in which economists, mostly in Europe but also in the US, debated 'the contours of a market-based society, which they believed was the best way to organize an economy and guarantee individual liberty' (Jones 2012: 6). Emerging as a hostile response to the 'collectivism' of social democracy, the New Deal and the Great Society in Europe and the US, as well as to fascism and communism, the neoliberal project initially found an institutional manifestation in the Mont Pelerin Society, which was first brought together by Friedrich Hayek in 1947 'to create, and then to synthesize, a neoliberal program and political strategy' (ibid.: 4; see Peck 2010a: Chapter 2, Mirowski and Piewhe 2009). The strategic kernel of their activity was for 'neoliberal thinkers' to establish links with 'the wider intelligentsia, journalists, experts, politicians, and policymakers' (Jones 2012: 4).

As the hub of neoliberal activity shifted across the Atlantic to the University of Chicago and Milton Friedman, energies were focused on building and acting through 'a transatlantic network of think-tanks, businessmen, journalists, and politicians, who spread an increasingly honed political message of the superiority of free markets' (ibid.: 4). The initial growth of this network took the form of think-tanks that emerged with economic support from business sources in the 1950s and 1960s. The intellectuals at the head of think-tanks such as the American Enterprise Institute in the US and the Institute of Economic Affairs in the UK 'used their institutions as engines of a renaissance of free market ideas in Britain, the United States, and beyond' (ibid.: 159). During the troubled decade of the 1970s, yet another generation of neoliberal think-tanks came into being, such as the Centre for Policy Studies and the Adam Smith Institute in Britain or the Heritage Foundation and the Cato Institute in the US. In this way, 'the intellectual infrastructure of neoliberalism' (ibid.: 170) was put into place.

This intellectual infrastructure was in turn linked to the collective agency of transnational capital. As Neil Davidson (2010: 23) notes, large business houses and corporations had generally been supportive of state intervention in boom years of the golden age. However, by the late 1960s, changes were afoot in the world economy that eroded this support. Firstly, accumulation and production was increasingly being oriented away from the strong focus on the nation state that had characterised organised capitalism. This was particularly so in the realm of finance, due to the formation of substantial financial markets 'outside the control of domestic banking regulations' (Kiely 2007: 60) during the 1960s – a tendency that was further amplified with the collapse of the Bretton Woods system in the early 1970s.

Manufacturing capital also had to relate to the increasing salience of global competitive pressures, which led transnational capital to advocate deregulation in order to be able to maximise profits in world markets (Davidson 2010: 23; see also Kotz 2002). The crisis years of 1973–74 further consolidated this reorientation towards a preference for deregulation as the Keynesian strategies that were initially mobilised in response to recession proved unable to revive growth (ibid.: 24). As transnational capital – with finance at the helm (Robinson 2004: 51) – searched for an alternative agenda that would enable them to pursue new accumulation strategies, their support for and advocacy of the policy prescriptions developed and propagated in and by the transatlantic network of think-tanks became more systematic and more pronounced (Kotz 2002: 70, Davidson 2010: 22–3).

The late 1970s witnessed the first departures from Keynesian orthodoxy in economic policy-making at the hands of beleaguered Labour governments and Democratic administrations in Britain and the US. However, the real political breakthrough of the neoliberal project in the global North was predicated on the construction of links between transnational capital, neoliberal think-tanks and conservative forces in British and American politics. During the crisis-ridden decade of the 1970s, factions among the British Conservatives and the American Republicans became increasingly vocal and organised in their desire to break with the post-war Keynesian consensus. Commonly referred to as 'the New Right', these factions collaborated closely with both business groups and think-tanks to articulate a new conservative policy regime that wedded sociocultural conservatism with the neoliberal critique of Keynesian economics (Jones 2012: Chapter 6, Harvey 2005: 48–62).

In the global North, the victories of Margaret Thatcher in 1979 and Ronald Reagan in 1980 enabled the neoliberal agenda to be transformed into 'state-authored restructuring projects' (Peck and Tickell 2002: 388). Conservatives and Republicans launched a series of reforms in the 1980s that aimed directly at disembedding the market from the regulations that had been imposed after 1945: privatisation of public goods, utilities and industries, financial liberalisation, and cutbacks in welfare spending (see Jessop et al. 1988, Hall 1983, Piven and Cloward 1982, Edsall 1985). Crucially, the advance of these reforms was predicated on concerted and successful efforts to break the structural power of labour in the economy, typically by provoking confrontations between state-backed employers and central trade unions. 'These defeats', Davidson argues, 'then acted as examples to other unions, against a background of multiplying legal restraints and increasing employer intransigence' (2010: 29). It was in Britain and the US, too, that neoliberalism's impact was fastest and deepest: other western states saw very different trajectories of change, and different strategic conflicts (Lash and Urry 1987).

During the 1980s, the reach of the neoliberal project was also extended beyond its transatlantic origins. Mediated through a variety of institutions – ranging from non-governmental initiatives, such as the Trilateral Commission and the World Economic Forum, via supranational political forums such as the G7 to existing international financial institutions like the World Bank and the IMF – this process brought together transnational capital, political elites and leading state managers around a global policy consensus centred on the key precepts of the neoliberal project (see Cox 1987: 253–65, Gill 1990: Chapter 5, van der Pijl 1998: 123–35).

The significance of the global extension of the neoliberal project became particularly clear when the hike in international interest rates following the Volcker shock of 1979 combined with recessionary tendencies in the world economy to push large parts of the global South into a debt crisis of massive proportions. As credit dried up in international financial markets, states in Latin America and Africa had to turn to the World Bank and the IMF to obtain loans. In doing so, they encountered an institutional couplet whose policy preferences had come to be shaped by the so-called 'Washington Consensus' – that is, a constellation which brought together the US Congress and senior members of the administration, the international financial institutions, the Federal Reserve Board and the economic agencies of the US government, and influential think-tanks around a specific interpretation of what had caused the crisis and how it could be resolved (Peet 2007: 109–13, Kiely 2005: 68–77).

According to this consensus, the debt crisis originated in the state-centred development strategies that had been pursued throughout the global South since decolonisation, rather than in the increasingly liberalised financial markets that had emerged after the collapse of the Bretton Woods system (McMichael 2004: 132). Consequently, the crisis had to be resolved through economic restructuring: loans were extended to indebted states on the condition that they implement Structural Adjustment Programmes (SAPs) centred on currency devaluation, reductions of public expenditure, deregulation of national markets and extensive privatisation schemes (Walton and Seddon 1994: 17–19).

Neoliberal restructuring through SAPs was crucial to the disembedding of accumulation in the global South. However, this was not a one-way process in which the global North forcibly incorporated the global South into the orbit of neoliberalism. Rather, as Adam Morton's (2011) study of Mexico's changing political economy has shown, the agency of (some) economic and political elites within states in the global South was integral to the orchestration of neoliberal restructuring. This illustrates a key feature of the transnational extension of the neoliberal project, namely that it has proceeded through the construction of horizontal alliances between transnational fractions of capital and the building of a concomitant consensus around 'ideas and policies conducive to transnational forces within major government bureaucracies and international organizations' (Gill 1990: 95).

As a social movement from above, then, neoliberalism was materially grounded in the changed conditions of accumulation that emerged in the context of the crisis of organised capitalism. Fusing together the collective agency of transnational capital, networked think-tanks, political parties and state managers, and operating through a wide array of institutional forms – some of which had to be created and others which had to be conquered – and across spatial scales from the local to the global, the neoliberal project established its dominance in the decades of the 1980s and 1990s. During the 1990s, the form of the project seemed to change its character – the New Right gave way to the 'Third Way' politics of New Labour, and in institutions like the World Bank, the language of structural adjustment was overtaken by the language of poverty reduction (see Kiely 2005: Chapter 4, Cammack 2004, 2009). As Peck and Tickell (2002: 389) have argued, this transition is best understood as a shift from a narrow focus on 'the mobilization and extension of markets' to a more encompassing focus on 'new forms of institution-building and governmental intervention' – typically centred on technocratic and depoliticised economic management – to secure the long-term consolidation of the initial achievements of the neoliberal project (see also Davidson 2010: 41–54).

The Political Economy of Neoliberalism

The neoliberal project has proceeded by disembedding the market from the institutionalised restrictions imposed upon the logic of commodification in the era of organised capitalism. This achievement expresses how neoliberalism as a movement from above has worked to restore the power of capital over labour. In this section, we investigate how this restoration of power is inscribed in the accumulation strategies and forms of state that characterise the political economy of neoliberalism.

This entails describing neoliberalism as system: but it is important to remember that it is no more self-sufficient or automatic than the political economy of capital (above). It is important to neoliberalism's legitimacy to describe itself as 'just the way things are' (neoliberalism as nature). Critical accounts deconstruct this to show its constructed reality in the form of institutions and mechanisms (neoliberalism as system), and of course, this is at one level how any successful movement from above can be described – as a routine, organised social reality.[18]

Yet if we do not place on the same ontological plane the political brutality with which this reality has been imposed against defenders of the old order and the other challengers of the late 1960s and early 1970s; the constant challenges to its power against which it has to assert itself in ways *external* to its natural routines; and the internal moments of doubt when neoliberal elites consider whether or not (for example) endless 'war on terror', particular financial mechanisms, partial suspensions of democracy in the EU, or the failure to respond to global warming are their only options, we see only the results of the construct and not the agency involved. This is not, of course, to deny the force of the repeatedly made point that neoliberalism has its own mechanisms for redefining individual identity, defusing popular struggles and coopting crises – as have all previous regimes which have lasted more than a few years. It is to say that if we do not see neoliberalism as a complex, contested, fragile and ultimately impermanent achievement of elite agency we are taking the *intentions* of its makers as *given fact* – and in essence conceding permanent defeat.

New Geographies of Production

The central economic dimension of the organic crisis of organised capitalism was a dramatic decline in profitability from the late 1960s to the early 1980s (Duménil and Levy 2004: 24). Restoring profitability for capitalist elites depended on *both* breaking the power of organised labour *and* reversing the processes of decommodification that had been so central to the reembedding of capitalist accumulation after 1945. The former objective was achieved through a restructuring of 'the geography of production' (Prashad 2012: 4) across the North-South axis and the latter objective through a range of practices that can best be understood as 'accumulation by dispossession' (Harvey 2005).

During the era of organised capitalism, the spatial structure of the world capitalist system was characterised by 'national circuits of accumulation that were linked to each other through commodity exchanges and capital flows' (Robinson 2004: 10). This spatial structure was in turn central to the reproduction of the social compact between capital and labour, as this was constituted in and through the bounded national state (Smith 2011: 17). The emergence of a new geography of production from the late 1970s onwards eroded this nation-centric spatial structure: the global North witnessed substantial processes of deindustrialisation as manufacturing plants were closed and industrial workforces downsized, while new centres of accumulation emerged, as transnational corporations relocated parts of the manufacturing process to the global South (McNally 2011: 50–57).

As a consequence of this spatial reorganisation, the circuit of capital accumulation was effectively transnationalised through

> ...the decentralization and functional integration around the world of vast chains of production and distribution, the instantaneous movement of values ... and the unprecedented concentration and centralization of worldwide economic management, control, and decision-making power in transnational capital and its agents. (Robinson 2003: 19)

This spatial reorganisation of capitalist accumulation has been integral to the restoration of the power of capital over labour in two ways.

Firstly, it enabled capital to break free from the compromises that had been struck with organised labour in the post-war era. Thus, parallel with the downsizing of industrial workforces and the rupturing of trade union power, production systems in the global North were reorganised according to the principles of 'flexible accumulation': new technologies were introduced, wage structures were tiered, employment was casualised, and working hours were extended (McNally 2011, Harvey 1990). These changes facilitated 'an enormous increase in exploitation', as the profits yielded by gains in productivity 'were claimed almost exclusively by capital' (McNally 2011: 48).

Secondly, by relocating labour-intensive phases of production to countries in the global South, capital has been able to benefit from 'the huge reserves of cheap labour ... which makes possible dramatic reductions in wage costs' (McNally 2011: 51; see also Taylor 2009: 156).[19] These reserves of labour are themselves the product of neoliberal restructuring. As Araghi (1995) points out, the period from 1973 to 1990 witnessed an acceleration of de-peasantisation that has to be understood in the context of the collapse of developmentalism. With the advent of structural adjustment, it was no longer possible to maintain subsidies, price supports, or protective tariffs for the agricultural sector (McMichael 2005, Araghi 2009).

Consequently, small and marginal peasants have been dispossessed in large numbers, and left with little option but to migrate to urban centres. Here, they join the ranks of those who have lost their jobs as a result of retrenchment in state industries and the public sector to form an 'informal working class' that feeds the fires of accumulation in the neoliberal world economy (Davis 2006: Chapter 8; see below).

Accumulation by Dispossession

As we noted above, the re-embedding of accumulation in the era of organised capitalism was closely associated with a process of decommodification that restricted the reach of market forces in certain crucial ways. The reversal of this process has been achieved through a multiplicity of practices that Harvey (2003, 2005) refers to as 'accumulation by dispossession' – that is, the conversion of resources that were previously available to subaltern groups as public goods and services, elements of a social wage, or common property into capital, and the insertion of these resources into the realm of accumulation.

Accumulation by dispossession has been propelled by economic practices that are at the very core of the neoliberal project. Privatisation – for example, of public housing, state-owned industries and natural resources – has been instrumental in reversing the thrust of decommodification and thus opening up 'new fields for capital accumulation in domains hitherto regarded off limits to the calculus of profitability' (Harvey 2005: 160). Financialisation – the fusion of financial deregulation and financial innovation that has swept across the world economy since the demise of the Bretton Woods system in the early 1970s – has similarly created vast opportunities for profit making through speculation, raiding, asset stripping and debt peonage (ibid.: 161). Privatisation and financialisation are in turn entwined in practices of crisis management, in which the convergence of national governments and international financial institutions around the restructuring of economies effectively redistributes 'assets and channel wealth and income either from the mass of the population to the upper classes or from vulnerable to richer countries' (Harvey 2007: 34). Finally, Harvey (2005: 62) notes, the state plays a key role in driving processes of accumulation by dispossession through the pursuit of privatisation offensives, by reducing state expenditures towards the social wage, and by implementing regressive tax regimes that favour high-income groups.

The effect of accumulation by dispossession has been 'to redistribute, rather than to generate, wealth and income' (ibid.: 159). This process of redistribution has been centrally predicated on commodification – in some cases by reinserting decommodified assets and resources (for example, public infrastructure, health care, or state-owned natural resources) into the realm of market exchange, and by creating new markets for common property resources that until the advent of the neoliberal onslaught had not been incorporated into the sphere of capitalist accumulation (for example, the extension of financialisation to the natural environment through carbon trading or the privatisation of agricultural knowledge systems through the institutionalisation of intellectual property rights). And this intensive expansion of commodification has in turn combined with the spatial restructuring of capitalist production to achieve 'the restoration of the power and income of capitalist classes' (Duménil and Levy 2011: 55). The largest and most organised sectors of capital have been strongly supportive of this process, which they have benefited disproportionately from and which resolves the strategic and political crisis in which Fordism and developmentalism had found themselves.

Profitability and Inequality

This achievement is manifest in the recovery of profitability that has characterised the period from 1982 to 2007 (McNally 2011: 40–42, Duménil and Levy 2011: 57–60).[20] This did not bring profits up to the levels witnessed in the 1950s and 1960s, but nevertheless constituted a departure from the crisis of profitability in the 1970s that was substantial enough 'to move the global economy out of crisis for a quarter-century' (McNally 2011: 49). Two features of this recovery are worth noting. First, it has been characterised by 'a new hierarchy in profit rates' in which the financial sector has reaped the highest rewards 'while the profit rates of the nonfinancial sector remained stagnant' (Duménil and Levy 2011: 69; see also Duménil and Levy 2004: Chapter 11). The recovery of profitability, then, is marked by a salience of financialisation in the political economy of neoliberalism. This is important in understanding the reconfiguration of capitalist elites behind the neoliberal project (Lash and Urry 1987): not all economic elites benefit equally, and indeed some – most notably, elements of national industrial capital which were not as mobile as multinational firms, but also national*ised* capital – have lost out, as of course have elements of the petty bourgeoisie. Other sectors have had to radically remake themselves or take substantial losses in order to survive.

Secondly, the revival of corporate profits has gone hand-in-hand with an ever-growing gap between productivity and wages. The combination of reorganisation of production in the global North with the increased exploitation of cheap labour in the global South has created a scenario in which there has occurred a 'huge allocation to capital of new wealth created by labor' (McNally 2011: 48).

These new equations of power between capital and labour find their expression in spiraling inequality. Between 1996 and 2007, the number of High Net-Worth Individuals (HNWIs) increased at an annual average of 7.6 per cent: 'In 2007, the total wealth of HNWIs reached $41 trillion' (Duménil and Levy 2011: 48). As we enter 2014, we confront a situation in which 1 per cent of the world's families own 46 per cent of the world's wealth: 'The bottom half of the world's population owns less than the richest 85 people in the world' (Oxfam 2014: 3). Inequality is not simply increasing between countries and along a North-South axis: income inequality has been persistently widening in the OECD countries between 1978 and 2008, and the impact of the financial crisis between 2008 and the present has exacerbated this trend (OECD 2011, 2013; see also UNDP 2014).

Indeed, in the US, the share of total income received by the upper 1 per cent of the national income bracket has skyrocketed during the neoliberal era, from a low of 9 per cent in the 1970s to an unprecedented 28 per cent in the late 2000s – the highest level since 1928 (Duménil and Levy 2011: Chapter 3, McNally 2011: 42–3). Britain has witnessed a similar trajectory of increasing inequality: the Gini coefficient has increased from 0.24 in 1977 to 0.34 in 2012, making Britain the country in the global North where income inequality has risen fastest since the late 1970s, a result of its early and accelerated switch to neoliberalism and its relationship to the financial industry (National Equality Panel 2010, Ramesh 2011). And in the emerging markets of the global South – China, India, and South Africa being cases in point – economic growth has coincided with dramatic increases in inequality between ascendant elites and the mass of the population (Ivins 2013, Prashad 2012: Chapter 3).

Across the North-South axis, the recovery of profit rates and the rise of inequality under neoliberalism is closely related to the emergence of a relative surplus population that is relegated 'to irregular, insecure, temporary and precarious forms of employment' (Neilson and Stubbs 2011: 436), or altogether marginalised from labour markets, in an age when an estimated 202 million people find themselves unemployed across the world (ILO 2014). In the global North, this relative surplus population is the product of industrial downsizing and restructuring since the early 1980s and consists of 'workers at the extreme edges, or completely outside of, restructured labour markets' (Gilmore 2007: 70).

As work has become unstable and precarious and incomes have declined, cities in the global North have witnessed the rise of a new form of urban poverty that is 'increasingly disconnected from cyclical fluctuations and global trends in the economy, so that expansionary phases in aggregate employment and income have little beneficial effect on it' (Wacquant 2008: 236). In the global South, the relative surplus population is at the centre of the mushrooming of what Mike Davis (2006: 178) refers to as 'the informal proletariat': a 1 billion-strong workforce that ekes out a living in an informal sector where employment is precarious and unstable, wages extremely low, and social protection altogether absent. Intrinsically linked to the exploitation of cheap labour in the new geography of production; the formation of this informal proletariat entrenches the power of capital over labour as it enables capital 'to subject workers to the most accelerated forms of exploitation possible to optimize profit' (McIntyre and Nast 2011: 1472; see also Araghi 2009). These processes have, of course, further undermined the numbers, confidence, strategic position and political legitimacy of the kinds of organised core labour force which were central to working-class power in the era of organised capitalism and whose defeat was a precondition for entry on the neoliberal path.

Market Discipline, Social Control and the Neoliberal State

As a social movement from above, neoliberalism has been fundamentally 'concerned ... with the challenge of first seizing and then retasking the state' (Peck 2010a: 4). Consequently, a new form of state – *the neoliberal state* – has crystallised, characterised by a definition of 'the limits and parameters of state purposes, and the modus operandi of state action' (Cox 1987: 105) that centres partly on facilitating the disembedding of capitalist accumulation across spatial scales and partly in governing new forms of social insecurity through models such as workfare and punitive containment (Jessop 2003, Gill 1995, Peck 2002, Wacquant 2004).

The economic modus operandi of the neoliberal state differs in fundamental ways from the forms of state that characterised the era of organised capitalism. Whereas the Keynesian welfare state centred its regulatory activities on counter-cyclical interventions and the developmental state was oriented towards economic modernisation through national planning, the neoliberal state pursues forms of macroeconomic regulation that are geared to 'create, restructure or reinforce ... the competitive advantages of its territory, population, built environment, social institutions and economic agents' in relation to the dynamics of global markets (Jessop 2003: 96). This is achieved through policy regimes that secure private property rights, liberalise national investment regimes and grant rights of access to transnational capital, impose fiscal prudence, create new spaces of accumulation through privatisation and ensure flexible labour markets (Gill 1995, Harvey 2005: Chapter 3, Jessop 2003: Chapter 3).

This process unfolds across spatial scales. Since the onset of the neoliberal counter-revolution in the 1980s, the 'market discipline' that constitutes the framework for national policy-making has been inscribed in legal and juridical forms of governance that are organised in and through transnational institutions as part of what Gill (1995) refers to as 'new constitutionalism'. New constitutionalism, Gill argues, represents a 'a political project to "lock in" the power gains of capital on a world scale' (ibid.: 164). This is achieved as international financial institutions like the World Bank and the IMF and transnational inter-governmental bodies like the G8 and the WTO attempt, against varying kinds of popular resistance and with varying degrees of success, to put in place policy frameworks and trade and investment treaties that ensure that the macro-economic policies of nation states conform to the prevailing market discipline. Significantly, these policy frameworks and trade and investment treaties have increasingly gained 'quasi-constitutional status' (ibid.: 168) at the nation-state level, and are in turn policed by the institutions and organisations through which they have been constructed. Furthermore, through the imposition of binding constraints on the conduct of macro-economic policy-making and governance, new constitutionalism has been instrumental in the attempt to insulate the economy from democratic decision-making processes (ibid.: 412–13).

This does not mean that nation states have been reduced to mere 'transmission belts and filtering devices for the transnational agenda' (Robinson 2004: 125; see also Cox 1987: 253–6). As Morton (2007: 148) has noted, to argue along such lines is to lapse into 'a flattened ontology that removes state forms as a significant spatial scale in the articulation of capitalism, levels out the spatial and territorial logics of capital accumulation, and elides the class struggles extant in specific locations' (see also Bieler and Morton 2014: 31–7). Rather, as Bieler and Morton have argued, transnational fractions of capital 'do not ... confront the state as an external actor, as a transnational state, but are closely involved in the class struggle over hegemonic projects within the state form' (ibid.:

42). A key achievement of the neoliberal project as a social movement from above has been the consolidation of the hegemonic position of transnational capital and the politico-administrative elites who nurture the most intimate links to this fraction of capital. Consequently, the emergence of the neoliberal state has been a process in which 'state policies and institutional arrangements are conditioned and changed by the power and mobility of transnational corporations' (Gill 1990: 94).

Across the North-South axis, the forms of state that were integral to the political economy of organised capitalism were – to different degrees and in different ways – characterised by the 'thickening' of social citizenship. With the emergence of the neoliberal state, this process has been reversed as social protection has given way to social control in the form of workfare and punitive containment that targets new surplus populations (see Wacquant 2009).

In the West, the post-war era had witnessed the emergence of 'entitlements-based welfare regimes' (Peck 2002: 341) that were centrally concerned with protecting the working population from the vicissitudes of labour markets: in other words, income transfers that were geared towards enabling citizens to maintain a basic standard of living countered the detrimental effects of unemployment. Under the aegis of neoliberal states that actively propel processes of recommodification, welfare regimes based on entitlements have increasingly given way to 'work-enforcing workfare regimes' (ibid.: 341; see also Peck 2001, Krinsky 2009).

At the heart of workfare is the principle that access to benefits and assistance from the state is made conditional upon participation in programmes that are oriented towards '*enforcing work while residualizing welfare*' (Peck 2001: 10; emphasis in original). As such, workfare represents a direct attack on 'the principle of social entitlement based on needs and social insurance based on progressive income transfers' that was at the heart of the concessions of the social compact that defined the political economy of organised capitalism (ibid.: 342). This attack has been launched in the context of labour markets that are increasingly characterised by 'falling wages, chronic underemployment, and job casualisation' (ibid.: 12) and a key effect of workfare has been to regulate the surplus population of unemployed and underemployed workers in relation to these markets. Workfare articulates with the restructuring of labour markets in the neoliberal era along three axes: (i) it disciplines welfare recipients into low-wage and flexible work; (ii) it undermines the ability of recipients to hold out and wait for better opportunities in the job market through the constant imposition of controls and conditions through the administrative apparatus, and (iii) it erodes claims to benefits and assistance by market-testing access to welfare services and restricting access to these services according to employability (Peck 2002: 347).

Workfare, then, is a modality through which market discipline is sought to be imposed at the level of individual bodies and everyday routines. This is not only evident in the turn away from welfare in the global North, but also in the increasing market orientation of development intervention in the global South. For example, as Rankin (2001: 20) has noted, the proliferation of micro-credit as an anti-poverty strategy specifically directed at women constitutes 'social citizenship and women's needs in a manner consistent with a neoliberal agenda' (see also Bateman 2010, Taylor 2012, Soederberg 2012). Similarly, the new global consensus around anti-poverty strategies related to the Millennium Development Goals – manifest, for example, in the rapid spread of Conditional Cash Transfer Schemes – is constructed in 'market-centric terms' (Peck 2011: 171): states in the global South are supposed to facilitate the ability of the poor to invest in their own human capital in such a way as to be able to contribute in a productive way to socioeconomic development. Dependency on state welfare is to be avoided, and the poor are made responsible for adopting the aptitudes of self-managing subjects participating in a market economy (ibid.: 173; see also Jayasuriya 2006).

The turn from social protection to social control is also manifest in 'the explosive growth of the scope and intensity of punishment' (Wacquant 2009: xvi) that has unfolded in the neoliberal era. The use of punitive containment as a mode of social control is most pronounced in the US, where the prison population has increased by some 450 per cent since the early 1980s. As a result, more than 7 million people are currently in prison, on probation, or on parole in a context where crime rates have in fact been falling consistently for the past three decades (Gilmore 2007: 17–18; see also Davis 2003, Alexander 2011: Chapter 1). There is a clear racial and social profile to the more than 2 million-strong inmate population in American prisons today: African Americans and Latinos make up more than half the prison population and 'as a class, convicts are deindustrialised cities' working or workless poor' (Gilmore 2007: 7).

Thus, coeval with the transition from workfare to welfare has been the intensive and extensive development of the penal and carceral powers of the neoliberal state. These powers have been put to use in forms of 'punitive containment' (Wacquant 2009: 41) of dispossessed subaltern groups that constitute the relative surplus population of the global North. This is amply demonstrated in Ruth Wilson Gilmore's (2007) compelling study of the rise of the prison-industrial complex in California – a state in which the prison population grew by 500 per cent between 1982 and 2000. From the late 1960s to the early 1990s, economic crisis and de-industrialisation combined to create a relative surplus population in which African American and Latino communities were over-represented. California's 'prison fix' – essentially a strategy that combined intensified criminalisation and policing with a prison-building programme that put surplus capital and surplus land to profitable use – has in turn produced a 160,000-strong inmate population which is overwhelmingly composed of 'working and workless poor, most of whom are not white' (ibid.: 15). This punitive containment of 'the human rejects of the market' (Wacquant, 2009: 70) combines with the discipline exerted through workfare to entrench the turn from social protection to social control under the neoliberal state.

If this huge rise in prison populations has US-specific features, the broader process of the penalisation of poverty has made inroads in Europe through transnational policy networks (ibid.: Chapters 8 and 9), as well as in the global South, where urban governance is becoming increasingly coercive (see, for example, Samara 2010, Wacquant 2008, Müller 2012, Campesi 2010). Furthermore, the imperative of controlling and containing surplus populations has been inscribed ever more firmly into global development discourses through an emphasis on 'security' – especially in relation to so-called 'failed states' (Duffield 2007, Taylor 2009, Bilgin and Morton 2002). Development interventions have therefore been increasingly reconstituted as technologies of containment and closely wedded to military interventions and the War on Terror (Duffield 2001). Finally, the border-zones between North and South are becoming increasingly more militarised and policed in order to ward off the 'global circulation typically associated with non-insured surplus populations' (Duffield 2007: 119).

Through the imposition of market discipline and social control, the neoliberal state has been integral to the restoration of the power of capital over labour and the disembedding of capitalist accumulation during the past three decades. The emergence of the neoliberal state is in turn socially moored in a historical bloc that differs in important ways from that which undergirded the political economy of organised capitalism (Smith 2011).

Neoliberalism as an Offensive Social Movement from Above

The political economy of organised capitalism is arguably best understood in terms of truce lines that congealed as subaltern groups mobilised around social movement projects that challenged the hegemonic constellations of the long nineteenth century. As we showed above, subaltern groups were integrated – both materially and politically – in new historical blocs across the North-South axis that formed the basis for 'expansive hegemony' (Smith 2011; see above). As an offensive social movement from above, the neoliberal project broke through these truce lines and the vertical alliances through which dominant groups elicited the consent of subaltern groups – both in the global North and in the global South. Consequently, the accommodation of subaltern groups in and through expansive forms of hegemony has increasingly given way to what Smith calls 'selective hegemony' (ibid.: 20) – that is, a form of hegemony that rests on a 'transnational historical bloc' (Gill 1990: 94) constructed through a set of horizontal alliances between economic and political elites.

The exclusionary nature of hegemony under neoliberalism in turn 'restricts the field of negotiable politics to selected participants' (Smith 2011: 4), while broadening the range of groups handled by coercion rather than the seeking of consent – a process accelerating in the current crisis. The consent of other subaltern groups has been elicited in particular along lines of ethnicity and gender (racism and nationalism, backlash and fundamentalist religion), often mobilised not in the form of political parties or street protest but rather as a vicious politics of opinion and media, as well, of course, as by the promise of financial gain and social mobility.

Movements from below were also terrains of struggle in this epochal shift, and this was not only a matter of bringing trade unions into line. The diversity of the women's movement in this period offers some particularly clear variants. For example, a liberal feminism which could operate effectively on the terrain of individual access to the labour market and indeed elite positions, in line with neoliberalism's own recommodifying tendencies; a socialist feminism which, highlighting issues like state-supported childcare, was largely marginalised, and a radical feminism many of whose best activists became eventually subcontracted and precarious welfare state employees in once-autonomous women's refuges and rape crisis centres, forced to compete for state funding on alien terms.

Similar stories could be told for other movements, along with their positive forms: the new kinds of feminism and labour struggle involved in today's anti-capitalist movements are, in part, the positive outcome of these conflicts, especially as activists have come to realise the broader political implications of particular forms of organising. It is important to note that neoliberalism did not *simply* roll over movements and squeeze them out of existence: from environmentalism to squatting and from anti-racism to disability rights, there are co-opted and contained forms of organisation as well as activists whose goals are wider than what can be attained within neoliberal parameters (Flesher Fominaya and Cox 2013).

More broadly, the coercive trend of neoliberalism is not necessarily a sign of strength. As Gramsci noted, when dominant groups come to rely on coercion over consent in their relationships with subaltern groups, this indicates that 'the great masses have become detached from their traditional ideologies, and no longer believe what they used to believe previously' (1998: 276). This is a crucial point to bear in mind as we move on to consider the current crisis of the neoliberal project.

The Economic Crisis of the Neoliberal Project

As a social movement from above, articulated and implemented through the collective agency of a historical bloc constituted around transnational capital, the neoliberal project has been successful in restoring the power of capital over labour across the North-South axis of the capitalist world-system. However, there is a very real sense in which this has been a Pyrrhic victory, for the very same accumulation strategies that have been at the heart of this restoration of power are also at the root of the economic crisis of the neoliberal project.

As we noted above, the recovery of profitability under neoliberalism has above all favoured finance capital (see Duménil and Levy 2011: Chapters 3 and 4). The 'explosion of profit rates of financial corporations' (ibid.: 70) is in turn rooted in the process of financialisation – that is, the combined effect of financial deregulation and financial innovation – that has been so central to the neoliberal project since the unravelling of the Bretton Woods system in the early 1970s. By the end of the 1980s, financial expansion had yielded a scenario in which 'the old structure of the economy, consisting of a production system served by a modest financial adjunct, had given way to a new structure in which a greatly expanded financial sector had achieved a high degree of independence and sat on top of the underlying production system' (Sweezy, cited in Foster and Magdoff 2009: 79). Through this process, corporations have come to rely less on banks and are increasingly engaged in financial markets; the nature of banking has changed as profits are progressively sought in fees, commissions and currency trading; and private households have become deeply enmeshed in financial markets both in terms of their assets and in terms of their liabilities (Foster and Magdoff 2009). Yet, whereas this economic structure has been the source of stupendous profits, it is also financialisation that has prepared the ground for the *internal* crisis of neoliberalism.

The story is well known, and will only be told in broad strokes here.[21] Between February 2007 and October 2008, a string of transatlantic bank collapses rooted in the market for US mortgage-backed securities shook the global financial system. This market had emerged in the 2000s as the trade in collateralised debt obligations (CDOs) – that is, bundles of consumer debt that combine high, medium and low-risk mortgages and other kinds of debt – had spiralled. CDOs represent a specific form of securitisation – a form of financial trading in which various forms of debt are repackaged as a 'security' that can be bought and sold on financial markets and where banks make profits from the fees they earn by selling loans to investors rather than from long-term lending. The increasing popularity of trading in CDOs 'created an incentive to find ever more exotic securitized instruments' (McNally 2011: 100).

One avenue for doing this was by expanding the US mortgage market. For such an expansion to occur, however, it was necessary for finance 'to spread its reach beyond the middle class to the poor and to bring racial minorities within circuits of credit' (Mahmud 2012: 477). In doing so, finance created a market in so-called subprime mortgages: '... banks pushed lending into more marginal markets, developed new financial instruments, and invented new ways to make mortgage loans to lower-income workers and racial minorities whom lenders had previously avoided' (ibid.: 477). By 2007, the market in subprime mortgages had reached a value of $1.3 trillion.

The dramatic expansion of the market in subprime mortgages and its relationship to the escalating trade in mortgage-backed securities have to be understood in relation to more general trends in the US economy over the past two-and-a-half decades. Firstly, since profitability peaked in 1997, asset price bubbles – that is, 'great speculative waves that [drive] prices for financial assets far above what any rational economic analysis [can] justify' (McNally 2011: 101) – have become increasingly important to sustaining economic growth in the US economy. The dotcom bubble that emerged in the late 1990s and then collapsed in the early 2000s is one example of this; the boom in trading in mortgage-backed securities is another and more recent one. Secondly, the expansion of subprime mortgages is expressive of how credit that has overtaken wages as the basis of consumption in the US. As we noted above, the neoliberal onslaught on labour generated declining real wages. The consequent loss in purchasing power and consumption has been partly offset through the expansion of credit: 'Gross debt of households rose from 50 percent of GDP in 1980 to 98 percent of GDP in 2007. Outstanding consumer debt as a percentage of disposable income grew from 62 percent in 1975 to 127.2 percent in 2005' (Mahmud 2012: 476). The combination of low interest rates and increased house prices in turn created a wealth effect which added further momentum to credit-fuelled consumption: during the early 2000s, US households extracted $750 billion in credit against the value of their homes.

The bubble in the US housing market eventually burst as interest rates were hiked a number of times between 2004 and 2006. House prices fell and mortgage defaults – especially in poor communities of colour that had been facing job losses and declining incomes[22] – escalated sharply. Consequently, the banks that had been taking on ever more debt to engage in trade with CDOs were faced with a substantial market collapse. Due to the fact that CDOs had spread throughout the financial system, the ensuing crisis was global in scope and prompted

> ... the largest coordinated financial bailout in world history ... All told, governments in the world's largest economies anted up something in the order of $20 trillion – an amount equivalent to one and a half times the U.S. gross domestic product – via a massive intervention without historical precedent' (McNally 2011: 2–3).

As a result of the massive bank bailout, the crisis transmogrified: public debts expanded rapidly as governments sold bonds in international markets to raise the funds needed to rescue the crisis-stricken bank sector. The increased debt burden combined with decreased tax revenues to create a sovereign debt crisis across the advanced capitalist countries of the global North. With this transition, the focus of governments changed from bailouts to austerity: 'Concerned to rein in government debts, they announced the age of austerity – of huge cuts to pensions, education budgets, social welfare programs, public sector wages, and jobs' (ibid.: 4). The politics of the austerity offensive in the global North echoes the politics of structural adjustment in the global South: whereas financial institutions were rescued through state interventions, 'the burden of adjusting to consequences of the crisis fell on populations whose supposedly reckless actions, or those of their governments, were primarily responsible for the harsh fallout from the crisis' (Heintz and Balakrishnan 2012: 397–8).

There is, then, a real sense in which 'the most perverse legacy of the global crisis has been a further retrenchment of neoliberal rationalities and disciplines' (Peck, Theodore and Brenner 2012: 266). However, while it is true that the austerity offensive of recent years bears witness to how the neoliberal project has 'once again demonstrated a capacity to capitalize on crisis conditions' by advancing 'a further retrenchment of market-disciplinary modes of governance' (ibid.: 212), this does not mean that neoliberalism is still going as strong as ever. While bailouts and austerity policies have been successful in salvaging the giants of the financial order and improving corporate profits, these interventions have also laid bare the nature of the neoliberal project more clearly than ever. The recession that resulted from government cuts and deleveraging by households and businesses has fuelled unemployment, and deepened poverty and inequality across the global North.

Significantly, these social consequences affect 'middle-class' groups whose support for the neoliberal project was predicated on promises of material benefits and upward social mobility. Hence, one of the central ideological tropes of the neoliberal project – the responsibility of the individual as an entrepreneurial financial subject to maximise their well-being through prudent investments in the marketplace (see Mahmud 2012: 483–4) – has been increasingly discredited, thus eroding one of its principal pillars of political support. The current signs of recovery – manifest in extraordinary levels of share prices in the US and the UK – are unlikely to do anything to change this. In fact, the resurgence of share prices is yet another bubble as a result of excess liquidity generated by quantitative easing, which is unlikely to have a positive impact on standards of living. Indeed, in the UK, incomes are not expected to recover to pre-crisis levels until 2022, and in the US, some 95 per cent of income gains between 2009 and 2012 accrued to the top 1 per cent of income earners (Chang 2014, Lowrey 2013, Inman 2014).

The current state of the neoliberal project, then, suggests that we are confronted with global elites who have no plan B, and who find it easier to resort to coercion than to construct consent in relation to subaltern groups. The ramifications of this crisis are arguably amplified by the fact that the capitalist world-system is witnessing the unravelling of US hegemony. The protracted waning of American economic supremacy has been widely noted (Harvey 2003: Chapters 2 and 5, Arrighi 2005a, 2005b, 2007: Chapters 6 and 7, Smith 2005, Wallerstein 2006, Desai 2013). American industry was decisively weakened during the 1970s, and by 1980, it was evident that US manufacturing was 'but one complex among many operating in a highly competitive global environment' (Harvey 2003: 65).

In order to compensate, the US sought to assert its hegemony in the realm of finance. If this shift offered substantial short-term gains, its long-term impacts have further eroded the hegemonic capacities of the American state as a steadily worsening balance-of-payments situation in relation to new centres of accumulation – particularly in Asia – has rendered the US economy highly vulnerable to capital flight and a collapse in the value of the dollar (Harvey 2003: 70–71).

Geopolitical Aspects of the Crisis

The turn to military unilateralism under the neoconservative administrations of George W. Bush is thus best understood as a coercive turn that sought to compensate for this erosion of hegemonic capacities in the economic domain (Smith 2005, Harvey 2003: Chapter 5). As signalled by the failure to garner substantial support for the invasion of Iraq in 2003 and the unravelling of support for the 'war on terror', this strategy was far from successful. Moreover, US failure to mobilise international support for interventions in Georgia, Syria and the Ukraine, combined with the fact that several significant Latin American states have distanced themselves from Washington's tutelage, suggests that a resort to coercion is unlikely to regain the hegemonic ground that the US has lost (see Desai 2013).

This is not to say that there is a clear and present alternative to US hegemony in the world-system. Although China has emerged as a major player in the world economy, this new prominence is constrained by the fact that its manufacturing industries remain dependent on export markets in the global North, and the US in particular. Although China's dollar reserves are the largest in the world, this in turn makes the country highly dependent on US fiscal policy (Kiely 2007: 215). Moreover, the wider process that the UNDP (2013: 13) dubs 'the rise of the South' – that is, the 'dramatic rebalancing of global economic power' that has been propelled by impressive growth rates in in the BRICS countries – cannot credibly be construed as an alternative to American hegemony. As

Prashad (2012: 222–3) has argued, the BRICS countries lack a military platform that is capable of challenging NATO dominance, and have failed to entrench recent growth processes in an institutional infrastructure that could rupture western dominance in the world economy. What is clear, however, is that the present moment is one of emerging 'systemic chaos' – that is, 'a situation of severe and seemingly irremediable systemic disorganization that cannot be controlled within the parameters of the regulatory capacity of existing structures' (Arrighi and Silver 1999: 33) – which further compounds the crisis of the neoliberal project as a social movement from above.

The erosion of the capacity of dominant groups to exercise leadership in this context of crisis has been paralleled by the development of a global arc of struggles from below. Originating in anti-austerity protests in the global South in the 1980s, this arc has been constructed through the conscious fusion of anti-systemic struggles during the 1990s and early 2000s into a movement of movements that declared another world to be possible. These movements have not only contributed to neoliberalism's crisis of political and intellectual hegemony but also, through the anti-war movement and uprisings in Latin America and the Middle East, to undermining US geopolitical hegemony. In neoliberalism's fiscal crisis, this movement has given rise to a new round of struggles. The next chapter discusses this trajectory and the strategic challenges that social movements from below face as they seek to develop a counter-hegemonic project that can bring neoliberalism to an end.

5

'The Point is to Change it': Movements From Below Against Neoliberalism

The philosophers have only interpreted *the world in various ways; the point is to* change *it.*

Marx, *Theses on Feuerbach*

Introduction: Premature Obituaries and Zombie Neoliberalism

Almost as soon as any new movement from below appears on the radar screen of the North's elites, writers proclaim it dead, irrelevant, or past its prime. This has been so for the Zapatistas (now celebrating the twentieth anniversary of their uprising), for the global 'movement of movements' against neoliberalism despite events in Latin America, for the movement against the wars in Afghanistan and Iraq (despite everything) and increasingly for anti-austerity movements. In part, of course, these are deliberate attempts to write off movements by apologists for our current regimes: to misquote Howard Zinn (1999), we might wonder *why* it is necessary to proclaim movements dead again and again.

Another reason for this obituary-writing lies in how journalists, academics, literary writers, and so on are trained. There is a natural tendency to defend one's own hard-won intellectual capital: where this consists of a particular way of writing about how things are at present, and of 'business as usual' tendencies into the future, anything which suggests that there may be more to the present than meets an eye focused on routines, and that the future may not yet be written in stone, will be unwelcome. There is also a need to have something to say about everything, and to appear to know something about any possible subject of conversation ('relevance', for a very media-oriented value of the word). Given the complexity of reality and how little of it anyone can know (not to mention how pressures for intellectual productivity squeeze the time available for exploring new areas of knowledge), what is most needed is a stock of ready-made dismissals for whatever falls outside one's own sphere of interest and actual knowledge (see Sotiris 2013).

For us, the most interesting part of the obituary-writing process is that engaged in by movement activists themselves. This too has multiple roots: frustration and despair, a sense of having lost particular internal or external battles, a desire to argue for different strategies (a return to trade union struggles, a return to communities, the construction of utopias), and the belief that today's movement is the strongest available argument for one's own flavour of theory. Perhaps the most significant, though, is the experience this chapter addresses, of stalemate: of having made huge efforts, having moved further in recent years than most of us would have thought possible in the 1990s, and yet of having in some terms achieved so little.

Organic Crisis and the Stalemate

This little is far from nothing. If Chapter 4 discussed the crisis of neoliberalism in internal terms, as the increasing limitations of the system's own operations, this chapter discusses the role of movements from below in *placing* neoliberalism in crisis and undermining its hegemony. This can be seen in various dimensions.

Geopolitically, the 'New World Order' which was once supposed to represent a permanent post-Cold War settlement is in serious trouble. The Latin American pink tide demonstrated US inability, for the first time in a century or more, to impose its will (in military, foreign policy, or economic terms) on its Latin American 'backyard'. The planned 'long war on terror' is basically over, with the original strategy for a rolling series of attacks on rogue states buried in the sand and political support for US wars collapsing not only among US elites, but also their European and Arab allies under the impact of the anti-war movements of 2003 in particular. This has fed into a broader weakness in relation to control of the strategically crucial Middle East and North African region manifested in the 'Arab Spring', in particular events in Egypt, and subsequent failure to secure support for war in Syria. Meanwhile, the Wikileaks and Snowden affairs have highlighted the legitimacy crisis of the supposedly all-powerful surveillance state.

It took the World Trade Organization 14 years since the Seattle protests to achieve its first comprehensive agreement; other global arrangements intended to institutionalise neoliberalism for good have collapsed (Multilateral Agreement on Investments) or stalled (Free Trade Area of the Americas); other agreements are increasingly negotiated in secret or on a purely bilateral basis. The democratic legitimacy of global elites has taken a massive hammering, with 'neoliberalism' now a dirty word and the EU regularly suspending the operations of democracy in order to keep the austerity show on the road (re-running a referendum here, co-opting parties elected on other mandates there, installing technical governments elsewhere). Internally, the financial crisis has hit many previous supporters of neoliberal politics, notably among western middle classes, badly; and the failure to develop an adequate response to climate change poses a medium-term threat to many fixed assets.

All of this also dramatises the inability of neoliberal elites to offer any effective leadership, or to manage any strategy more complex than 'hold on tight and cross your fingers'. The tentative criticisms of neoliberalism made at the start of the current crisis by isolated elite members have had no real implication beyond the narrowly technical ('quantitative easing', and so on). There is no significant dissent within elites – political and financial, or their allies in academia and journalism – about the proposal that the only way forward is more austerity, more neoliberalism, more privatisations. Unless, of course, we stop it; and the fact that elites are so resistant to alternatives is one of the major factors forcing ordinary people into radical resistance. As Chapter 4 has shown, we are increasingly in a zombie-like phase of capitalist development (Peck 2010b), in which elites are incapable of solving contradictions through new hegemonic projects. This signals the onset of the twilight of neoliberalism.

This twilight is not simply an internal crisis: indeed, many of the reversals mentioned above can be traced back to movements that *pre-date* the financial crisis – Zapatismo, 'pink tide', summit protests, anti-war movement, Maoist guerilla insurgency in India, worker unrest in China. More recent movements – protests over climate change and against the energy companies, southern European *indignados*, 'Arab Spring', Anglo-American Occupy, the gradual secession of the South African working class from the ANC's neoliberal hegemony, and other crises from Turkey to Thailand – represent a massive and sustained presence on the world stage of collective action from below of a very dramatic kind, and a powerful undermining of neoliberal hegemony.

A Retreat to Versailles

Since Seattle, this has been symbolised by an elite 'retreat to Versailles'. Where in the period of multilateralism world leaders such as Clinton had 'bathed in the crowd', now the world's most powerful people could only hold their summits behind massive barricades, in remote venues, or in dictatorships. Even personally popular figures such as Obama require a near-complete lockdown of a *friendly* city such as Dublin in order to appear. The 'leaders of the free world' are no longer able to meet their own populations except under the most tightly controlled circumstances: we are not far from the Red Square parade. Part of this loss of legitimacy was a direct result of movement activity. Not only have movements turned neoliberalism into a dirty word for much of the world, they have also de-legitimised much of the militarist and security state agendas, and for that matter, popular trust in corporations and governments generally.

As elites slowly retreat from attempts to gain popular consent, popular institution-formation has grown. This is perhaps most visibly the case with the twenty-year-old Zapatista revolution, and the various attempts at reshaping the state in a movement-inflected direction in South America, particularly Bolivia and Ecuador, but also in the exploration of various pan-Latin American economic and political alliances as explicit alternatives to US and neoliberal hegemony in the region.

In the global North, beyond the remarkable Icelandic 'saucepan revolution' (Júlíusson and Helgason 2013), the practices of the Spanish *indignados* movement in particular (Romanos 2013) and those of the 2011 'Occupy' wave show a new confidence in street-based direct democracy and the formation of alternative bases of popular legitimacy. These are rooted in the longer history of the movement of movements, particularly its decision-making processes (Maeckelbergh 2009, Gordon 2007, Szolucha 2013) and the World Social Forum experience (Sen and Waterman 2012, de Sousa Santos 2006, Conway 2005) as well as the development of Indymedia, giving rise to new forms of depoliticised social media which are now in turn being repurposed for movement purposes (Mattoni 2012). Finally, alternative economic institutions – particularly occupied workplaces, land occupations and networks of exchange outside the formal economy – are playing an important symbolic role (and locally a practical one) in Latin America and parts of Europe.

Given this flourishing of popular agency, the stalemate represents a paradoxical moment in world history. We have built movements – even a movement of movements – which have challenged the powerful and constructed solidarity on historical scales (the anti-war protests of 15 February 2003 were probably the biggest single event ever organised by actors other than states, commercial interests, sports, or religion). And yet we have not won: with the important exception of Latin America, neoliberalism continues to be 'rolled out' (perhaps in the way of tanks rather than carpets), and this raises exactly the kinds of questions this book tackles: how *can* we understand this coincidence of what would once have been seen as an irresistible force with what still appears as an immovable object?

It is in such moments that we need theory most. There are times of advance when 'build something, anything' is a sufficient starting-point; and times of retreat when 'defend what you can' is enough. But what of times of stalemate, when we are doing everything we can, they are clearly on the defensive, and yet we are not moving forward? How can we find ways of identifying potentials for change and underlying moments of crisis which are something more than wishful thinking and projection?

The current situation is marked by a stalemate of historically unusual duration, starting around the turn of the twenty-first century. By comparison with some earlier movement waves, such as those associated with the dates of 1848, 1919, or 1968, this period of stalemate and opposing institutions has been exceptionally long and again underlines elite weakness. If so, however, why stalemate? Why not a more transformative outcome?

Leaving aside some important exceptions in Latin America, the hegemonic crisis and movement strength we have outlined has not translated into fundamental social change. A thought experiment illustrates the point: if we had seen current Greek or Spanish levels of mobilisation in the 1990s, we would have expected to see a much larger scale of social transformation. Why is this not happening?

We have certainly seen a concerted elite attempt to demobilise the movement from Seattle onwards. This was manifested through strategies of criminalisation and increasingly aggressive protest policing (Wood 2007); through the shift to a strategy of 'permanent war' which in the US had the effect of detaching unions from the global justice movement and was equally damaging in Australia (Humphrys 2013) but backfired elsewhere, giving rise to the remarkable protest of 15 February 2003 (and incidentally making links between western anti-capitalists and radicals in the Arab world); through strategic interventions, such as the 2002 attempted coup against Chávez, and through co-option, such as the 2005 attempt to rebrand the G8 through 'Make Poverty History'.

On the whole, however, these attempts at demobilisation have not been hugely effective – two decades of low-level counter-insurgency have not defeated the Zapatistas. The killing of Carlo Giuliani at the Genoa protest in 2001 did not intimidate Europeans off the streets (Cox 2014b), while the breaking of movement alliances in the US after 2001 was comprehensively reversed with Occupy. War as the 'last refuge of the scoundrel' did not boost US hegemony, and attempts to co-opt and commodify the movement have not been notably successful.

The hopeful theme we would take from this is that perhaps the single biggest reason for the apparent immovability of neoliberalism is the limited mobilisation capacity of the movement of movements. As events in Latin America and North Africa (or Iceland, Spain and Greece) show, this is not a given: under the right circumstances, these movements can have far more impact. A key explanation of different national levels of mobilisation is certainly the legacy of earlier movement waves, in particular the relationship between unions and moderate left parties (in some countries including NGOs), offering alternatives to direct popular participation, with a limited professional leadership visibly 'in the game' – hence demobilising and deradicalising under most circumstances. We identify this situation as hopeful because it is more within our power as activists to affect.

A second reason for immovability, of course, is both the *real* de-territorialisation of power (as with the relationship between the EU and the 'Troika' and individual nation states) and the popular *belief* that power is de-territorialised and that (for example) 'the market' or 'EU rules' stand above human action. The latter is obviously easier to tackle – the former requires greater international solidarity and awareness of struggles abroad. It is particularly important in Europe to resist *right-wing* populist responses to this situation, which are among other things a historical revenge for the institutional left's visceral loyalty to the EU, giving the impression on the ground that all progressive actors necessarily support an intensification of EU neoliberalism.

However, an equally important reason for the apparent immovability of neoliberalism, which is key to a radical reading of the crisis, lies in the increasingly small intellectual gene pool of elites. Few members of contemporary elites have a background as organisers; the days of mass parties and unions are firmly in the past, and elites are far more adept at securing the goodwill of other elite members than at mobilising consent. All of this penalises elite members who even suggest abandonment of core orthodoxies and the gains of neoliberalism, which is what major concessions to popular movements would entail. These are not the hallmarks of a flexible leadership group capable of riding out the storm: they are signs of brittleness, of an *ancien régime* on the way out.

To summarise, the horizontal alliance-building strategies of neoliberal elites are increasingly rickety, with allied elites more likely to consider defection or strategic non-participation; vertically, popular consent is eroding in a wide range of contexts. At present, the main factor supporting its continuation is surely the absence of a plan B, an alternative strategy capable of creating a new hegemonic alliance – something evidenced in the complete failure of neo-Keynesian responses to the crisis to gain traction among political, economic, or intellectual elites. There is no obvious place from within contemporary leaderships to develop an alternative capitalist strategy beyond 'more of the same'. This fact, and the consequent privileging of coercive responses to challenges, are signs of a strategic *incapacity* to survive, and underpin our analysis that we are already in the twilight of neoliberalism.

Such changes of regime are not unusual; indeed, from a historical perspective we are now overdue a shift. The absence of internal support for a shift of gear such as that which marked the shift from organised capitalism to neoliberal capitalism in the 1970s thus represents a particular window of opportunity. Geopolitically identified alternatives such as a China-centred global order or the rise of Islamic radicalism, for their part, lack the hegemonic capacity needed to organise such an order. In this context, movements from below have a significant opportunity: a hegemonic order which is past its sell-by date, incapable of reorienting itself and where there are no other credible capitalist strategies currently capable of gaining elite consent is a good situation for movements to find themselves in.

Once we see neoliberalism as a *movement* from above, and place our analysis of the collective agency and alliance-building of elites on the same plane as the actions of popular movements, we can ask a different set of questions – crucially, questions about *action* that go beyond the disempowering analysis of structure as omnipotent, or simple celebration of the existence of popular agency. In particular, we can ask 'how can we win?'

How Can We Win?

We started work on this project because of our own experience of movements in Ireland, India, Norway and globally, their struggles to develop better understandings of their practice and the difficulties they face in doing this. In this chapter, we want to ask a fairly simple question: what should the movement of movements do if we want to win?

Obviously there are many answers out there, and different answers tend to convince different people for a range of reasons: relevance to their own struggles, ability to answer immediate questions, ideological affinities, language and sheer style are obviously part of the package, and what we have to say will be judged in these terms. We think, though, that there are two reasons why the approach outlined in Chapter 3 may have something to offer beyond these.

One is that it draws on the experience of previous generations of activists in movements which had some success in both confronting and changing existing power relations on a broad scale. Rather than borrowing from academic theory (which is often second-hand activist theory minus the good parts), or making up something completely new in order to compete in a marketplace of intellectual style and celebrity, we feel that activist theorising has real value because of its orientation to 'this-worldly' practice. While our main shared point of reference is the workers' movement and Marxist theories, we are also drawing substantially on the experiences of women's movements, of anti-colonial movements and the movements of 1968 and their successors. No one movement or tradition has a monopoly on popular struggles for change, or on what people have learnt in the process, but that learning should be our starting-point, rather than the internal logics of academia or media; this is an 'ecology of knowledges' (de Sousa Santos 2006) rather than a hierarchy or a marketplace.

A second reason has to do with alliance-building and good sense: combining and reflecting on the experience and thinking of many different elements of the movement of movements – what works to bring us together and sets us off from the systems we are challenging – is better than pulling a rabbit out of a theoretical hat based on the processes of a small elite within part of a movement, whether those involve the accommodation processes of NGOs, the possession of theoretically correct knowledge on the part of political sects, the radicalisation of stylised violence, or competition within a globalised 'radical celebrity' marketplace. This is a 'democratic epistemology' (Wainwright 1994) in which the most valid source of knowledge about what movements need to do is the shared experience gathered by their *different* participants from a wide range of starting-points, distilled and developed in their debates and alliance-forming processes.

Thus in this chapter, we are trying to draw on as broad a range of what activists already know as possible, in order to make sense of what we should do next – and broaden that out in the discussion to bring in the knowledge of other participants. We start by outlining what is at stake and what winning means for a social movement project from below, looking at some of the key strategic points within these movements. Following this, we draw on the experience of Irish anti-capitalist and anti-austerity movements as well as the more positive experiences of movements and states in Latin America to look at the process of 'insurgent architecture' in practice, and explore the nature of the wider stalemate in the twilight of neoliberalism – and possible outcomes beyond neoliberalism.

The Movement of Movements and the Crisis

Thinking Movement Boundaries

Academic social movements research has had little to say about the question of movement boundaries. The supposed object of study is routinely taken for granted, whether defined by actor (women's movement, workers' movement) or by issue (environmental movement, peace movement). Questions such as 'how does the concept of an anti-nuclear power movement relate to that of an environmental movement?' are rarely tackled beyond asides about what is 'really' environmental. Discussions about movement continuity and whether certain movements are 'new' or not are also rarely thought through.

Melucci's (1989) answer – in effect, that movements construct their own boundaries in practice – does not resolve the problem for participants, much of whose internal conflicts revolve around *how* movements should define themselves and *where* they should construct boundaries – who to ally with or dissociate from, what origin myths to present, how to relate to events abroad, and so on. As will be clear from Chapter 3, we see this as a (potentially) developmental process: activists take time not only to understand and articulate their own situation, struggles and goals, but also to abstract from the specific, create wider alliances, or develop broader movement processes. One implication of this is that any given movement does not *necessarily* or *automatically* reach a particular level of development, or 'mean' this or that: these things are the objects of struggle, and can go in different directions. At present, for example, Irish conflicts over the closures of hospitals or cuts to third-level education are routinely framed in particularist terms by campaign leaderships, while their Spanish equivalents are typically set within a wider rejection of austerity, in the 'colour tides' model.

Our usage of 'movement', then, is not the fixed one often assumed in the supposedly scientific social movements literature. It is one which, precisely, *moves* – wins or loses, falls back into particularism, becomes part of other movements, creates states, and so on. One purpose of our specific vocabulary of situated needs and experiences, local rationalities, campaigns, militant particularisms and movement projects is to restore this sense of potential, development, change and dialectics to the wider process as we live it.

A Movement of Movements

Having said this, we want to deploy two particular concepts to characterise movements from below in the present crisis: 'movement of movements' and 'movement waves'. The term 'a movement of movements' was perhaps first introduced by Italian activists to describe the processes of the anti-capitalist, global justice, or alter-globalisation movement from the late 1990s on (Cox and Nilsen 2007). Its conceptual strength lay in recognising the coming together of a diversity of independently constituted movements which had overcome a purely particularist identity politics but had no intention of submitting to the leadership of a single party or lining up behind the *left* identity politics of privileging a narrow definition of working-class interests.[1]

The moment (c. 1999–2001) when this image became widespread reflected a long organisational prehistory, starting with the defensive struggles of the 1980s – 'IMF riots' (Walton and Seddon 1994) in the global South, trade union and welfare struggles in the North. In the 1990s, the remarkable inspiration of the 1994 Zapatista uprising was followed by conscious attempts to bring movements together in the 1995 and 1996 *encuentros*, the latter giving birth to People's Global Action, a key mover behind the summit protests from 1999 on. This, however, was just one of a series of movement processes, ranging from the Narmada Bachao Andolan to the counter-cultural milieu around Italian social centres (Membretti and Mudu 2013) or British roads protests (Flesher Fominaya 2013), which saw the articulation of local rationalities as militant particularisms, alliances between such particularisms as broader (often transnational) campaigns, and the development of far-reaching movement projects.

Around the turn of the millennium, a series of protests against the key institutions of neoliberalism – the World Trade Organization, the G8, the World Bank/IMF, the EU and so on – gave rise to a shared repertoire around summit protests (Scholl 2013), new modes of radical-democratic decision making (Gordon 2007), communication structures such as Indymedia and discussion fora such as the World Social Forum (de Sousa Santos 2006, Sen and Waterman 2012). Parallel with this, the Bolivian 'water war' of 2000 (Zibechi 2010), the Argentinian uprising of 2000–01 and the 2002 defeat of the anti-Chávez coup in Venezuela ushered in a new and dramatic period of struggle.

Of course the 'movement of movements' did not itself remain fixed. The nationalist backlash enabled by the events of 9/11 broke apart its alliances in the US (leading some writers to conclude that the movement had ceased to exist everywhere; it remained perfectly active in Europe), while the Bush regime's new wars led to the inclusion of new groups (and better links with much of the Arab world). The 'pink tide' in Latin America, meanwhile, saw these movements becoming substantially *more* significant, and engaging in various kinds of effective relationships with state power. The global crisis from 2007–08 onwards induced a shift in focus, particularly towards austerity politics at the national level and the crisis of democratic legitimacy – and new forms of activism in the Arab world, in opposition to austerity in Europe and as Occupy in the Anglophone world.

Perhaps the most important shift over these last ten years, and one which authors have variously celebrated or condemned depending on their own theoretical preferences, has been one from a primary focus on global economic and political institutions (and hence a series of relatively visible forms of movement coordination) to a primary focus on events and struggles at the national level (hence making it harder to identify international coordination in institutional forms). Yet nobody familiar with contemporary movement struggles in Europe, Latin America, or the Arab world could plausibly claim that they take place in national bubbles.

What do we mean by using this phrase 'movement of movements' – across movements, across countries, and over time? In 2014, as in 2000, movements are seeking to coordinate their actions and support one another, nationally and transnationally; they are developing appropriate forms of internal communication and meeting; they are attempting to articulate analyses of the present and projects for the future. Now as then, there are a multiplicity of competing approaches to this, and much innovation. We have mentioned the extension of earlier direct democratic and consensus decision-making processes to Occupy and *indignados* encampments; we could also mention attempts at European-level days of action and coordinated 'Blockupy' events at the European Central Bank, or the 'colour tides' model in Spain, which seems to draw on the 'colour blocs' of earlier summit protests to enable combined action between a multiplicity of campaigns and militant particularisms.

As in 2000, both 'we' and 'they' are understood in ways which routinely transcend national boundaries – not only in protests against Troika-mandated austerity or in elements of the Arab Spring but equally in activism around online surveillance, climate justice, or the West's wars abroad. In 2000, the exact language by which issues were identified was contested; today, too, the question of whether the real target is austerity, neoliberalism, or capitalism is up for grabs, as is the question of whether the political problem is corruption and elite takeover of an otherwise acceptable parliamentary system or whether the representative model itself is fundamentally broken. As usual in movements, what is defining is not any specific position but rather the argument itself and what it represents – a determined move beyond single-issue politics of any kind to challenging economic and political fundamentals, and the willingness to do so in alliance with other social groups and people elsewhere around the world.

It seems clear, however, that the core strengths of contemporary popular movements build on earlier struggles. Flesher Fominaya and Cox (2013) have shown for Europe how current anti-austerity protests grow out of networks and practices already developed in the anti-war movement and the struggles of the 2000s – which in turn brought earlier movements together in ways that make the phrase 'a movement of movements' a particularly useful conceptual one. In Latin America, social movements and communities in struggle have come together in very dramatic ways (Zibechi 2010), with a range of states either developing new relationships with movements or subject to movement pressure 'from below and the left' (Prevost, Campos and Vanden 2012, Petras and Veltmeyer 2005, Cannon and Kirby 2012). In North America, the post-9/11 fragmentation noted earlier has to some degree been repaired in alliances around Occupy, Idle No More, tar sands/Keystone XL and other struggles.

Struggles from Below in China and India

As Chapter 4 noted, the disembedding of accumulation under the neoliberal project – and, consequently, the restoration of capital's power over labour – has revolved around the crafting of a new geography of production and the expansion of commodification through accumulation by dispossession. However, the advance of these processes has also given rise to some of the most significant sites of resistance to the neoliberal project.

China's emergence as a major new centre of accumulation in the capitalist world-system has been characterised by intense labour struggles (Lee and Selden 2008). These struggles have in part been animated by workers in state-owned enterprises who have resisted labour reforms, bankruptcies, privatisation and unemployment through petitioning, arbitration and protest. Combining Maoist idioms and slogans with legal discourses centred on notions of citizenship and rule by law, these struggles are typically based on single work-units and subgroups within a specific factory who target local enterprise management and local government, and only scale up to the provincial and national level of government if these initial efforts do not yield results (Lee 2007).

More recently, however, mobilisations have targeted transnational corporations, challenging the labour regimes that have emerged in the global factories that have been integral to China's turn to market socialism (Chan 2012). Strikes in the Honda and Foxconn factories are only two examples of a new wave of industrial mobilisation in southern China where workers – very often drawn from the country's vast migratory workforce – have been successful in forcing significant concessions from both corporations and the Chinese government (Dongfang 2013). The fact that this wave of strikes has been successful in driving up industrial wages expresses the capacity of labour to boost its bargaining power in relation to capital through collective action (Barboza and Tabuchi 2010, Tsui 2012).[2]

Corporate takeover of natural resources such as land, mineral, fossil fuels, forests and water has been one of the key manifestations of accumulation by dispossession in the neoliberal era (see, for example, Swyngedouw 2002, McMichael 2012, Bumpus and Liverman 2009, Perreault 2010). Neoliberalisation in India has pushed conflicts over natural resources to the forefront of subaltern resistance over the past two decades – particularly around the establishment of Special Economic Zones (SEZs) and the opening up of the country's mining sector to foreign direct investments (see Sampat 2010, Padel and Das 2010). As Levien (2011, 2012, 2013a, 2013b) has pointed out, India's political economy is characterised by a neoliberal 'regime of dispossession' in which the state is facilitating land acquisition for private capital, provoking a series of 'land wars' energised by the mobilisation of peasant producers across the country.

These land wars span a wide variety of mobilising strategies – from democratic social movements to Maoist guerilla warfare in India's 'Red Corridor' – and has often been met with violent coercion by the state (Menon and Nigam 2007). Several SEZs have been cancelled as a result of this mobilisation, and in the eastern state of Orissa, a major victory was won by Dongria Kondh Adivasis as the transnational mining firm Vedanta was forced to cancel a multi-million dollar project in the Niyamgiri hills after several years of campaigning and mobilisation – locally, nationally, and globally (Sethi 2013, Woodman 2014). In the 'Red Corridor', where conflicts over dispossession are compounded by abject poverty among Adivasi communities, the state has resorted to paramilitary and military warfare against a Maoist movement that the country's last prime minister dubbed the biggest threat to India's internal security (Sundar 2012, Mukherji 2012).[3]

Uneven and Combined Development of Social Movements

Elsewhere, the new wave of struggles in the Middle East and North Africa (Shihade, Flesher Fominaya and Cox 2012) and in sub-Saharan Africa (Manji and Ekine 2011) have found the process of alliance formation and the articulation of movement projects harder going for a variety of reasons, despite the very dramatic nature of some of these struggles. In particular, it has been difficult for movements from below to escape from being drawn into the logic of supporting competing elites and to articulate their own projects. This contrast, of course, mirrors the geography of the early 2000s quite closely, and underlines the importance of the movement process in enabling popular power. At present, and absent some other effective movement process from below, the movement of movements remains the most powerful single actor within the current movement wave and that most capable of articulating a shared strategy beyond neoliberalism.

The shape of this movement of movements is of course constantly changing, as the potted history above indicates: we are talking about the complex struggle of ordinary people to articulate their own collective agency in the teeth of massive police repression, entrenched power relations, global economic elites, deep-seated structural processes, clientelist networks, the merchants of official culture and the practices of everyday common sense. To borrow a phrase from Bond, Desai and Ngwane (2013), we are seeing the 'uneven and combined development of social movements' – and what else should we expect?

The common criticism that, because movements do not have a homogenous base, disagree among themselves about strategy and tactics, contain various political tendencies and work differently in different countries, they are therefore somehow 'not a movement' is one which could only really be levelled on the basis of a caricatured notion of movement. Thompson's (1963) English working class was a complex and contested achievement of bringing together hugely diverse groups within a very loose cultural and political identity; as Barker (2013b) has pointed out, movements are necessarily fields of conflict as well as collaboration; while the historiography of 1968 no less than the Resistance or the Comintern (Daniele and Vacca 1999, Pavone 1991, Klimke 2008) has shown just how diverse these movement waves – flattened in memory and representation – actually were. Indeed, the image of what a 'real global movement' would be implied by these criticisms is not one grounded in historical experience at all, but rather an image of a global advertising campaign or sports event – actors homogenised and simplified as consumers or spectators, reduced to buying or cheering, and as far as possible conceptualised with no sense of context.

Communication and collaboration, a shared sense of 'we' and 'they', compatible strategies and analyses are all *achievements* of shared struggle: they do not precede it but are part and parcel of how people remake themselves in movement, as they articulate their local rationalities to one another, combine their militant particularisms into campaigns and articulate movement projects. This does not mean that the movement of movements is bound to win; the fragile constructions of solidarity, cooperation and debate can become irretrievably ruptured, just as opposing forces may be capable of rallying and deploying effective resistance or reasserting their hegemony: the huge difference between the movement of movements' experience in Latin America and in western Europe in the 2000s is testimony enough to that. But for now, those links remain, between individual movements as well as internationally, and we have seen one movement wave develop into another and then another, in a historically long cycle. This of course begs the question of how to understand such cycles.

Understanding Movement Waves

Global capitalism generates waves of resistance, 'anti-systemic movements', and has done so for a quarter of a millennium at least (Arrighi, Hopkins and Wallerstein 1989). It does not do so uniformly, but rather in particular sectors of the world-system: for example, the Atlantic Revolutions (late eighteenth century), the Latin American wars of independence (1800–20s), the failed liberal revolutions of the early nineteenth century in Europe and the Greek wars of independence, Europe's 'revolutionary years' 1848 and 1919 (in practice, 1916–24), the democratic revolutions of 1905–10 from Mexico and Argentina to Russia and Turkey, anti-fascist resistance in continental Europe and Asia (1940s), decolonisation and revolutionary movements in Asia, Africa and Latin America (1940s–70s), popular uprisings in Europe, North America, Mexico and Japan (1968), the end of an era in Eastern Europe, Soviet Union and China (1989), the 'movement of movements' in Latin America, North America and western Europe (early 2000s), and now Latin America, the Middle East and southern Europe.

We do not intend this as a complete list, but rather as a heuristic tool to start laying out the problem, which can be put as follows. With some regularity (but not very frequently), capitalism generates such 'waves of movements', which span at least one region of the world-system, often more but never (to date) all. An adequate explanation then has to be global, but one which takes account of the relationships between different parts of the world-system, whether this is understood in terms of the strength of popular agency, the weakness of elites, or otherwise. The movements generated are not identical across a whole region; just as regions are structured differently within the world-system, so too are states, provinces and even cities structured differently within a given region in terms of the particular configuration of forces from above and below.

In such waves, popular mobilisation increases by one or two orders of magnitude, including normally passive groups.[4] They are thus fundamental for restructuring popular agency, in that they reorganise the question of 'who is active?' in social movements, political parties, and so on – something which in routine times is normally more predictable; indeed, relatively few movement organisations survive such waves in anything like the form in which they entered them. They do not remain confined to a single nation state, but are diffused transnationally, with actors in other countries recognising themselves in earlier events elsewhere and taking advantage of what they hope will be a historical opportunity to make gains. The gains sought for typically include *both* the unfinished business of earlier waves (reflecting the re-mobilisation of the resigned) *and* new kinds of issues (reflecting the participation of new social actors).

The large-scale mobilisation of the population means, almost by definition, that previous forms of hegemony are no longer working. Groups which have previously been resigned or had not yet become coherent political actors (re-)enter the political contest; some of those which had been unenthusiastic members of hegemonic coalitions detach themselves, and long-time opponents of the hegemonic order are able to make substantial alternatives visible to wide sectors of the population.

Sometimes these waves involve revolutionary situations or indeed outcomes as parliamentary democracies replace monarchies, nation states replace imperial rule, state socialism replaces capitalism, and so on (most states in the world today are the product of one or another of these waves). Often states resort to coercion to put down such movements, but the restoration of consent involves the substantial reorganisation of hegemony with major concessions such as the extension of voting rights, a shift from dynastic to national-state structure or decolonisation, the construction or extension of welfare systems, the extension of rights to women or ethnic minorities, the opening up of the cultural space, and so on.

On occasion, of course, such waves are defeated by the mobilisation of popular forces behind elites (European fascism from the 1920s to the 1940s, for example), or elites change the rules of the game (neoliberalism as a response to the movements of 1968). More commonly, however, popular forces make substantial gains because the maintenance of hegemony or the production of a new hegemony requires including them to some degree.

Thus these global waves of social movements have been among the major social forces in the history of recent centuries. Decolonisation – whether the US in the eighteenth century, Latin America in the nineteenth, Ireland in the 1920s or Asia after the Second World War – is one major outcome. Democracy – in the French Revolution, the European resistance to fascism, or the events of 1989–90 – is another. Social justice has been a common theme, from the Haitian revolution via the European uprisings at the end of the First World War to the Latin American 'pink tide'. A democratisation of everyday life – in particular after 1968 – is another.

The extent to which such waves result in revolutions or 'social movement cycles' is not one which can easily be answered a priori: revolutionary situations are a common, but not ubiquitous, part of such waves; while by no means all revolutionary situations have revolutionary outcomes. Our concern here is with the large-scale, transnationally connected articulation of popular power, whatever the shape of its encounter with the state.

Explaining Movement Waves

A range of explanations are possible for why such waves develop. A conventional left explanation might involve Kondratieff wave theory, positing a declining rate of profit and hence a political crisis for the ruling fraction of capital;[5] in a sense, Skocpol's (1979) argument, identifying weakened states, often as a product of wars or other competition within the international state system, is a variant of this. Such arguments – highlighting the relative weakness of hegemonic relations within a particular region of the world economy – may have an explanatory value for why such waves hit where and when they do. Another set of arguments include Katsiaficas' (1987) 'eros effect', combining contagion (or as we might now say 'networking') with de-routinisation (Koopmans 2004) to explain the mobilisation of new groups within individual countries and the spread of contestation between countries. None of these arguments have been fully developed in relation to movement waves, however, which remain in some ways one of those massive facts of world history that are hidden in plain sight and rarely discussed.

We would like to propose the following analytic framework, drawing on the general arguments made in Chapter 3. Firstly, it is the capitalist world-system itself which creates the conditions for global popular agency (Linebaugh and Rediker 2000) through the interconnections it creates, whether the sailors and migrants of the early modern Atlantic or the IT technicians and migrants of the twenty-first century. In capitalism, very large numbers of people experience themselves as to some degree connected to others at great distances, share some operative control of the means of communication, transport, coordination, and so on, and develop common identities (whether radical-democratic ideologies, or the imagery of Che Guevara or Bob Marley). The potential for interconnected popular uprisings is constantly regenerated in ways that do not describe earlier forms of society: this not only enables practical networking but also contagion effects, when movements in one place inspire others who identify with them. In our terms, the movement process has a particularly strong potential to develop in capitalist society, not only locally but also transnationally.

Secondly, weakened hegemonic alliances in particular regions are key to movement waves. A variety of things can weaken such alliances: an accumulation crisis leading to a failure to continue producing economic gains for core actors, failure to keep subordinate members of the alliance onside, and failure to maintain effective coercion over those not in the alliance or to integrate new social actors. Moments of possibility are thus generated which are made visible by a breach in one country or even just one city, leading to defections from the hegemonic alliance, not only from below but also from above (Lash and Urry 1987). Hence, an explanation of revolutionary waves is also an account of movements from above in crisis.

Multiple outcomes are thus possible: in the early 2000s, predictions for the outcome of what was thought to be a terminal crisis of neoliberalism included not only the success of the global justice movement but the rise of a new, Chinese geopolitical hegemony (Arrighi 2005a, 2005b), the success of transnational Islamic movements, or a new regulatory era; and none of these were entirely impossible. It is perhaps a tautology to say that a genuinely long-running or major crisis, such as the present, indicates the long-term incapacity of the current accumulation strategy and its associated hegemonic alliance to continue.

There is nothing surprising in this in terms of the analysis set out in Chapter 3. At the outset of any new arrangement, relatively high gains can be generated for participating groups and concessions offered (not only because of whatever economic switch has been made but also because the use of force, or the generation of a new alliance, offers the dominant group an unexpected degree of freedom for an opening period). However, as such arrangements continue, their benefits naturally decline (for some groups, if not for all). Increasingly, actors who have previously participated within hegemonic arrangements (such as the US 'middle class') remain more or less loyal out of fear of an unknown alternative or because of the exit costs rather than because they are positively benefiting.

Such groups are therefore likely to defect if there is any substantial internal rearrangement, with the result that the hegemonic alliance becomes more and more rigid and less able to reorganise itself to deal with challengers (consider the failure of neoliberal elites to offer any plan B in response to the financial crisis). On occasion (as with the end of Keynesianism), it is elite actors who come to the conclusion that the long-term cost of remaining within is higher than the exit cost. The varying weights of such components, as of new actors entering the field or previously resigned opponents gaining confidence, is not a foregone conclusion, and this is part of what makes the study of revolutions interesting as a field of study. 1917 in Russia and 1919 in Ireland, 1945 or 1989 in Europe, 1994 in South Africa or what may be happening in Greece today – these are not all identical processes which can be neatly dismissed with the same set of clichés.

Sooner or later, therefore, something will have to break; and this is one major reason why accumulation strategies do not last very long (typically 30–50 years in recent European history, if we consider Keynesianism, fascism and state socialism; the figures for national developmentalism or for that matter the period of high imperial rule in the majority world are not all that different). A 'passive revolution', where a new faction within the dominant force reconstructs a new hegemonic alliance from above, is one possible outcome. Monarchies may be abandoned to preserve capitalism, or democracy may be abandoned in favour of fascism. Another is the arrival in power of an 'alternative elite', such as neoliberalism or for that matter conservative national independence movements. Other possibilities are more positive, and include the variety of what we might call revolutionary outcomes.

The really transformative moments often involve new social groups becoming political subjects, moving towards articulating their local rationalities as militant particularisms and taking a conscious hand in collective political agency on their own behalf. This is a standard observation in the study of historical revolutions, and it is equally obvious in movement 'waves' such as 1968. However we categorise the present, one of the differences between (say) Ireland and Spain or Greece is that these groups are not active (yet) in Ireland; and one of the challenges we face on a European scale is that they are only active in a few countries, while in others such mobilisation seems almost impossibly far away. Part of the difference here, of course, is the different modes of capitalism in operation in different European countries, and the different relationships between movement institutions such as trade unions and political parties with austerity politics.

Put another way, the key question is the extent to which popular actors move from being fundamentally passive – giving tacit acceptance to overall structures and passive support to particular institutions of interest representation – to becoming active in their own right (Cox 2001a). In this sense, Gramsci's account of civil society as the secondary trenches behind the formalities of the state is illuminating. If – when people come to feel that enough is enough and something has to be done at the level of economic structure, state power, or, for that matter, culture – they are happy to entrust the business of doing so to parties, unions and NGOs which specialise in this kind of mediation and reproduce the structures of passivity and constitutionality, that fact will in itself structure much of what follows. Of course, at times people come to realise this mistake, or follow more convincing practical suggestions that seem closer to their own experience.

When these groups do burst into the political sphere as active agents in their own right, they have a double learning process. Partly they use a language inherited from above – nationalism, football, constitutionalism, facebook, hostility to movements. Partly they struggle to find a suitable language to express what they know, on a practical level, about how to do things – the experience of survival in the modern workplace, the loose network of friends with shared interests scattered around a city, design and media skills, and all the discontents they are aware of but for which politics does not yet have a language. It is naturally challenging as well as exhilarating for activists who are not on their first engagement with politics to navigate this terrain. Such events bring out *part-time* activists, as well as people who had dropped out of politics for decades but now think it worthwhile re-engaging, and people who are finally finding a way to act on things they have felt for a long time (Davies and Flett 2009). Not everyone involved in the protests is 19 years old, though it is a good sign that so many are.

An Activist Perspective

To say this is to sketch out a research programme for several years: how can contagion or networking be demonstrated, locally or internationally? How can we demonstrate mechanisms of translation or appropriation? How can we give convincing explanations as to which regions of the world-system are affected in a given wave? Why, under most conditions, do major power structures remain so stable outside of these waves? What are the limits of popular mobilisation in such situations? What groups offer passive solidarity, limiting the scope of repression? How can we identify the long-term impact of the fact of mobilisation itself, successful or otherwise? How does the current wave relate to earlier movements? Perhaps most importantly, how can we ensure that we are not simply telling the kinds of stories we prefer, those we are equipped to research, or those that suit our own movements' level of action?

Movements, for their part, do not have the luxury of waiting for monster research programmes (even if the funding was available for this kind of project). They have to make up their minds, in the usual processes of internal argument and politics, as to how they see their situation and what they think they should do about it: 'Are we in a moment of possibility or not? Are large numbers of newcomers becoming mobilised and radicalised as agents in their own right? Are such moves on the cards?' Here, we feel, radical researchers have often let movements down. Specifically, it is often taken as a mark of true radicalism to show that all possible problems are structurally generated, ideally at so deep a level as to be barely accessible to human action. This is often very welcome for the senior academics who act as professional gatekeepers, as it combines the display of great cleverness with the practical conclusion that there is nothing to be done – prefiguring a transition to a resigned worldly wisdom. For the younger researcher, the temptation is to invest in a theoretical vocabulary inaccessible to all but a few initiates but with an appropriately political pedigree, thus restricting 'radical theory' to a small and self-selected group. This plays into the hands of elite attempts to intimidate and disempower, to use the failures of past movements to discredit the possibility of real change, and encourages us to rationalise our own depression, paranoia, or cynicism as theory rather than see it for what it is.

Conversely, other researchers are so concerned to *legitimate* their movements' politics within academia that they retreat to a position of celebrating what (some participants in) movements are already doing anyway. This theoretical celebration may be very welcome, but is unlikely to convince other participants, or to help those already pursuing the desired path, when the 'latest advances' (it is telling that newness is seen as a virtue) of radical theory are in effect saying 'if everyone did this everywhere capitalism would collapse' – something which could be true of almost any significant act of dissent, but is unhelpful in coordinating the variety of movements, strategies, social groups, tactics and regional situations involved in actual revolutionary waves. Often, the practical movement activity of such thinkers is far in advance of their theoretical contribution: put another way, their activist good sense does not translate sufficiently into theory.

If some of the comments above are disappointingly banal, it is because we are convinced that the single most important thing people in movements can do is to talk to each other, *across* their differences, and see how they can 'learn from each other's struggles', without trying to get everyone else to follow their own mode of acting (or, as sometimes seems to be more important, to use the same language).[6] Put another way, we would rather win than look cool. What we need most is a stronger sense of *agency* – 'theirs', in understanding not just how the system works but how the *alliances* which underpin it work and how they can come to be taken apart, and 'ours', in understanding how we can form the kinds of alliances that are capable of bringing about the change we say we want.

By looking at how forms of capitalism come to an end, we can see two important aspects of agency. One is hope: this is a normal process, it happens frequently enough for many of us to have already lived through one such set of changes if not more. That does not mean that what happens afterwards is always good; that is up to us. It *can* be worthwhile, even if it is not always what we want: feminism, the end of dictatorships, welfare states, the withdrawal of empires – these are not trivial things for those of us whose lives are affected by them.

The other is to focus closely on these *alliance processes*. To the extent that we have seen a long 'phoney war' – the existence of well-developed challenges to neoliberalism which for all their repression have not gone away (and have not been crushed by tanks and torture chambers as they would have been in earlier periods) – this represents 'their' inability to mobilise enough consent to squash 'us'; and both the extent and the weakness of US control of Latin America and the Arab world are illuminating in this respect too. We are seeing a system which has no plan B, and which finds it easier to coerce than to gain consent – but which then has to gain the consent of those who have to support the coercion. This was, as we have seen internationally, easier in Afghanistan than in Iraq; internally, it was easier in the US after 9/11 than in Western Europe; and there are real limits, in Europe or Latin America at least, to its hegemony. Winning involves taking this weakness and pushing it further, finding ways to make new allies and to disaggregate existing hegemonic alliances.

What Does it Mean for a Movement From Below to Win?

Almost every activist in the movement of movements is outraged at the global state of affairs. Most of us have thought things through and realised that the problem is structural, not accidental, and have become determined to bring about large-scale change. But many people remain very reluctant to talk about *winning* – in other words, to consider what it means to bring about that change against the determined and powerful opposition of those who run, or benefit from, current arrangements.

Partly this is because of a fear that thinking like this means acting like 'the system' and is bound to lead to a cynical instrumentalism, attempting to replace one set of elites with another. Partly it is because of a belief that we could bring about dramatic change without having to confront current elites. Here we want to look at these ideas directly, and ask how they contribute to the current stalemate between the institutions of the 'New World Order' and the movement of movements. We also go on to ask what 'winning' might actually mean: what happens when a movement from below achieves its goal of 'constructing another world'?

In answering these questions, we draw on the experience of popular movements in the past and on other continents – movements which have come up against these issues first-hand and have had to tackle them practically. It is only by looking at other activists' experience, and trying to learn from them, that we can hope to do more than 'act out' – our own beliefs, our own subculture, our own 'issues' – and that we can have an effect on the world other than by accident.

This section talks about unpleasant things (such as state power) which are likely to upset many people. In some ways, this underlines our basic point, which is that most ordinary people dislike real violence, so that when social movements win, the main issue is rarely about physical force. We do not need to be afraid of each other; we need to look the situation in the face and find our courage despite what states might do (or try to do) to us.

The Fear of Leninism

One concern when people talk about winning is the 'fear of Leninism': the assumption that winning means a military insurrection which would inevitably lead to an authoritarian state. In some ways, this misrepresents the actual events of 1917, but the difficulty here is the *myth* of 1917. One possible response to the myth is the factoid that more people were killed when Eisenstein filmed the storming of the Winter Palace than in the real thing.[7] At least the general sense of this is true: like most successful revolutions, October 1917 was a relatively mild event, whose drama paled into insignificance by comparison with the violence of the First World War, which it extricated Russia from. The key factors in violence were the civil war which followed, the intervention by other states and the development of the new Soviet state; not revolution itself.

More generally, large-scale, systematic violence has almost always been the territory not of revolutionary movements[8] but of *states*: states fighting major wars, states repressing revolutionary movements, or post-revolutionary states fighting intervention and repressing dissent (Halperin 2004). In the four major waves of twentieth-century revolutions in Europe (1916–24, 1943–47, 1965–70, 1989–91), by far the most violent were those of the European Resistance, in countries such as France, Italy, Poland and Yugoslavia. These levels of violence, which were dwarfed by the more general violence of the war and the Holocaust, were made possible by that broader violence and by the assistance of Allied states, who understood them primarily as part of their own war efforts.

There is a simple reason for this overall peacefulness of revolutions, which is that ordinary people are generally reluctant to engage in systematic violence, so that it is a serious practical problem for armies (or police forces) to train them to kill on command. It is rare for popular movements to be in any position to commit the kinds of mass killing that states can organise;[9] and it is less and less relevant to the question of political power. Power, for movements from below at least, only rarely comes out of the barrel of a gun.

A related, but more realistic, concern, can be called the 'fear of reaction': that after a popular uprising is *defeated*, there will be a counter-revolutionary bloodbath aimed at terrorising the population into submission. This happens all too frequently, as the examples of the repression of the Paris Commune, of fascism in power in Europe (after the mostly failed revolutions of 1916–24), or the Latin American 'dirty wars' (after the left-wing and peasant movements of the 1960s and 1970s) remind us.

We draw a slightly different lesson from this history: if we want to create movements that pose a serious threat to those in power, we had better be very serious about winning. The costs of only getting halfway (scaring them but leaving them in place, or winning only temporarily) are too horrifying to be contemplated. To say 'another world is possible' and effectively resist the system, while planning to leave those in power in control of armies, prisons and police forces is to risk the lives not only of activists, but of their partners, families and friends, and of anyone who might be seen to be supporting them.

Finally, and perhaps more trivially, we should note that there is often a reaction to strategic arguments which responds more to activist experience of, for example, groups with a habit of instrumentalising popular movements for party-political ends dressed up as 'real politics'. While it is all too clear why non-aligned activists who have had negative experiences at the hands of such organisations have no desire to see them take state power, it is giving such groups too much credit to take their self-image seriously and imagine such an outcome. Almost by definition, the outcomes of revolutionary situations favour groups which are *good* at alliance-building, not those which make a habit of burning their bridges with social movements.

Refusals to Win

This brings us to the position of consciously 'refusing to win'. One version of this is attempting to replace one elite or policy with another within the institutions of the New World Order (see, for example, Cammack 2004 on the World Bank), whether because this is seen as a real step forward, or because it is seen as the only game in town. This is the reformist strategy of insider critics of the G8, WTO, World Bank, and so on – whether NGOs committed to 'constructive criticism', products of the system such as Stiglitz, Soros and Sachs, or celebrities such as Bob Geldof and Bono. Its starting assumption is TINA – 'there is no alternative', at best, mild improvements on the facts of neoliberalism, as though they fell from the sky.

Another version is 'decoupling' strategies which are against 'globalisation', but broadly in favour of existing local power structures, however modified. This strategy runs from (some) local currency schemes, eco-villages and 'downshifters' via small business and various brands of nationalism through to religious fundamentalism (Starr 2001).

Both strategies are honest in their limited aims. We doubt their feasibility – of reformism because neoliberalism leaves little room for anything other than profit, and of localism because it undermines its own ability to resist the power of the market and the state. But our main objection is to their overall goals: to leave things fundamentally as they are and tinker on the margins, whether by increasing aid within a massively exploitative and ecologically destructive system or by creating small lifestyle niches within that system.

A more serious problem is raised by Holloway's (2002) slogan of 'changing the world without taking power'. One reading of this is to say that the main power relations, and so the main terrain where movement struggles need to win, are social rather than political. It is possible to broadly agree with this (as we do) without ignoring the need for a political victory on the back of a social one.

A more damaging reading is to treat the state as either irrelevant or just given, and has deliberately feeble aspirations (like Bey's (1991) 'temporary autonomous zone'). This approach is similar to the liberal celebration of 'civil society'[10] as a good thing, but scores style points because it looks far more radical. Such celebrations of defeat have a history: they come from the post-1968 context where activists came to accept that the power of the state could not be challenged because it was ultimately backed up by tanks (as was demonstrated variously in Prague, Paris and Derry).

From this defeat, activists deliberately limited their aims to what they could achieve within those large-scale power relations. For many people, this enabled them to get on with politics on a small scale or locally, rather than giving up in despair. But we are now moving out of that long defeat of the movements of the 1960s, which was symbolised by the coming to power of neoliberalism in the decades that followed. And we have seen the movements of 1989 in the Soviet bloc demonstrate the constraints on the effectiveness of state violence – or, more specifically, that military power always rests on political and social power. Movements that cut deep enough into society are capable of bringing about huge changes, even if not always the ones they hoped for.

Day's *Gramsci is Dead*, with its call for 'permanent autonomous zones' and its attack on what it presents as the Gramscian 'assumption that effective social change can only be achieved simultaneously and *en masse*, across an entire national or supranational space' (2005: 8) fits into this same perspective (and fills the academic market niche previously occupied by Laclau and Mouffe's 2001 *Hegemony and Socialist Strategy*, in other respects a rather different book).

Briefly: yes, neoliberal capitalism, capitalist patriarchy, and so on have a powerful logic of their own which does indeed reach 'across an entire national or supranational space'. While it is possible, and important, to develop counter-cultural spaces of resistance from which movements can gain inspiration and where they can network (Cox 1999a), the history of such projects – for example, the commodification of European social centres (Consorzio Aaster et al. 1996) – underlines the limitations of such strategies when they are cut off from wider social change. Broader social logics *do* have power over such spaces, and in neoliberalism in particular the scope for severing links with the outside world is severely reduced.

It is certainly possible, as it always has been, for advances to be made in one area and not in others; indeed the continued maintenance of hegemony depends on the ability to co-opt popular movements *selectively*. However, some things – the fundamental shape of class, gender and race relationships in a given society – are not equally amenable to change, still less to piecemeal or exemplary strategies, and can only be tackled on a large scale by major popular alliances. The defeat of absolute monarchy, fascism, empire, or Stalinist rule; the end of institutionalised racism in the US or South Africa; women's right to vote and the (partial) defeat of religious controls on sex, marriage and childbirth; peasant control of the land in France or Ireland; the institutionalisation of welfare states across the global North – these are not the products of isolated autonomous zones, minor concessions to single-issue movements, or separate struggles in affinity. With all their flaws and limitations, it nevertheless took mass struggle around shared goals, large-scale alliances and at times revolutions to achieve these.

So What Does *Winning Mean?*

Given our general understanding of the social movement process as the widening and deepening of the scope and direction of collective skilled activity, winning consists of society *defeating* the state, breaking up at least some of the existing power relations, and starting to create and substitute its own, democratically controlled, institutions in place of the old ones.[11] Some such experiences – the French Revolution of 1789, the Paris Commune of 1871, the 'two red years' in Italy, the Spanish Revolution, the institutions of the European Resistance in 1943–45, the dissident agenda of 1956 in Hungary or 1968 in Prague, the 'utopian moment' of the 1960s, the Zapatista movement in southeast Mexico – are well known, others less so.

In such cases, revolution is not something imposed by a vanguard elite, but a collective achievement of ordinary people going far beyond what they previously believed to be possible. These situations share a potential for human self-development to flourish beyond the normal limits set by exploitation, oppression, ignorance and isolation, creating institutions driven by human need rather than by profit and power. This tends to give rise to self-management in workplaces and direct democracy in communities, while on a wider scale, it has usually been connected with a strong internationalism, a refusal of racism and advances in women's power.

As Chapter 3 argued, this does not come from nowhere. The 'political economy of labour' (Lebowitz 2003) – the way ordinary people try to meet their needs in the face of capital and the state – is something which people are constantly struggling towards, even if it is usually less dramatic. In 'revolutionary moments', people see, and grab, the opportunity to push things further – but what they are doing grows out of this broader, everyday struggle.

Such organic crises are not the outcomes of the mysterious workings of the objective laws of capital (Cleaver 2000), or of something utterly new that allows us to view the past with contempt; they are the result of popular struggle and the weaknesses of existing movements from above. These in turn go back to previous struggles against capitalism, which forced elites to re-organise along neoliberal lines – which are now pushing ordinary people to their limits and showing us that we need to turn to each other to survive in this new world.

Rather than try to brand these revolutionary experiences for some political party, we want to stress that these core elements do not belong to any organisation; they are part of the aspirations which ordinary people consistently express whenever they see a real change to do so. These 'everyday utopias' do not need to be installed from above by decree; what they do need is a breaking of the power relations within communities, workplaces, state institutions and globally, which stand in their way. To quote Zibechi:

> The new society [in Marx] is not a place that one arrives; it is not something to be conquered and therefore is not out there; and it is even less something implanted. The image that Marx offers us of revolutionary change is that of a latent power that lies dormant within the world of the oppressed, and grows out like a flower. That is why he uses the expression 'to set free'. (Zibechi 2010: 3)

These transformations (and the personal transformations which go along with them) are part and parcel of the *process* of developing movements from below that can challenge existing power relations (as Sewell 1996 has argued, for example, revolution in the modern sense was *invented* at the Bastille). Winning, then, is about human development in many dimensions: in changing social relations on a micro-scale; in creating new ways of working, of living in places, of gender relations; in constructing broader global connections – and in creating movements which can carry this change forward against the determined, even 'last-ditch' opposition, of powerful elites. This is difficult, and success is not guaranteed.

But it is also not impossible. Tilly (1996) calculates that Europe alone experienced roughly one revolutionary situation a year over the last half-millennium. Put another way, in the twentieth century, most people in most countries could expect to experience on average one revolutionary moment in their lifetimes, even if most were either defeated or recuperated by new states. It is possible to win, in other words; people try to do so with some regularity, and this experience – of ordinary people reshaping their world in the face of state opposition – is one which our movements have to reclaim as our own.

For activists in the privileged North, who often look at our societies with despair, this means not only making links with our sisters and brothers in the South, who have often been far more successful at building large movements rooted in poor urban and rural communities,[12] but learning from a history of movement struggles that reaches back beyond our own lifetimes – and building links with people here and now who are struggling in their own communities and workplaces. This is far more personally challenging than travelling halfway around the world to support struggles elsewhere, important though that is – it involves looking closely at the relations of social class, gender and race which we are caught up in at home, and making links across difference with people whose experiences of 'people like us' have not always been comfortable. In the process (we are speaking from experience), we may find out a lot about ourselves and our society which we would never have known from within activist subcultures.

Building Movements: The Irish Experience of Insurgent Architecture

Revolution, then, is a development of the collective skilled activity of ordinary people to the point where it can successfully challenge power structures. Harvey (2000) has used the metaphor of 'insurgent architecture' to describe the same process of human development against opposition which we have conceptualised in earlier chapters, and we want briefly to identify the elements contained within this, using some Irish movements as a way of identifying the issues involved and reframing some problems facing the movement such as institution-building and strategic thinking.

The period since 1968 has been one of almost uninterrupted movement struggles in the Republic of Ireland, in an uneasy interplay with the conflict in Northern Ireland – which at times facilitated the radicalisation of popular movements in the South, at others enabled their corralling within a logic of the state's conflict with paramilitaries and hierarchical party leaderships. Despite long periods of relatively high trade union membership and their continuing ability to mobilise large numbers, the labour movement's double subordination to a conservative Labour Party (routinely junior partner in right-wing governments) and the logic of national competitivity have kept it even more restricted to questions of distribution rather than power than some of its counterparts elsewhere in western Europe.

Three movement alliances were particularly important in these years. Firstly and most obviously, the women's movement, together with GLBTQ movements, survivors of abuse in religious-run institutions, secular activists and some religious minorities, challenged the nexus of Catholic power and private patriarchy across a wide range of fields, including women's access to employment, church control of education, contraception, divorce, the legalisation of homosexuality, abortion and responsibility for the horrors of Ireland's carceral past (O'Sullivan and O'Donnell 2012). If the conflict is far from over, as the death of Savita Halappanavar highlighted,[13] there can be little doubt that things have changed radically in many of these fields. Put another way, a modernising alliance oriented to international capital and credentialising strategies has substantially displaced the earlier hegemonic role of religion in a society structured around inheritance and the associated gender regimes (Inglis 1998). The shift has been far faster than in most European societies, not least because the left substantially agreed that this was a key issue for Irish society as a whole, and supported a wide range of campaigns.

A second movement alliance was that around rural conflicts over industrial development, mostly by multinational corporations (Allen and Jones 1990). The highpoint of this was the multiple parallel campaigns in opposition to the proposed nuclear power plant at Carnsore in 1979

(Dalby 1984), which saw Ireland become one of the few states in Europe to defeat nuclear power outright. Existing in an uneasy relationship with an elite-oriented, technocratic environmentalism (Tovey 1993), since 2005 the centre of this conflict has been Shell's gas pipeline project in the peripheral region of Erris, which has seen massive use of state violence against an alliance of local residents, ecological campaigners, anarchists, socialists, republicans and trade unionists. The arrival of fracking projects spanning the north-south border and the development of links with the Erris campaign are extending this conflict further.

Third is the long history of urban working-class community organising since the 1960s, discussed in Chapter 2. This saw widespread self-organisation and self-provision of basic needs as well as large-scale direct action. In the 1970s and early 1980s, great effort was put into developing independent community education and the transmission of skills from majority world experiences as well as within Ireland.

We have already discussed the process of 'social partnership' which the state, employers, unions and farmers' organisations entered into in the late 1980s, and which from the 1990s was extended, partly in response to movement demand, to offer consultative rights and funding to 'community and voluntary' groups – in practice, the NGO end of social movements, with predictable results in terms of professionalisation, demobilisation and the fragmentation of earlier alliances between movements. Once this result had been achieved and the state was no longer under political pressure to defuse mass movements, community and NGO participants in partnership processes came under increased pressure with loss of funding, increased competition, a narrowing of criteria in all fields from service provision to legal structure, forced amalgamation of organisations and sanctions for political advocacy – a process which began before the financial crash provided public justification.

It was, perhaps not coincidentally, during the period of partnership that activists increasingly came to question the credibility of developmentalist nationalism, as the practical limits of a top-down, legislative and distributive inclusion of movements became clearer. In particular, the Irish wing of the movement of movements was centred around the primacy of a bottom-up politics of direct action, grass-roots organising, radical democracy, and a scepticism as to both social-democrat/NGO and authoritarian/Leninist modes of organising. That both Labour-linked and Trotskyist front groups felt impelled to adopt the language and style of this new politics underlines this (comparatively late) generational shift in Irish movement politics. A combination of summit protests, direct action against the use of Irish airports by US military and 'rendition' flights, a new wave of direct-action feminism and engagement with rural community struggles gave this movement considerable purchase for a time, and inscribed a logic of alliance-building and radicalisation at the heart of anti-systemic struggles (Cox 2006).

However, the substantial demobilisation of community activism during this same period has meant that – unlike, for example, the Italian situation (de Sario 2009) – relationships between alter-globalisation activists and community struggles have been not so much fraught as tenuous, outside specific conflicts such as the Erris conflict mentioned earlier or urban opposition to incinerator projects. As with trade unionism, there are overlaps and individual connections, but attempts by activists from either side to build links on a wider scale have tended to run into the sand, for now.

In the face of the crisis, surviving professionals in NGOs and community organisations have adopted a defensive line, seeking a return to the previous status quo of partnership, defending 'their projects' despite the manifest lack of mobilising capacity to force concessions from the state. The search for an organisation-focused solution was also tempting for the traditionalist left, who saw the crisis as an opportunity to reassert their own leadership and preferred themes around the state and economics – leading to an ever-decreasing cycle of struggle which was unable to break from the logic of demonstrating their own small numbers in any protest not organised by the state's loyal opposition in the trade unions.

The net result was a prioritising of organisation over movement on (almost) all sides,[14] with the partial exception of the 2012 campaign that successfully convinced about half the population not to pay a new household tax (in 2013, however, the campaign's Trotskyist leadership was comprehensively outmanoeuvred by the state and it collapsed). At present, legislation is finalising the process of subsuming community organisations within the structures of local government, symbolising the endpoint of this particular strategy.

Laurence has argued elsewhere (Cox 2010c, 2011b, 2012, 2013b) that the way out must lie not in a further reassertion of the narrow interests of organisational elites, be they community, NGO, or Trotskyist, but in strategies aimed at supporting the development of active *movement* participation and alliance-building on our own terrain. This is obviously easier said than done; in all likelihood, the next moves in action from below will not come from increasingly isolated movement organisations but from new mobilisations below the radar.

The most obvious cases of this were the massive mobilisations which forced new legislation on abortion (but were easily corralled into a legislative framework and rapidly became dormant) and the strong showing of Irish Occupy – which was particularly long-lasting, visible and widespread, but (as elsewhere) struggled to find adequate expressions for the forces it expressed once the camps were shut down. At time of writing (April 2014), it is only around opposition to Shell in Erris and fracking elsewhere in the north-west that there are significant *alliances* of movements with any degree of willingness to act outside the institutional frameworks of routine politics. This does not mean, of course, that this situation will last; given the failures of *organisational* movement politics, however, there is every reason to believe that the new wave will, like the Italian 1977, come from outside existing organisational contexts.

The NBA and the State

The dilemma over how social movements from below should relate to the state can be illuminated by revisiting the movement process of the Narmada Bachao Andolan. As we noted in Chapter 3, the anti-dam movement's origins can be traced to local grass-roots struggles against the everyday tyranny that the local state enacted in Bhil Adivasi communities in the western parts of Madhya Pradesh. In these struggles, the Khedut Mazdoor Chetna Sangath (KMCS) challenged corruption, malpractice and violence by holding the local state and its representatives accountable to basic democratic precepts. The struggle ultimately – and significantly – democratised local state-society relations as Bhil communities lost their fear of the state, came to understand its procedural workings, and developed an understanding of themselves as rights-bearing citizens.

However, the trajectory of the anti-dam campaign presents us with a different experience of engaging with the state. From the onset of the campaign, the NBA demanded that the state should conduct a review of the Sardar Sarovar Project (SSP), and if the project was found to be in violation of official norms relating to resettlement and rehabilitation, it should be scrapped. This strategy – a form of 'jury politics' (Dwivedi 2006) in which the state is posited as a neutral arbiter between two opposing parties – never bore fruit: both state and federal governments bowed to pressure from the supporters of the dam, and ultimately the construction of the SSP was approved by the Indian Supreme Court (Nilsen 2010: Chapters 3 and 6).

At the heart of these contrasting experiences lies the fact that whereas the KMCS challenged *local* power structures and the *local* state, the anti-dam campaign was both pitted directly against the vested interests of dominant groups in the economically prosperous state of Gujarat and embedded in a wider critique of India's post-colonial development project. In other words, the anti-dam campaign militated against the fundamental modalities through which the Indian state had worked to expand capitalist relations in post-colonial India. In pursuing this campaign through a strategy centred on jury politics, the NBA ultimately came up against structural constraints that circumscribe the scope for subaltern action in and through the state (Nilsen 2008b).

Developing Strategic Thinking

We have rehearsed these particular experiences to underline the ways in which strategic thinking is necessarily tied into specific organising histories, both within individual campaigns and movements and between them. The 'insurgent architecture' of the movement of movements operates on a particular terrain, in which global processes of neoliberalism from above are provoking a revival of movements from below. Yet the different vernacular styles of building – existing institutions, traditions of struggle, movement landscapes and local truce lines with the powerful – cannot be wished away, only remade in the process of attempting to find solidarity with one another and win against what is still, for now, a more powerful opponent. This is one major reason why the reification and uncritical celebration of any specific local style of activism is less than helpful.

We feel that it is important to hold both aspects – the wider social picture and the narrower organisational situation – in view simultaneously. If we only look at the problem in macro-social terms, we lose a sense of how the movement of movements is rooted in existing struggles. If we only look at those groups which are already mobilised, we lose the movement's commitment to broadening participation – not simply numerically, but in terms of power. This process implies the movement remaking itself, or constantly dying and being reborn: a serious challenge to individuals and groups who have only just staked out positions for themselves within the movement.

Strategic questions are always easiest to pose in abstract terms, constructing an unhelpful relationship between 'objective reality' and organisational action ('the movement must …'). Instead, the logic of our argument is to do what we can, and encourage others to do what they can, to support the process of radicalisation of the 'movement within society' (which is what 'social movement' originally meant) – supporting what are as yet less articulated, less 'radical', or less 'organised' layers of conflict, reaching out to what people *are already doing* in broader social groups than those we can currently connect with, and always listening.[15]

We start from a Gramscian commitment to good sense as against common sense, hence to the processes whereby expressions of local rationalities can articulate themselves in struggle and encounter one another in alliance – paying attention *both* to the further development of already-organised forms of struggle *and* to the self-expression and self-organisation of new groups, within, around and outside those movements. The developmental process whereby local rationalities come to express themselves as militant particularisms, in open conflict with hegemonic relationships; where alliances are made across such particularisms into broader campaigns, and where such campaigns come to articulate far-reaching movement projects that question the fundamentals of the social order, is not a linear one. At each stage – together with defeats, particularist temptations and alliance offers from elites – we find not only a moving forward of the existing movement but a mobilisation and radicalisation of new participants, whose perspectives are crucial to include if the movement is to grow and win – but whose involvement simultaneously requires a rethinking on all levels, threatening existing hierarchies.

The history of the genesis of the Zapatistas – urban radicals seeking to rouse the peasantry, finding that indigenous communities had been resisting capitalism and imperialism for some time, and starting to listen to and learn from them before proposing processes through which this resistance could develop further – is one which the 'movement of movements' can still learn a lot from in this context. Bringing the movement home consists in learning from each other, not just tactically but also strategically, in constant interaction with our own developing practical sense of the local situation and its possibilities. We need to construct, almost within ourselves and our movements, a dialogue between these two touchstones, not privilege one over the other.

Beyond the Stalemate: How Can the Movement Develop in the Crisis?

If we are right – that is, if the neoliberal hegemonic alliance has reached its twilight years and if elites are struggling to articulate an alternative strategy which could restore profitability and underpin a new hegemony – we can ask what the movement of movements might do under these circumstances.

A movement capable of remaking the world needs to develop a substantial degree of (counter-) hegemony; that is, it needs to form long-term, strategic alliances (in which, Gramsci tells us, the leading group distinguishes itself both by its capacity to understand and include the perspectives of its internal opponents and by its ability to make concessions in terms of its own corporate self-interest) around a different way of organising the social world, grounded in the life-activity of subaltern social groups.

It is of the nature of things (and the experience of previous movement waves) that such a situation will not reach a point of universality or homogeneity, but will be marked by all kinds of complexities, and will be in process at the point where – having posed a sufficiently dramatic threat to the powers that be – serious efforts are made to defend the most threatened interests by destroying the movement. As noted above in relation to repression, however, what determines both the outcome of such confrontations and the degree of bloodiness of attempted reaction is the extent to which the movement has built widespread alliances and legitimacy and is already substantially recognised as the bearer of popular interests in strategic areas.

This means that such a movement project will need to have a complex engagement with movements representing a range of class interests, gender positions and ethnic or racial identities – and show a genuine ability to engage with new expressions of the exploited, oppressed and stigmatised as they come to articulation – even if the decisive moment in terms of conflict is likely to arise before all such issues can be resolved. Similarly, it will need to have a real presence if not in all global regions, then at least in a number of strategic ones, including those which at present operate as the core and from which power is exercised.

Within this broad field of alliance and argument, there will naturally be a vast range of conflicting ideas and interests expressed in tension with one another. Politically central is the extent to which participant groups are willing and able to resolve or at least express and explore these conflicts with each other rather than seek individual alliances within existing arrangements.

The experience of revolutionary moments from 1789 onwards is that the articulation of counter-hegemonic projects and dual-power institutions *does* provoke a reaction from those whose interests are centrally tied up with the current order; that such a reaction takes place at the point where the outcome is not a foregone conclusion (the current order is seriously threatened but not yet out for the count), and that the defenders of the status quo will not shrink from the use of violence but may be unable to deploy it effectively if their hegemony is already seriously compromised.

Moments of confrontation are unpredictable, involve a wide range of actors, and are only rarely under the control of a single agent, on either side. In line with our position, one of the most important 'revolutions within the revolution' is the extent to which popular power is strengthened in the process: in the construction of dual-power institutions, in the relationship between events on the street and those in the halls of power, in the shape of the institutions which emerge from a confrontation, and, perhaps above all, in the strengthening or weakening of alliances between movements in the process. We can illustrate this by looking at events in Latin America.

Movements and States in Latin America

In the last decade and a half, Latin America has witnessed a so-called 'pink tide' – that is, a series of electoral victories by political parties of various left-wing hues, ranging from the mildly social democratic in the case of Bachelet's Chile, Kirchner's Argentina, and Lula's and Rouseff's Brazil to the more explicitly socialist in the case of Chávez in Venezuela, Morales in Bolivia, and Correa in Ecuador (see, for example, Burbach, Wilpert and Fox 2013, Sader 2011, Petras and Veltmeyer 2005, 2009, 2013, Dangl 2010). The pink tide constitutes a significant break with Latin America's recent political and economic past, in which an elite-controlled transition from dictatorship to democracy combined with the consolidation of neoliberalism in the region to create structures of extreme inequality and political disenfranchisement (see Robinson 1996, Panizza 2009, Green 2003, Taylor 2006). The key features of this break with the neoliberal project are a turn to a more interventionist approach to economic policy-making, the introduction of more generous social policies, and attempts to build regional alliances capable of loosening the grip of US hegemony in the region (Kellogg 2007, Rigirozzi 2012).

Crucially, the electoral victories of left-wing political parties has been paralleled by and closely related to the surfacing of radical social movements from below that have developed and advanced radical counter-hegemonic projects. In Brazil, for example, the rise to power of the Partido dos Trabalhadores (Workers' Party, PT) has been coeval with the emergence of the Movimento dos Trabalhadores Sem Terra (Landless Workers' Movement, MST), which has challenged the entrenched inequalities of landownership that are foundational to the power structures that undergird the country's political economy (see Branford and Rocha 2002, Wright and Wolford 2003, Wolford 2010). In the Andean region, both Morales in Bolivia and Correa in Ecuador were ushered into power by the movements of workers and indigenous peoples against dispossession of natural resources wrought by neoliberal restructuring (see Webber 2012a, Lazar 2010, Schaefer 2009, Becker 2012).

Argentina and Venezuela have witnessed the growth of substantial urban social movements: in Argentina, this has taken the form of the Movimiento de Trabajadores Desocupados (Unemployed Workers' Movements, MTD), factory occupations by workers' collectives, and the emergence of neighbourhood assemblies (see Dinerstein 2002, Sitrin 2012, Schaumberg 2008); in Venezuela, the promotion of participatory democracy through the Bolivarian Constitution of 1999 gave rise to Comités de Tierra Urbana (Urban Land Committees, CTU), which have developed into significant sites of mobilisation and organisation for the urban poor and working classes (Motta 2011, Garciá-Guadilla 2011).

The new pink tide regimes have been referred to as 'post-neoliberal' and 'neo-developmentalist' to signal their departure from the policy regimes of the Washington Consensus (Grugel and Rigirozzi 2012, Bebbington and Bebbington 2012, Féliz 2012, Ban 2013). Chávez's presidency in Venezuela – lasting from 1999 to his death in 2013 – was arguably the first harbinger of this turn away from neoliberal orthodoxy, pioneering both the nationalisation of natural resources and expansive anti-poverty programmes (Wilpert 2007, Ellner 2008, Ciccarello-Maher 2013). In Brazil, this has been most clearly manifest after 2006, when the onset of Lula's second presidential term was marked by a decisive turn from neoliberal policies through the adoption of an interventionist economic policy geared to boost growth and the introduction of targeted welfare programmes such as the Bolsa Familia cash transfer scheme (Ban 2013, Morais and

Saad-Filho 2011, 2012). Similarly, in Argentina, the presidencies of Nestor Kirchner from 2003 to 2007 and Cristina Kirchner from 2007 onwards have been associated with greater state intervention in the economy and the adoption of redistributive social policies (Féliz 2012, Wylde 2013). And in Bolivia and Ecuador, the electoral victories of Morales and Correa have been associated with the introduction of new constitutions that have sought to entrench greater state control over the countries' natural resources, especially oil and gas (Arsel 2012, Kennemore and Weeks 2011, Becker 2010).

The positive results of these new policy regimes cannot be denied. Across Venezuela, Brazil, Argentina, Bolivia and Ecuador, economic growth has reached impressive heights after decades of stagnation, thus boosting employment, incomes and state revenues. In combination with redistributive social policies, economic growth has in turn been translated into reduced levels of poverty and decreased inequalities (Huber and Stephens 2012). But to what extent has this new constellation of leftist political rule in Latin America enabled social movements from below to articulate and advance their oppositional projects?

There is no unambiguous answer to this question. Certainly, pink tide regimes have demonstrated their affinity with social movements from below through the introduction of policies that make concessions to key movement demands and by including movement representatives in policy dialogues and policy implementation. For example, in Brazil, Lula's PT government – which benefited greatly from the support of the MST – made efforts to promote land reform by settling landless families, and in Argentina, Kirchner's government moved to regularise and support factories that had been taken over by workers' collectives (Wolford 2010, Dinerstein 2010, Hirtz and Giacone 2013). In Venezuela, the mushrooming of Urban Land Committees in slums in urban centres has in fact followed a decree by the Chávez government, which responded to slumdwellers' concerns by offering the possibility of regularising ownership of homes (see Motta 2011). In Bolivia and Ecuador, the introduction of new constitutions that secured national control over natural resources expressed a recognition of long-standing demands of indigenous peoples' movements in the two countries (Kohl and Farthing 2006, Becker 2012).

However, there are also clear limitations to the extent to which the left turn in electoral politics has created a more favourable context for social movements from below in the region. Firstly, the concessions that have been granted by pink tide governments often fall far short of the substance of movement demands. In Brazil, the MST has openly criticised the PT's agricultural policy for favouring agribusiness interests and for failing to create space for the implementation of a radical agenda of land reform (Stedile 2007). Similarly, in Bolivia and Ecuador, indigenous social movements have been disappointed by the actual ramifications of the new constitutional parameters for the control and use of natural resources, which has sparked new conflicts between subaltern groups and the governments of Morales and Correa (Kennemore and Weeks 2011, Becker 2010, Hesketh and Morton 2014, Webber 2012b).

Secondly, the incorporation of social movements from below in the development and implementation of policies contains the potential for demobilisation and depoliticisation of movement agendas. This is arguably most evident in the Argentinian case, where the Kirchner government moved to accommodate the wave of militant factory takeovers by granting formal recognition to recovered companies. As Hirtz and Giacone (2013) have shown, this meant that formal recognition was made conditional upon the introduction of specific modes of organising production and management that went against the grain of the horizontal practices developed through the initial factory occupations. Furthermore, dependence on the state for loans and subsidies led to an erosion of the militancy of collective workers' organisations. At the same time, their involvement in protracted judicial processes for the legal expropriation of factories created significant instability as well as weakening their market position, as they were prevented from accessing credit during this period. Thus Hirtz and Giacone conclude:

> The way in which recovered companies were institutionalized was aimed not at repressing their development but at forcing workers to compete in a market in which they had to use all their efforts to maintain productivity, abandoning antisystemic elements developed in the process of struggle such as direct democracy and solidarity. (Ibid.: 98)

The Latin American experience over the past one-and-a-half decades has given rise to an intense debate on the left between social democratic perspectives (for example, Huber and Stephens 2012, Weyland, Madrid and Hunter 2010) that see current leftist reformism as a sustainable path towards more equitable human development in the region; Marxist critiques of the pink tide (for example, Petras and Veltmeyer 2005, 2009,

Webber 2011, 2012b) that call for a reorientation towards revolutionary strategies capable of breaking decisively with the neoliberal past; and autonomist or anarchist approaches (for example, Sitrin 2012, Zibechi 2012) which eschew engagement with the state in favour of the construction of autonomous spaces of resistance through horizontal mobilising strategies. As significant and interesting as this debate has been, the polarised terms on which it has been conducted arguably prevent us from moving beyond unhelpful either/or binaries as we think strategically about how to relate to state power when mobilising against the neoliberal project.

Engagement with the state seems to be an intrinsic aspect of the mobilisation of subaltern resistance; even in the case of the Unemployed Workers' Movement in Argentina – often portrayed as a model of autonomist politics – contentious negotiations with the state over the implementation of workfare programmes constitutes an important part of the movement's strategic register (Dinerstein 2010). And in the context of a region that witnessed poverty and inequality escalate dramatically during the neoliberal decades of the 1980s and the 1990s, it would be arrogant to dismiss the significance of reforms that have reversed these processes – at least in part – and secured subaltern groups access to basic public goods such as education and healthcare. However, the fact that social movements from below have not refrained from challenging the regimes which they themselves have been instrumental in bringing to power should simultaneously alert us to think critically about the limits to the extent to which social movement projects can be pursued in and through the state and the domain of electoral democracy.

A possible way of navigating between the Scylla of state-centrism and the Charybdis of anti-statism in this debate is to call for an *instrumental* rather than a *committed* engagement with the state. This entails, on the one hand, recognising that the form of the state can be transformed – up to a point – through mobilisation from below, and that the victories that can be gained from such transformations – whether regime change or progressive reforms – can prepare the ground for further counter-hegemonic advances. On the other hand, this recognition does not entail positing interaction and negotiation with the state as the be-all and end-all of movement activity. Rather, drawing on an awareness of the fact that the structuring of state power ultimately undergirds and reproduces the hegemony of dominant groups, the recognition of potential gains in engaging with the state should be joined to an equally clear perception of what is risked in a strategy that does not seek to move beyond the institutionalisation of political power in the state.

Ultimately, what flows from this way of thinking is a commitment to a multi-scalar strategic repertoire that corresponds to the multiple scales on which social movements from below operate – ranging from everyday conflicts that only occasionally reach the level of state intervention or a challenge to the political order, via the development of needs and capacities for which interaction with the state is only a means, to anti-systemic efforts to challenge the principles of power from above on which the capitalist state rests. Within the parameters of such a multi-scalar approach to strategy, engagements with the state and the gains that can be had from such engagements remain coupled to the construction of a social movement project which seeks to develop the collective skilled activity of subaltern groups to the point where it can successfully challenge extant power structures and their entrenched institutional manifestations.

Of Parties and Princes

The question has often been asked (indeed, since the 1880s) whether 'revolution is a meaningful concept today' (Foran 2003). There is no doubt that 1871 was neither 1848 nor (as Marx observed) was 1848 1789. The Russian Revolution, like the Chinese and Cuban after it, were widely recognised as having changed the rules of the game. The events of 1968 and 1989, the end of apartheid and the Zapatista rebellion, the *Argentinazo* and the 'pink tide'; the Arab Spring and *indignados* all present new possibilities – understandably, since the commonality is not simply the developing characteristics of states, capitalism, culture, and so on, but the ongoing process of popular self-development, the 'political economy of labour' together with the changing meanings of gender and the rewriting of the rules of race and ethnicity.

Yet the most recent round of events – from the anti-Chávez coup to the Icelandic saucepan revolution, from the Egyptian struggle to the bloodshed of Bahrain, from the Ukrainian crisis to the jungles of South Asia – gives no grounds for the proposition that the state form has reached its endpoint, that societies will cease attempting to remake their states (and sometimes succeed), or that such processes will sometimes bring into question apparently fixed geopolitical orders.

States are important; but this book argues strongly against a state-*centric* view of things (one which treats the reified products of movements from above as givens). This does not make it an anarchist book, but this distinction seems sometimes hard to grasp. It is natural that those who have invested heavily in researching and writing about policy and institutions should treat states as we know them as the uttermost bound of the Real. So too with members of once-reformist parties and their allied trade unions, who would face immense contradictions were they to envisage a broader historical perspective. In fact, of course, in recent decades such bodies – and their surviving cadres – have moved wholeheartedly onto neoliberal terrain in most countries.

It is more surprising that Marxists, with a broader perspective on social structure, potential and history, should so often treat an orientation to 'party' or 'state' as defining Marxism. Leaving aside the enormous variations in what constitutes states historically, or state-ness in the present era, 'party' is not a single thing. For Marx and Engels in 1848, *Partei* meant something more like what we would call 'tendency', 'faction', or 'ideology' – so much so that in the book which uses *Partei* in its title they noted:

- The Communists do not form a separate party opposed to the other working-class parties.
- They have no interests separate and apart from those of the proletariat as a whole.
- They do not set up any sectarian principles of their own, by which to shape and mould the proletarian movement.
- The Communists are distinguished from the other working-class parties by this only: 1. In the national struggles of the proletarians of the different countries, they point out and bring to the front the common interests of the entire proletariat, independently of all nationality. 2. In the various stages of development which the struggle of the working class against the bourgeoisie has to pass through, they always and everywhere represent the interests of the movement as a whole.
- The Communists, therefore, are on the one hand, practically, the most advanced and resolute section of the working-class parties of every country, that section which pushes forward all others; on the other hand, theoretically, they have over the great mass of the proletariat the advantage of clearly understanding the line of march, the conditions, and the ultimate general results of the proletarian movement. (Marx and Engels 1888)

The meaning of 'party' in this period – when only a handful of elected parliaments existed and deputies formed their own alliances – was radically altered by the late nineteenth-century SPD model of the highly structured mass-membership party, from 1917 onwards by the prestige of the Bolshevik model, and in the post-war period by successful post-independence nationalist parties – to say nothing of western catch-all parties, the massive drop-off in popular participation in recent decades, or the last surviving flickers of post-1968 left sects.

To treat these different usages of 'party' as having the same real referent, let alone defining of what constitutes Marxism, is in our view indicative of the impoverishment of much contemporary Marxist thought. Rather than Gramsci's 'Modern Prince', it sometimes seems that many Marxists are on a desperate search for a Prince Charming, as though if there were no party to identify with they could no longer be Marxists. Where Prince Charming is not available at home, he is sought elsewhere: in southern Europe (Rifondazione Comunista, Front de Gauche, die Linke, Syriza ...), or in Latin America (Castro, Ortega, Lula, Chávez ...).

In developing this book, we have been asked 'What is your position on the state?' (or, by one publisher, which Latin American left model we would endorse), as though this was the crucial fact and all else would follow from that. This might once have made sense, in the era of massive Internationals with shared platforms and sister parties across the globe – and when such parties were often within shouting distance of actual political power, in states where control of national economic and foreign policy was at least partly available to winners of elections.

Today, however, it marks far more the impoverishment of this form of 'Marxism' and its inability to grapple in any historically minded way with the question of popular agency. Marxism is *not* the position that in all times and all places the political party is the best way to organise (counterposed, presumably, to anarchism).[16] Rather, we would argue that its defining feature in a much deeper sense is a commitment to structured popular agency, to representing 'the interests of the movement as a whole', and hence to strategies of alliance-building between movements, of identifying the most radical common potential, and of close attention to the interests underlying different tendencies within movements, not as a means of dismissal but as a means of understanding and preventing movement capture by elites.

The history of the last hundred years – reformist and Leninist alike – highlights the extent to which political parties have become mechanisms to capture and channel popular movements. This is not to say that they need always be that, but that the Marxist emphasis has to be on the *movement*, not the party: a party is worthy of Marxist interest only to the extent that it is successful in placing the movement first. More broadly, the Marxist question should be one about how popular agency is currently structured – or the competing types of structure which movements adopt. Rather than fetishising a particular mode of organising either as universally valid (and hence defining a new Marxist 'tradition'), or as sweeping all before it because it is new, the useful question is one of the *relationships* between different types of popular organising in a given time and place, and how they reinforce one another or cancel each other out, not only in the struggle against capital and the state but also in the internal struggle to articulate 'good sense' against 'common sense' and to become political subjects rather than objects.

In this book, we have argued that it is this developmental process from local rationalities to movement projects – which necessarily involves external struggle, internal learning and complex processes of building alliances and counter-hegemony – that matters most. The value or otherwise of any given political party or leader has to be evaluated in these terms, of their contribution or otherwise to this process. All too often, enthusiasm for the individual or collective Prince Charming represents a falling back into simplicity: the macho simplicity of 'hard-edged realism', the reductionist simplicity which uses parties and international relations to boil everything down to coercive power, or the populist simplicity of the heroic narrative and the dramatic gesture.

This very simplicity often amounts to the anti-intellectualism of left intellectuals: dismissing problems of consent and culture, ignoring the popular struggle to find adequate forms for movement development, writing off potential allies who do not fit into the easy narrative, and above all, arguing *against* the need for movements to learn. This last point – the most destructive from the point of view of anyone committed to popular agency – is perhaps the key point of purchase for anti-intellectualism. The position we have argued here is that popular needs, situated experiences, local rationalities and militant particularisms *cannot* be read off a potted history of past Left debates, today's media, online noise or the current fads in academia.

There is no Book which contains them, in advance, any more than there is a Book that tells us how we can successfully make a revolution against neoliberalism. All these books are written and rewritten inside people's heads and in their conversations as they struggle to make a better world; the attempt to short-circuit this process and leap in from outside armed with a particular form of cultural capital is readily recognisable as a variant of how commercial culture – or service-class managerialism – operates. It has nothing of Marxism but the name.

The essence of Marxist politics is *not* the proposition that participation in elections is a touchstone for orthodoxy, nor that the (revolutionary) state will set us free, nor that internal authoritarianism and enforced orthodoxy define revolutionary seriousness. It is the connected set of propositions that it is important to make links between the most advanced and most articulate *movements* of the day; that a new social order will also create its own institutions, grounded in popular self-organisation in struggle, and that the essence of 'revolution' – or social change – can be measured in the extent to which popular power as against elite power grows.

This commitment to the process of movement development is worth the candle – from the viewpoint of the local rationalities which it expresses – whether or not it arrives at such a moment, and whether or not such revolutionary moments are successful (if nothing else, the last century has taught us that even a 'successful' revolution is the start of a new round of conflicts rather than the end of history). The process of organising and articulating popular power in opposition to the interests, power and common sense expressed by the hegemonic order itself shifts the balance within the ruling order, and (as after 1848 or 1968) even a victorious reaction typically has to include the popular forces which it has just defeated, at least to some extent. Barring a counter-revolutionary 'white terror' aimed at eradicating popular power – whose feasibility is partly a function of how far a failed revolution was *isolated* – movement development is not time wasted. If the last hundred years contain any 'lessons' for movements, it should be that the strategy of canalising all popular energies into a demobilising, top-down (the two are synonymous) political monolith constitutes an immense hostage to fortune which has rarely been liberating, even after successful revolutions.

Comrades, What Should We Be Doing?

This book has, we hope, had a clear political as well as intellectual direction. Our position is, firstly, that the forms of opinion politics – in which issues and, sometimes, principles are discussed in isolation from serious reflection on social agency and interests – are deeply mystifying.

There is also a fundamental confusion in the sort of 'critical' analysis which simply dissects the existing structures of society in isolation from the agency which created and maintains them, and which divorces calls for change from any sense of conversation with popular agency. To argue about change in any honest way is to engage with *collective agency* – the more so for anyone who agrees that popular participation in shaping society is important in itself (a position which used to be called, simply, democratic).

Secondly, to take this 'this-worldly' position does *not* imply an uncritical celebration of everything movements do (or the kinds of movement activity which reflect one's own political preferences). It overestimates the power of traditional intellectuals within movements or as allies to imagine that such celebration, in itself, will make any practical difference (it may of course make a difference within particular intellectual fields). The *organic* intellectual activity of a movement is shaped differently – in propositions for action which gain more or less support, in the construction of alliances, in encouraging the articulation of other people's voices and so on: here 'this-worldliness' is another word for a critical sociology of how knowledge works within movements (Barker and Cox 2002).

The specific kind of strategy we have articulated here is a developmental one, which proposes that the most effective orientation is one which is both deeply rooted in the local rationalities of the subaltern and actively seeks to develop and extend those rationalities in the articulation of militant particularisms, alliances between those into campaigns, and the development of movement projects that make another world socially, not simply technically, possible. This means arguing *both* against quick-fix solutions which entail the capitulation of good sense before hegemonic common sense *and* against strategies which see development as inherently a bad thing. As noted, however, winning these arguments is a practical matter.

To support the articulation of good sense and subaltern rationalities is no linear matter:

> Working-class revolutions ... constantly criticise themselves, they continually interrupt their own course, return to what has apparently already been achieved to start it from scratch again. Cruelly and thoroughly they mock the shortcomings, weaknesses and pitiful nature of their first attempts; they seem to throw their opponent down, only

> for him to draw new strength from the earth and rise up once more against them, yet more gigantic than ever. They shrink back again and again in the face of the undetermined vastness of their own aims, until a situation has been created which makes any turning back impossible, and the conditions themselves cry out: 'Hic Rhodus, hic salta! Here is the rose, dance here!' (Marx 1984)

To shortcut the painful articulation of agency from below is almost inevitably to accept a definition of the terms of struggle by those who are already privileged; the shape of present-day social democratic parties – fundamentally captured by professionals oriented to centre votes and elite acceptability at the expense of popular needs and interests, let alone working-class power within their organisations – makes this point clear. There is no shortcut that leads around engagement with popular struggles.

Conversely, the argument in favour of movement development requires above all a practice which convinces other activists that the goal is not to elevate a new leadership above internal democracy. Again there is no quick fix: to commit to the practice of making links between movements, learning from each other's struggles and finding wider perspectives *while bringing other activists with us* is a perspective marked in years or decades, not in weeks or months. This rubs up against the urgency of the present crisis – a crisis which in this sense is always with us as an argument against taking the time needed to build solidarity and mutual trust and to come to see each other's perspectives and situations more fully.

Finally, to the extent that movements are successful in articulating radical needs and developing movement projects, they will challenge existing hegemonic coalitions and find themselves in a *hic rhodus, hic salta*. It is understandable – given the scale of past repressions and the memory of revolutions gone wrong – that many activists prefer to shy away from serious considerations of these situations and take refuge either in liberal fantasy or in radical nostalgia. The strategy that we are proposing here has no built-in guarantees of success either. However, to the extent that a grounding in good sense entails the kind of self-confidence that encourages self-organising, it also enables the construction of dual-power institutions. To the extent that a developmental movement politics entails the building of movement coalitions around a shared project and the disaggregation of existing hegemonic relations, it also enables effective political acting in a crisis.

... And Afterwards?

Confidence, and effective action, are often outcomes of seeing a larger picture, looking beyond the present so as not to be paralysed by its hopes and horrors, its threats and choices. In this context, it is helpful to ground movement organising and thinking in our own good sense, and to recognise that the point of politics is, often, to allow a reassertion of the best logics of an everyday life lived well – a terrain which goes deeper and with which we are more familiar.

The goal is, for example, to extend the everyday solidarity which we already practice to a greater or lesser degree with friends and family outwards, within our communities and globally. It is to take the skilled practice and respectful discussion with peers which we already practice in some areas of our life (perhaps in a small corner of our workplace, perhaps in our organising) as a wider principle for collective cooperation and how we make the world together. It is also to allow the humanity which we hope to embody in our encounters with suffering close to us – terminal sickness, ageing, loneliness, ordinary heartbreak, our hopes and fears for our children – to focus on this emotional reality rather than having to fight endless battles for service delivery or against professional power, around discrimination on grounds of ethnicity, sexuality, or disability, or against the stupidities of everyday ideology.

Activists do not, after all, seek conflict and its inevitable costs for its own sake – nor would we expect to find many allies if we did. But neither do we seek refuge in a rose-tinted cocoon which fails to acknowledge the reality of deeply entrenched economic, political, cultural, professional, religious and other interests and their reactions to threats. As adults, we expect conflict without seeking it out; we face it with the confidence that comes from movement practice and a practical orientation to winning for the sake of the needs which the struggle articulates.

Neoliberalism, like all other forms of capitalism before it, will come to an end; we are already living through its twilight. The question is rather what will come next: in particular, if our movements can contribute to broadening the conflict beyond neoliberalism to capitalism, patriarchy and the racialised global order altogether. These are big pictures, but not insuperable ones: class societies too come and go, as do forms of patriarchy and racism. On the widest, archaeological perspective, such societies are themselves a blip on the human timespan – at most 10,000 years in their oldest locations, a few hundred years in many places and in a few still in conflict with non-class societies.

Within the belly of the beast, social relations shaped around internationalism and the encounter between different ways of being are far from unusual, even while they struggle against racism and nationalist stupidity. So too are practices of childrearing, relationship and family which point far beyond patriarchy – and again find themselves in conflict with ethno-religious ideologies and broader social power structures. Social relationships that privilege solidarity, equality and self-determination are equally a constant gadfly within class society. The task of articulating a different world which takes these local rationalities seriously and names their opponents is painful, exhausting, mentally and emotionally challenging and riven with conflict. It need not be overwhelming – or doomed to failure. It is also, as humanist Marxism underlines, a process of experiencing ourselves as we can be, engaged to the fullest with the other people we share our world with, remaking ourselves and our world.

We make our own history: and movements from below have helped to create much of what makes our everyday lives worth living. Overcoming alienation is also this: recognising both the successes and the limitations of our movements' past efforts, and the ways in which we ourselves are formed by this history, able to draw on the 'good sense' of previous movements, including their fossilised academic expressions, to articulate today's needs and struggles against the hegemony of 'common sense' shaped from above. As we become political subjects on our own behalf, recognise ourselves in each other and see the connections between our different movements, we come closer to being able not only to articulate the hope of 'another world', but also to bring it about.

Notes

Preface

1. Marx normally writes *Mensch*, 'human being', although English translations usually render this as 'man'. We have checked and corrected translations throughout.

Chapter 1 'The This-Worldliness of their Thought': Social Movements and Theory

1. In Chapters 4 and 5, we develop an extended analysis of this crisis in terms of its internal problems and movement opponents.
2. By 'system', we are not offering an analysis of social relationships, but describing activists' experience of a reified power structure which is neither responsive to our 'communicative logics' (Habermas 1987), nor to its own stated forms and legitimating claims about democracy, human needs, and so on.
3. The first, and bloodier, war of that name took place between Iran and Iraq in the 1980s; the same western powers who later went to war on Iraq twice spent much of the first Gulf War funnelling weapons to Iraq.
4. Eschle et al. (2011) attempt a sketch of what this might look like in relation to feminism, women's movements and women in movement.
5. This understanding of theory as *consciously generated knowledge* is of course also the point of departure for much radical adult education (Mayo 1999), community development (Hope and Timmel 1984), humanist Marxism (Thompson 1997) and cultural studies (Williams 1965), all of which have reflected on how subaltern groups generate their own ways of understanding the world.
6. Gramsci tends to use *uomo*, 'man'. Latin *homo*, however, means 'human being' as opposed to *vir*, 'man'.
7. Not all autonomists within the tradition derived from Italian *operaismo* describe themselves as Marxists; there are also theorists of autonomous movements (that is, those on the non-institutional left) who are not *autonomists* in this sense (for example, Katsiaficas 2006). Lastly, there are great variations within the field of theoretical production: quite naturally, since it is also a field of cultural capital and 'small differences'.
8. Dinerstein (2014) is a welcome attempt to reverse this trend.

9. When we offered a paper on winning to an autonomist journal, we were informed that it was terribly Leninist to suggest that it might involve actually defeating a powerful opponent.

Chapter 2 'History Does Nothing': The Primacy of Praxis in Movement Theorising

1. See Baviskar 1995, Nilsen 2010 and Whitehead 2010 for in-depth analyses of the trajectory of the NBA.
2. Although these needs are a universal and constant aspect of human existence, they are 'always satisfied in socio-culturally specific ways' and subject to 'socio-cultural refinement or mediation' (Fracchia 2005: 50, 51). Our relationship to food is a good example. Moreover, our 'higher' needs are also shaped in corporeal ways – our need to learn or communicate, our appreciation of stories and music, or of smell and touch, are all rooted in our specific human embodiment and thus distinct from other species' relationship to each other and the natural world.
3. In German, *der Mensch* is linguistically masculine and so the relevant pronoun is *er*. English, however, forces a choice of pronoun between 'he' and 'she' (or perhaps 'it', 'they', 'hir', and so on). We use 'she' by way of reversing the unreflected usage in which Marx's *Mensch* has regularly been translated 'man'.
4. We focus here on changes in needs and capacities over time. However, the indeterminacy also applies to cultural diversity. With Fracchia (2005: 37) we can say that while 'human universals, such as biological needs, are malleable and socio-culturally mediated ... the particularity of their manifestations does not abrogate the universality of needs: if some people refuse to eat what others consider a delicacy, the fact is that both have a minimum caloric requirement.' In any given social and cultural context, such things are often anything but indeterminate – human beings are in principle flexible but their developing needs and capacities, the *different* ways in which these develop and the conflicts around how they are met combine to produce locally determinate needs and capacities.
5. We do not mean to suggest that consciousness is separate from needs and capacities as such. Consciousness is itself a capacity – the capacity for conscious reflection, itself embodied and tied to other determinate aspects of our species such as language or our particular capacities for memory. Furthermore, it is a capacity profoundly linked to the corporeal; it did not appear fully formed and ready to make sense of the world, but rather it emerged in tandem with the development of corporeal needs and capacities (see Heller 1976: 41–3, McNally 2001: 87–93).
6. This sentence paraphrases Ken Cole (1999: 161).

7. The disclaimer 'might' is important: the articulation of new needs and practices may well be stymied if they militate against the workings of extant social structures. We discuss this further below.
8. A brief footnote on what kind of understanding of culture this produces and its theoretical advantages: in his critique of Geertz' conception of 'culture as text', William Roseberry (1989: 25) argues that what is lacking in Geertz is 'a concept of culture as material social process'. He continues: 'Without a sense of culture as a material social process or creation … we once again have a conception of culture as product but not as production' (ibid.: 26). With an understanding of culture as a material social process that is simultaneously socially constituted and socially constituting, we can move beyond such a static conception of culture. Geertz, however, is not alone in proposing a static conception of culture; a similar idea can be found in the base–superstructure opposition in some Marxisms. Much as with the debates over forces and relations of production, their interrelationship, and their relationship to the mode of production, this approach revolves around the question of what exactly makes up the material base and the ideational superstructure, and how the relationship between the two should be conceived of. As Williams (1977: 75) notes, 'In the transition from Marx to Marxism … the proposition of the determining base and the determined superstructure has been commonly held to be the key to Marxist cultural analysis.' This proposition essentially views the relationship between base and superstructure as unidirectional. The material base constitutes the active and the real whereas the ideational superstructure is viewed as a passive epiphenomenon; thus when the base says 'jump' the superstructure says 'how high?' The result – an understanding of base and superstructure as either 'relatively enclosed categories' or 'relatively enclosed areas of activity' (ibid.: 78) – ironically led back to what Marx's *Aufhebung* of philosophy had sought to move away from: 'the *separation* of "areas" of thought and activity' and 'the related evacuation of specific content – real human activities – by the imposition of abstract categories' (ibid.). This dualism can be avoided by conceiving of culture as a material social process and, conversely, of material social processes as always already culturally mediated. The base–superstructure couplet is profoundly useless in this context, and we do not employ it.
9. The definite rejection of Althusser's claim is Geras, who writes: '… if the nature of man [*sic*] depends upon the ensemble of social relations, it does not depend wholly on them, it is conditioned but not determined by them, because they themselves depend on, that is, are partly explained by human nature, which is a component of the nature of man' (Geras 1983: 68).
10. These relations take on an exploitative character with the development of a capacity to regularly produce a surplus and where 'one part of society ceases to perform productive labour, in part or in whole, and obtains leisure at the

expense of the remaining working population' (Smith 1990: 39), as with class societies, patriarchy and racialised divisions of labour such as slavery.

11. Once dominant arrangements have been replaced by an emergent formation, they may persist in residual forms.
12. Capitalism – and modernity in general – exhibits an extraordinary dynamism in terms of the development of needs and capacities (see Berman 1982). However, we need to recognise the internal dynamism of non-modern social formations, rather than seeing them as essentially static entities that required some kind of external impulse in order to change, and to consider them on a comparable ontological basis. This is implicit in Marx's understanding of the change from feudalism to capitalism.

    Opting for a generic conception of radical needs also entails that the radicalism of needs is context-dependent and historical. For instance, a demand for citizenship and liberal democratic rights in general as an expression for the need for 'voice', recognition and representation in processes of authoritative decision making will be radical in a totalitarian context as the satisfaction of this need entails structural change. In a liberal democratic context, however, such demands from minority groups can be accommodated within the extant system without a fundamental change in the basic structural workings of that system; in such a case, we see the modification of a dominant structure of entrenched needs and capacities.

    Heller (1976: 93) indicates this when she writes that 'It would be a mistake … to think that the mature Marx relates the structure of radical needs exclusively to modern industrial production' and points to the *Grundrisse* where 'the idea of radical needs has a more universal character than in any of the earlier works'. However, she does not elaborate on this assertion in *The Theory of Need in Marx* (see Grumley 1999 for a discussion of the career of the concept after Heller's turn to 'reflexive postmodernism').
13. See, for example, Lysgaard's (1985) study of 'the worker's collective', Melucci (1989) on submerged networks in Italy in the 1980s, Genovese (1976) on 'the world the slaves made' and Scott (1985, 1990) on everyday resistance for examples of the carving-out of spaces where emergent needs may be satisfied.
14. Calhoun makes the following important qualification: '… their orientation was not simply conservative, or even restorationist, but was aimed at the creation of a radically different social order from that in which they lived, one in which traditional values would better be realized' (1982: 8). We should also note that the communities in question were not timeless, but were themselves ongoing achievements of, for example, weavers structured around putting-out systems.
15. This is, incidentally, one of the practical purposes of class analysis.
16. Drawing on Cole (1999: 66) and Callinicos (1988: 52), forces of production can be defined generally as 'the productive capacity [of human beings] to transform the natural environment into use values' and as consisting of 'the

labour process, the particular technical combination of labour-power and means of production employed in order to transform nature and to produce use-values, thereby determining a particular level of productivity'. Relations of production are 'the social relations through which people interact to be able to produce' and consist of 'the relationship of the direct producers to the means of production and their labour-power, the nature of any non-producing owners and the mode of appropriation of surplus-labour from the direct producers by any such owners'. The mode of production, finally, is made up of '[t]he dialectical unity of the forces and relations of production' (Cole 1999: 67).

17. Geras (1983: 67) formulates a similar argument: '... if diversity in the character of human beings is in large measure set down by Marx to historical variation in their social relations of production, the very fact that they entertain this sort of relations, the fact that they produce and that they have a history, he explains in turn by some of their general and constant, intrinsic, constitutional characteristics; in short by their human nature.' Much ink has been spilt among and between Marxists over these concepts. Here we will simply point to Sayer's argument that material objects and social relations cannot be thought of as universally and inherently existing as productive forces and relations: 'they become so only by dint of the relations ... in which they stand' (1987: 26–7). They are thus 'an attribute of human beings in association, their collective capacities, not a set of things as such at all' (ibid: 27). Similarly, the debate over whether forces or relations of production are the driving force in history (see Wood 2002 and Harman 1998a for overviews) leapfrogs over Larrain's fundamental point that 'both productive forces and relations of production are social results produced by human practice; they are crystallizations of the process whereby human beings produce their material existence' (1986: 115).

Chapter 3 'The Authors and the Actors of their Own Drama': A Marxist Theory of Social Movements

1. Touraine, 1981: 1.
2. Gillan (2010) makes a similar argument in relation to working-class community media as in the first instance expressions of *class* rather than forms of *media*.
3. This, incidentally, is why different societies have characteristically different 'social movement landscapes' (Cox 2011b). If the circumstances under which we make our own history are not of our own choosing, neither are they external to human agency; rather, they are its reified and naturalised products. This naturalisation is, of course, reproduced by critics such as Andreas Bieler who misunderstand our position as voluntarist.
4. See Ste. Croix (1981: 44, 57–66) on the ubiquity of resistance to exploitation.

5. See our discussion of primitive accumulation in Chapter 4 for an example of this.
6. See Chapter 4 for an extended discussion of accumulation strategies in historical capitalism.
7. Thanks are due to Ariel Salleh for debate and discussion around this point.
8. To anticipate the second half of this chapter, our attempted reclaiming and reconstruction of the activist reflection on movements from below contained within the Marxist tradition is not intended to deny the value of performing a similar operation on other traditions (see, for example, Eschle et al. 2011 in relation to feminism); it is, however, to recognise that this reclaiming and reconstruction is a huge task even for one movement, and deserves a similar degree of attention for others, before any kind of overarching synthesis can be achieved. It cannot simply be a matter of 'agentifying' existing structuralist syntheses: because human agency is complex, developmental and often ambiguous in its outcomes, each movement tradition is likely to preserve specific learning points as particularly salient, which cannot simply be 'read off' from structure in an academic mode. Of course, as movements develop their alliances with each other there is a slow process of communication between different 'ecologies of knowledge', or of developing a shared activist 'good sense' rooted in multiple movement knowledges. This book is intended as a contribution to this conversation.
9. We are focusing in particular on how this privileged access is structured in modern, capitalist societies.
10. It also justifies the kind of strategy we are advocating here against those who accuse it of being arbitrary, or of seeking to fit movements into pre-established agendas. The point of acting so as to enable movements' greater development is precisely to make good sense 'more unitary and coherent' – and to give it greater impact on reality as against hegemonic common sense. This is also, of course, what motivates other movement participants *not* to take the path of least resistance (fitting movements into existing structures) but rather to support strategies that go in this direction, despite the huge forces arrayed against these strategies.
11. See, for example, the critiques of 'resistance studies' by Abu-Lughod (1990) and Ortner (1995). See also the critiques of the Subaltern Studies project by Sarkar (1997), Moore (1998, 2000), and Nilsen (2009b). Similarly, see Harvey's (2006: 81–2) critique of Habermas's Manichean conception of 'system' and 'lifeworld'.
12. This, incidentally, is why 'just as [the living] seem to be occupied with revolutionizing themselves and things, creating something that did not exist before, precisely in such epochs of revolutionary crisis they anxiously conjure up the spirits of the past to their service, borrowing from them names, battle slogans, and costumes in order to present this new scene of world history in time-honored disguise and borrowed language' (Marx 1984: 10).

13. Here and elsewhere, we use the phrases 'middle class' and 'middle classes' to represent recognisable political-cultural formations, not to define an economic position, which of course varies greatly among those self-identifying in this way.
14. We are not here proposing a missionary role for 'educated outsiders' as agents of salvation; these activists could act as catalysts because they drew in different ways on the theoretical knowledge generated by other movements, in the past or elsewhere – whether this knowledge was drawn directly from such movements or (for example) from the accounts sedimented in the official histories of the Indian independence movement and paid lip service to by the state which draws its legitimacy from that movement.
15. A point often forgotten by 'post-Marxists' who talk about the diversity of contemporary political subjects as if this was something new is that the relatively homogenous working class of the Fordist period was itself the product of a long process of organisation from below (Thompson 1966) and from above (Lash and Urry 1987). Political subjects make themselves; they do not start out ready-made.
16. In the NBA's repertoire of contention, the term *satyagraha* is associated with the annual protest events that took place during the monsoon months (June, July, August, September) every year from 1991 onwards until 2002. Basically, what the *satyagraha* revolved around was a braving of the rising of the waters of the Narmada which set in with the monsoon rains and the closing of the floodgates of the SSP. The *satyagrahas* are centred on one or two villages in the tribal areas of Maharashtra and Madhya Pradesh, where the resident families, Andolan activists, and domestic and international supporters of the movement stand their ground as the waters rise. The braving of the waters thus signals a defiance of the displacement wrought by the project and constitutes an emotive image of the opposition to dam building on the Narmada.
17. As noted earlier, where mobilisation is not taking place on a 'blank canvas' in terms of the availability of previous movement learning processes, people do not necessarily have to go through this experience directly (or again).
18. See also Steinberg's (1999) analysis of how nineteenth-century English cotton-spinners developed a discursive repertoire based on an appropriation of the mill-owners' ideology of dominance, and Lee's (2007) analysis of how Chinese factory workers fuse Communist ideology with discourses of law to contest dispossession and unemployment in China's rustbelt.
19. See in this connection also Gilroy's discussion of 'the black Atlantic', which he posits as a 'modern political and cultural formation' characterized by 'the desire to transcend both the structures of the nation state and the constraints of ethnicity and national particularity' (1993: 19).
20. See Macintyre (1987) for a fascinating contrast between how self-taught working-class activists used Marx on the British left and the ways in which

this was displaced in the 1920s and 1930s by a new Moscow-trained, often university-educated leadership.

21. We might add the early nineteenth-century Latin American wars of independence, the period of anti-fascist resistance in Europe and the anti-colonial struggles of the post-Second World War period in Asia and Africa.

Chapter 4 'The Bourgeoisie, Historically, Has Played a Most Revolutionary Part': Social Movements from Above and Below in Historical Capitalism

1. Marx (1990: 874) conceptualized the freedom of the worker under capitalism in a double sense: 'Free labourers, in the double sense that neither they themselves form part and parcel of the means of production, as in the case of slaves, bondsmen, etc., nor do the means of production belong to them, as in the case of peasant-proprietors; they are, therefore, free from, unencumbered by, any means of production of their own.'
2. This view of capitalist development entails a critique of those historical analyses that see capitalism as first developing within Europe, on the basis of processes of economic change internal to the European region, and then extending its reach to cover the rest of the world (see, for example, Brenner 1976, 1977). Drawing on authors like Blaut (1993), Heller (2010), Bhambra (2011) and Pradella (2013), we see the genesis of capitalist development as a thoroughly global process.
3. In this section, we draw on some of the classic accounts of early modern English social history, a discipline in large part defined by Marxists. This account was and remains highly significant politically, not only in this specific historiographical context but because of the role of the Hanoverian 'Glorious Revolution' in grounding the legitimacy of the contemporary British state – and the enthusiastic reference to regicide, religious radicalism, popular democracy, the Levellers and the Diggers by subsequent generations of English radicals (for one example, Leon Rosselson's 1972 song 'The World Turned Upside Down', inspired by Hill's book, is still widely heard in British protests and occupations).

   Because of this significance, a major assault was mounted on this 'Marxist orthodoxy' in the 1980s and early 1990s. Other than a generalised critique of Marxism, this included a Namierist emphasis on written sources and a postmodern 'linguistic turn', both prioritising the voices of those who controlled the intellectual means of production and whose records have been best preserved, as against the painstaking work of reconstructing the often fragmentary record of *popular* experience and resistance. Wood (1991) has mounted a substantial defence of the Marxist account of early modern England, while Holstun (2000) has shown that a textual analysis of *radical* texts also supports this account. The resurgence of Marxist scholarship on the English Revolution also encompasses the work of researchers such as Wood (2001, 2007), Heller (2010), Kennedy (2008), Gurney (2012) and Davidson (2012).

4. In this period, church attendance – the central form of collective assembly – was obligatory and church courts had significant powers over day-to-day matters of 'morals'. Anglicans, Presbyterians and Catholics held different views over how this coercive power should be structured, while 'sectarians' were such because they stood for the independent self-organisation of those adopting a particular perspective, with no claim to impose that on others.
5. This definition draws on Callinicos (1988); Fine and Saad-Filho (2004); Lebowitz (2003); Wolf (1982); and Harvey (1999). In defining capitalism this way, we are not suggesting that actual capitalist development entails the simple universalisation of this essence. The actual historical development of capitalism is fundamentally uneven process in various ways – how capitalist and non-capitalist modes of production articulate (see, for example, Banaji 2010b); how capitalist dynamics related to non-commodified spheres of societies and lifeworlds (Habermas 1987, Offe 1984, Gibson-Graham 2006); and in terms of its spatial dynamics (Harvey 1999, Smith 1990). These relations and dynamics have to be conceptualised in relation to specific phases and regions of capitalist development. As we noted in Chapter 2, a full account of this process would also include discussion of the development of particular forms of patriarchy and racialised divisions of labour.
6. Marx discusses the circuit of capital under the rubric of 'the general formula for capital' in Chapter 4 of *Capital*. This outline also draws on Fine and Saad-Filho (2004: 31–6) and Harvey (2010: 87–92).
7. This is in contrast to the extraction of surplus under feudalism, which was based on 'politico-legal relations of compulsion' that enabled feudal lords to extract surplus from the peasantry through 'labour services, rents in kind, or customary dues owed to the individual lord by the peasant' (Morton 2005: 498).
8. For this analysis, we focus on *capitalist* social formations and the struggles that shape them, without wishing to deny their interdependence with *patriarchal* and *racialised* formations and their struggles. As we have argued elsewhere (Barker et al. 2013, Eschle et al. 2011), fuller theorisations both of movements around race and ethnicity and of women's movements and GLTBQ movements, offering a conceptualisation of collective agency grounded in those movements' own theorising, are badly needed, not least as counterpositions to purely structural analyses of patriarchy and race.

   While considerable work has been done, in particular from socialist and Marxist feminist positions and from anti-racist and anti-imperial positions, in working towards an integrated analysis of how racial, patriarchal and capitalist structures co-constitute one another and mark particular periods, this has not yet been matched by equivalent attention to the other side of the coin. To start from activist knowledge in order to develop a classed account of collective agency from above and below, and of the consequent structuring and restructuring of historical periods from the point of view of capitalist relationships, is not to deny that the same needs to be done in relation to gender and race, or that these three dimensions then need to be brought into a single frame of reference; it is to make a first step along this road, which we hope others will follow in a task which is surely beyond the capacities of any one individual. None the less, we hope that the *shape* of the approach developed here may be useful for activists and theorists trying to explore these other dimensions with a view to bringing about a different kind of society.

9. In economic terms, the 1857 depression amounted to little more than 'an interruption of the golden era of capitalist growth which resumed on an even larger scale in the 1860s and reached its peak in the boom of 1871–3' (Hobsbawm 2004: 46).
10. See Halperin (2004: 95–9) for a detailed discussion of wages, productivity and consumption in nineteenth-century Europe.
11. See Morton (2007) for an insightful and instructive analysis of Gramsci's concept of passive revolution.
12. However, as Halperin (2004: 159–60) notes, democratisation remained partial throughout much of Europe until after 1945, both in terms of the extension of universal suffrage and in terms of the full recognition of political parties representing the working class.
13. Space does not permit an adequate examination of the Russian Revolution and the post-war Soviet bloc comparable to what we offer here for the one-time First and Third Worlds. An adequate analysis would trace a similar arc of movements from below arising out of the revolutionary wave of 1916–23, and in parts of eastern Europe and East and South-East Asia, resistance to imperialism and fascism. In some cases (Russia, China), this generated movement-become-state, massively powerful forms of movement from above (whether endogenous or imposed) comparable to our discussion below of national-developmentalist regimes, followed by a second round of crises in eastern Europe in particular from 1968 to 1989 and (again for eastern Europe in particular) a particularly aggressive form of neoliberalism introduced after the collapse of the old regimes.
14. This does not mean that international trade was insignificant under organised capitalism. As Glyn et al. (1991: 50–51) point out, world trade grew strongly after the Second World War. However, it was only towards the end of the 1960s that an increasing proportion of labour in the global North came to be involved in production for international commodity markets. It is in this sense that economic growth during the golden age years can 'be regarded as primarily domestically based' (ibid.: 51).

15. Food imports were organised through what Friedmann (1982) has called 'the food-aid complex'. Within this framework, the US government would buy surplus grain from private grain companies and sell these surpluses on to countries in the global South in return for foreign currencies that were mostly inconvertible. These payments were then held in bank accounts in the recipient countries, and were spent as loans to recipient countries, which would in turn use these funds to finance development projects, to pay for US obligations, and to procure military equipment. The food-aid complex played a central role in American strategy towards the Third World during the Cold War, and simultaneously allowed the US government to solve the problem of overproduction in domestic agriculture.
16. See Harvey (1990: 135–6) on variations in the form of state interventionism.
17. Of course, the actual organisation of welfare state regimes was highly differentiated from region to region in the global North (see Esping-Andersen 1990). See Mann (2012: Chapter 9) for a history of the development of the welfare state, and Halperin (2004: 245–6) for perceptive comments on the development of welfare regimes in Europe.
18. One thing which neoliberalism happily takes from its Fordist predecessor is the relative power of highly organised, top-down structures in the state and economy, and the 'gains' of popular demobilisation. Indeed, it is plausible that neoliberalism's success *could not have happened* had power not already been so centralised within the international financial order, corporations, nation states, political parties, trade unions, and so on. In some ways, the neoliberal takeover previously described depends on being able to win within these organisations and to use their relative legitimacy as well as their power to defeat popular challenges. Actual popular majorities for neoliberalism per se have been hard if not impossible to achieve (throughout the Thatcher years, the British NHS remained massively popular, for example) and of course neoliberalism itself seeks a definition of legitimacy external to any popular vote.
19. The relocation of industrial manufacturing to the global South has not resulted in anything like developmental convergence in the world economy. As Kiely (2007: 147–57) has shown in great detail, high value-added production is still concentrated in the Northern core of the world economy, and to the extent that an increasing share of investment, trade and financial flows accrues to the South, this is concentrated to a limited range of emerging economies, particularly in the Asian region. The capitalist world-system, therefore, is still dominated by an entrenched 'Northern-dominated hierarchy of wealth' (Arrighi, Silver and Brewer 2003: 3).
20. The issue of profit rates under neoliberalism has generated some controversy among Marxists. Brenner (2006) is among those who have argued most forcefully that neoliberalism has failed to revive profit rates to the levels witnessed during the golden age of capitalism, and his assertions have

recently been backed by Callinicos (2010). Conversely, Duménil and Levy (2004, 2011) and McNally (2011) – the primary sources for our argument in this section – maintain that neoliberalism has in fact boosted profit rates, albeit not to the levels witnessed in the post-war era of expansion. The argument of the failure to bring profit rates back up to the level of the golden age seems to us to be flawed, as it tends to disregard the unusual circumstances of the post-war boom – for example, the impacts of post-war reconstruction and the significance of the permanent arms economy in driving economic growth. Moreover, as Davidson has put it, the tendency to use the boom years of organised capitalism as a yardstick when making these assessments is problematic because it fails to recognise how the recovery of profits under neoliberalism – despite its shortfall compared to the 1950s and 1960s – has been structured in such a way as to benefit 'individual members of the capitalist class by increasing their personal wealth, at the expense of the poor and the working class' (Davidson 2010: 63).

21. The following account draws on Gowan (2009), Blackburn (2008, 2011), Foster and Magdoff (2009), Callinicos (2010), Dumenil and Levy (2011), McNally (2011); Mahmud (2012) and Heintz and Balakrishnan (2012).
22. Heintz and Balakrishnan (2012: 396) notes that 'approximately one-quarter of African American and Latino borrowers who took out loans from 2004 to 2008 lost their homes to foreclosure or were seriously delinquent by February 2011, compared with just under 12 percent of white borrowers.'

Chapter 5 'The Point is to Change It': Movements From Below Against Neoliberalism

1. Mass radical left parties had always grappled, more or less well, with issues of gender, race, colonialism, war and culture; it reflects the one-dimensionality, and university bases, of their post-1968 imitations when they treat these as identitarian diversions rather than a normal response to the complexity of actual working classes.
2. The rise in labour struggles in China has been paralleled by a steep increase in rural protest, often targeting illegal and forced land acquisitions by nexuses of officials and investors for 'development zones' (see Walker 2006, 2008, Li and O'Brien 1996, Guo 2001).
3. The Maoist movement is intensely debated on the Indian left, between those who see the Maoists as representing an authentic expression of Adivasi political agency (see Giri 2009, D'Souza 2009, Roy 2010) and those who see the Adivasis as caught in a bind between state violence and the violence of the Maoist guerillas (Banaji 2010a, Nigam 2010).
4. By way of illustration, Barker (1996b: 19) quotes figures of 2.2 per cent and 1.8 per cent of the population involved in early 1980s movements in West Germany and the Netherlands respectively. These were – by German

and Dutch standards and by comparison with, say, France (0.2 per cent) – relatively high levels of movement mobilisation; by contrast, individual revolutionary organisations such as Solidarity in Poland had perhaps 10 million members in 1981 out of a population of c. 36 million – around a 27 per cent level of participation. The French general strike of 1968 also involved perhaps 10 million workers, in this case out of a population of c. 50 million – around a 20 per cent level of participation in the strike alone. These are differences of orders of magnitude.

5. Barker (1996b) critiques this.
6. This is the basic position of the journal *Interface*, founded by activists and scholars involved in contemporary movements.
7. <http://news.bbc.co.uk/1/hi/programmes/from_our_own_correspondent/4268064.stm>
8. One partial exception is conspiratorial, 'substitutionist' groups. Some historical examples include the Blanquist tradition in France, the 1916 Rising in Ireland and the Red Army Faction in Germany; even in these cases, the scale of violence which they were capable of organising was small by comparison with that of the states they confronted. Compare, most dramatically, the 1916 Rising with the almost-contemporary Battle of the Somme.
9. Conversely, of course, movements which have successfully become states with their own armies are fully capable of unleashing state-scale violence, internally or externally.
10. Obviously there are other, and more useful, meanings of 'civil society', starting with that used by Gramsci.
11. In another historical period, the phrase 'dictatorship of the proletariat' was used to define this – in ancient Rome (and before Mussolini), a 'dictator' was someone to whom power was given for a limited period of time to act outside constitutional limits. In other words, the 'dictatorship of the proletariat' consisted, in cases such as the Paris Commune, of ordinary people directly taking power, outside the legal bounds set by a collapsed regime, while they put a new kind of social order in place. In this sense, *any* change of regime is dictatorial in that it is a temporary period of non-constitutional rule. Obviously, in the twentieth century, the phrase has come to have very different connotations, and we are not suggesting reviving it.
12. See, for example, Polet and CETRI (2003).
13. Ms Halappavanar entered a Galway hospital suffering from a miscarriage. She was refused an abortion, apparently on the grounds that 'This is a Catholic country' and died of septicemia as a result. Massive protests forced the state to finally legislate (inadequately) on abortion, twenty years after a court case and referenda had established constitutional rights in this respect.
14. See <http://anarchism.pageabode.com/andrewnflood/solidarity-engagement-revolutionary-organisation> for a very reflective analysis of internal data on libertarian organising in Ireland.

15. 'On the Southern Question' (1978) highlights Gramsci's commitment to supporting the development of *independent* peasant organising in the South: the Turin communists were prepared to support even anti-communist candidates who represented a break with the hegemonic power relations of rural Italy.
16. See Prichard et al. (2012) for a useful rethinking of the relationship between the two traditions.

Bibliography

Abu-Lughod, L. (1990): 'The Romance of Resistance', pp. 41–55 in *American Ethnologist*, Vol. 17 no. 1.

Alexander, M. (2011): *The New Jim Crow*, New York: New Press.

Alinsky, S. (1971): *Rules for Radicals*, New York: Random.

Allen, K. (1997): *Fianna Fáil and Irish Labour*, London: Pluto.

Allen, R. (2004): *No Global*, London: Pluto.

—— and Jones, T. (1990): *Guests of the Nation*, London: Earthscan.

Althusser, L. (1969): *For Marx*, London: Allen Lane.

Araghi, F.A. (1995): 'Global Depeasantization, 1945–1990', pp. 337–68 in *Sociological Quarterly*, Vol. 36 no. 2.

—— (2009): 'Accumulation by Displacement: Global Enclosures, Food Crisis, and the Ecological Contradictions of Capitalism', pp. 113–46 in *Review*, Vol. 32 no. 1.

Armstrong, P., Glyn, A. and Harrison, J. (1991): *Capitalism since 1945*, Oxford: Basil Blackwell.

Aronowitz, S. (1983): *Crisis in Historical Materialism*, Minneapolis: University of Minnesota Press.

Arrighi, G. (1994): *The Long Twentieth Century*, London: Verso.

—— (2005a): 'Hegemony Unravelling – 1', pp. 23–80 in *New Left Review*, Vol. 32.

—— (2005b): 'Hegemony Unravelling – 2', pp. 83–116 in *New Left Review*, Vol. 33.

—— (2007): *Adam Smith in Beijing*, London: Verso.

—— and Silver, B. (1999): 'Introduction', pp. 1–36 in Arrighi, G. and Silver, B. (eds): *Chaos and Governance in the Modern World System*, Minneapolis: University of Minnesota Press.

—— and Silver, B. (2003): 'Polanyi's "Double Movement"', pp. 325–55 in *Politics and Society*, Vol. 31 no. 2.

——, Hopkins, T. and Wallerstein, I. (1989): *Anti-Systemic Movements*, London: Verso.

——, Silver, B. and Brewer, B.D. (2003): 'Industrial convergence, globalization, and the persistence of the North–South divide', pp. 3–31 in *Studies in Comparative International Development*, Vol. 38 no. 1.

Arsel, M. (2012): 'Between "Marx and Markets"?', pp. 150–63 in *Tidsschrift for Economische en Sociale Geografie*, Vol. 103 no. 2.

Bakhurst, D. (1990): 'Social Memory in Soviet Thought', pp. 202–226 in Middleton, D. and Edwards, D. (eds): *Collective Remembering*, London: Sage.

Ban, C. (2013): 'Brazil's liberal neo-developmentalism', pp. 298–331 in *Review of International Political Economy*, Vol. 20 no. 2.

Banaji, J. (2010a): *The Ironies of Indian Maoism* <http://www.isj.org.uk/?id=684>.

—— (2010b): *Theory as History*, Leiden: Brill.

Barboza, D. and Tabuchi, H. (2010): 'Power Grows for Striking Chinese Workers' <http://www.nytimes.com/2010/06/09/business/global/09labor.html?pagewanted=all&_r=0>.

Barker, C. (1996a): '"What Is To Be Done?"', pp. 25–44 in Barker, C. and Kennedy, P. (eds): *To Make Another World*, Aldershot: Avebury.

—— (1996b): '"The Mass Strike" and "The Cycle of Protest"', paper to Alternative Futures and Popular Protest conference, available at <https://sites.google.com/site/colinbarkersite/>.

—— (2002): '"A Modern Moral Economy?"', paper to Making Social Movements conference, available at <https://sites.google.com/site/colinbarkersite/>.

—— (2013a): 'Class Struggle and Social Movements', in Barker, C., Cox, L., Krinsky, J. and Nilsen, A.G. (eds): *Marxism and Social Movements*, Leiden: Brill.

—— (2013b): 'Marxism and Social Movements', in Snow, D. et al. (eds), *The Wiley-Blackwell Encyclopedia of Social Movements*, Chichester: Wiley-Blackwell.

—— and Cox, L. (2002): '"What Have the Romans Ever Done for Us?"', available at <http://eprints.nuim.ie>.

——, Cox, L., Krinsky, J. and Nilsen, A.G. (2013): 'Marxism and Social Movements', in Barker, C., Cox, L., Krinsky, J. and Nilsen, A.G. (eds): *Marxism and Social Movements*, Leiden: Brill.

Bateman, M. (2010): *Why Doesn't Microfinance Work?*, London: Zed.

Baviskar, A. (1995): *In the Belly of the River*, Delhi: Oxford University Press.

Bebbington, A. and Bebbington, D.H. (2012): 'An Andean Avatar', pp. 131–45 in *New Political Economy*, Vol. 16 no. 1.

Becker, M. (2010): 'Correa, Indigenous Movements, and the Writing of a New Constitution in Ecuador', pp. 47–62 in *Latin American Perspectives*, Vol. 38 no. 1.

—— (2012): *Pachakutik*, Lanham, MD: Rowman & Littlefield.

Bensaïd, D. (2002): *Marx for our Times*, London: Verso.

Berger, M.T. (2004): 'After the Third World', pp. 9–39 in *Third World Quarterly*, Vol. 25 no. 1.

Berman, M. (1982): *All That Is Solid Melts Into Air*, New York: Simon and Schuster.

Bevington, D. and Dixon, C. (2005): 'Movement-Relevant Theory', pp. 185–208 in *Social Movement Studies*, Vol. 4 no. 3.

Bey, H. (1991): *TAZ*, New York: Autonomedia.

Bhambra, G. (2011): *Rethinking Modernity*, Basingstoke: Palgrave.

Bieler, A. and Morton, A.D. (2004): 'A Critical Theory Route to Hegemony, World Order and Historical Change', pp. 85–113 in *Capital and Class*, Vol. 28 no. 1.

—— (2014): '"The Will-O-The-Wisp of the Transnational State"', pp. 23–51 in *Journal of Australian Political Economy*, vol. 72.

Bilgin, P. and Morton, A.D. (2002): 'Historicising Representations of "Failed States"', pp. 55–80 in *Third World Quarterly*, Vol. 23 no. 1.

Blackburn, R. (1988): *The Overthrow of Colonial Slavery*, London: Verso.

—— (2008): 'The Subprime Crisis', pp. 63–106 in *New Left Review*, Vol. 50.

—— (2011): 'Crisis 2.0', pp. 33–62 in *New Left Review*, Vol. 72.

Blaut, J.M. (1993): *The Colonizer's Model of the World*, London: Guildford Press.

Blomley, N. (2007): 'Making Private Property', pp. 1–21 in *Rural History*, Vol. 18 no. 1.

Bond, P., Desai, A. and Ngwane, T. (2013): 'Uneven and Combined Marxism within South Africa's Urban Social Movements', in Barker, C. et al. (eds), *Marxism and Social Movements*, Leiden: Brill.

Boyle, M. (2005): 'Sartre's Circular Dialectic and the Empires of Abstract Space', Dublin, pp. 181–201 in *Annals of the Association of American Geographers*, Vol. 95 no. 1.

Branford, S. and Rocha, J. (2002): *Cutting the Wire*, London: Latin America Bureau.

Brenner, R. (1976): 'Agrarian Class Structure and Economic Development in Pre-Industrial Europe', pp. 30–75 in *Past and Present*, Vol. 70.

——(1977): 'The Origins of Capitalist Development', pp. 25–92 in *New Left Review*, Vol. 104.

——(2006): *The Economics of Global Turbulence*, London: Verso.

Brewer, J. (1989): *The Sinews of Power*, Boston, MA: Harvard University Press.

Broad, R. and Heckscher, Z. (2003): 'Before Seattle', pp. 713–728 in *Third World Quarterly*, Vol. 24 no. 4.

Bumpus, A.G. and Liverman, D.M. (2009): 'Accumulation by Decarbonization and the Governance of Carbon Offsets', pp. 127–55 in *Economic Geography*, Vol. 84 no. 2.

Burbach, R., Wilpert, G. and Fox, M. (2013): *Latin America's Turbulent Transitions*, London: Zed.

Calhoun, C. (1982): *The Question of Class Struggle*, Chicago, IL: University of Chicago Press.

Callinicos, A. (1988): *Making History*, Cambridge, Polity.

——(2008): *Imperialism and Global Political Economy*, Cambridge: Polity.

——(2010): *The Bonfire of Illusions*, Cambridge: Polity.

Cammack, P. (2004): 'What the World Bank Means by Poverty Reduction, and Why it Matters', pp. 189–211 in *New Political Economy*, Vol. 9 no. 2.

——(2009): 'Making Poverty Work', pp. 193–210 in *Socialist Register*, 2009.

Campesi, G. (2010): 'Policing, urban poverty and insecurity in Latin America', pp. 447–71 in *Theoretical Criminology*, Vol. 14 no. 4.

Cannon, B. and Kirby, P. (eds) (2012): *Civil Society and the State in Left-led Latin America*, London: Zed.

Cardoso, F.H. and Faletto, E. (1979): *Dependency and Development in Latin America*, Berkeley: University of California Press.

Chan, C.K. (2012): *The Challenge of Labour in China*, London: Routledge.

Chang, H.-J. (2014): 'This is no recovery, this is a bubble – and it will burst', <http://www.theguardian.com/commentisfree/2014/feb/24/recovery–bubble–crash–uk–us–investors>.

Chatterjee, P. (1993): *The Nation and its Fragments*, Princeton, NJ: Princeton University Press.

Chibber, V. (2003): *Locked in Place*, Princeton, NJ: Princeton University Press.

—— (2004): *Reviving the Developmental State*, pp. 226–246 in *Socialist Register*, 2004.

Chomsky, N. (2007): *Failed States*, London: Penguin.

Choudry, A. and Kapoor, D. (2010): *Learning from the Ground Up*, London: Palgrave.

Ciccarello-Maher, G. (2013): *We Created Chávez: A People's History of the Venezuelan Revolution*, Durham, NC: Duke University Press.

Cleaver, H. (2000): *Reading Capital Politically*, Leeds: Anti/Theses.

Cohen, G.A. (1978): *Karl Marx's Theory of History*, Princeton, NJ: Princeton University Press.

Cole. K. (1999): *Economy – Environment – Development – Knowledge*, London: Routledge.

Collins, C. (2013): 'Language, Marxism and the Grasping of Policy-Agendas', in Barker, C., Cox, L., Krinsky, J. and Nilsen, A.G. (eds): *Marxism and Social Movements*, Leiden: Brill.

Consorzio Aaster, CSOA Cox 18, CSOA Leoncavallo, Moroni, P. (1996): *Centri Sociali*, Milano: ShaKe.

Conway, J. (2005): *Praxis and Politics*, New York: Routledge.

Cooper, F. (2000): 'Back to Work', pp. 213–35 in Alexander, P. and Halpern, R. (eds): *Racializing Class, Classifying Race*, Basingstoke: Macmillan.

Coulter, C. (1993): *The Hidden Tradition*, Cork: Cork University Press.

Cox, L. (1998): 'Gramsci, Movements and Method', presented to the Alternative Futures and Popular Protest conference, available at <http://eprints.nuim.ie>.

—— (1999a): 'Building Counter Culture', unpublished PhD dissertation, Trinity College, Dublin.

—— (1999b): 'Power, Politics and Everyday Life', pp. 46–66 in Bagguley, P. and Hearn, J. (eds): *Transforming Politics: Power and Resistance*, Basingstoke: Macmillan.

—— (2001a): 'Globalisation from Below?', paper to William Thompson Weekend School, available at <http://eprints.nuim.ie>.

—— (2001b): 'Barbarian resistance and rebel alliances', pp. 155–67 in Rethinking Marxism, Vol. 13 nos 3/4.

—— (2006): 'News from Nowhere', in Hourigan, N. and Connolly, L. (eds), *Social Movements and Ireland*, Manchester: Manchester University Press.

—— (2009): 'Hearts with one Purpose Alone?', pp. 52–61 in *Emotion, Space and Society*, Vol. 2.

—— (2010a): 'The Interests of the Movement as a Whole', pp. 298–308 in *Interface*, Vol. 2 no. 1.

—— (2010b): 'The Politics of Buddhist Revival', pp. 173–227 in *Contemporary Buddhism*, Vol. 11 no. 2.

—— (2010c): 'Another World is Under Construction?', *Irish Left Review*, available at <http://www.irishleftreview.org/2010/05/17/world-construction-social-movement-responses-inequality-crisis/>.

—— (2011a): 'There Must be Some Kind of Way out of Here', pp. 23–5 in CrisisJam, Greek Left Review, New Left Project and ZNet (eds), May Day International ebook, available at <http://www.newleftproject.org/index.php/mayday/article/there_must_be_some_kind_of_way_out_of_here_social_movements_and_the_crisis>.

—— (2011b): 'Gramsci in Mayo', paper to New Agendas in Social Movement Studies conference, Maynooth, available at <http://eprints.nuim.ie>.

—— (2012): 'Challenging Austerity in Ireland', in *Concept: the Journal of Community Education Practice Theory*, Vol. 3 no. 2.

—— (2013a): 'Eppur si Muove', in Barker, C., Cox, L., Krinsky, J. and Nilsen, A.G. (eds): *Marxism and Social Movements*, Leiden: Brill.

—— (2013b): 'Why are the Irish not Resisting Austerity?', in *OpenDemocracy*, 11 October.

—— (2014a): 'Movements Making Knowledge', in *Sociology*, Vol. 48 no. 5.

—— (2014b): 'Changing the World without Getting Shot', in M. Lakitsch (ed.), *Political Power Reconsidered*, Wien: LIT-Verlag.

—— (2014c): 'Challenging Toxic Hegemony', forthcoming in *Social Justice*, Vol. 41.

—— and Flesher Fominaya, C. (2009): 'Movement knowledge', pp. 1–20 in *Interface*, Vol. 1 no. 1.

—— and Flesher Fominaya, C. (2013): 'European Movements and Social Theory', in C. Flesher Fominaya and L. Cox (eds), *Understanding European Movements*, London: Routledge.

—— and Mullan, C. (2001): 'Social Movements Never Died', paper to ISA/BSA social movements conference, available at <http://eprints.nuim.ie>.

—— and Nilsen, A.G. (2007): 'Social movements research and the "movement of movements"', pp. 424–442 in *Sociological Compass*, Vol. 1 no. 2.

—— and Szolucha, A. (2013): 'Social Movement Research in Europe', pp. 59–63 in *Perspectives on Europe*, Vol. 43 no. 2.

Cox, R.W. (1987): *Production, Power and World Order*, New York: Columbia University Press.

Cresswell, M. and Spandler, H. (2012): 'The Engaged Academic', pp. 138–54 in *Social Movement Studies*, Vol. 12 no. 2.

Dalby, S. (1984): 'The Nuclear Syndrome', in *Dawn Train*, No. 3, available at <www.innatenonviolence.org>.

Dale, G. (2010): *Karl Polanyi*, Cambridge: Polity Press.

Dangl, B. (2010): *Dancing with Dynamite*, Oakland, CA: AK Press.

Daniele, C. and Vacca, G. (1999): 'Gramsci a Roma, Togliatti a Mosca', Torino: Einaudi.

Davidson, N. (2010): 'What Was Neoliberalism?', in Davidson, N., McCafferty, P. and Miller, D. (eds), *Neoliberal Scotland*, Newcastle: Cambridge Scholars.

—— (2012): *How Revolutionary Were the Bourgeois Revolutions?*, Chicago, IL: Haymarket.

Davies, M. and Flett, K. (2009): 'The Tenacity of Activism', paper to Alternative Futures and Popular Protest conference.

Dávila, J. (2013): *Dictatorship in South America*, Oxford: Wiley-Blackwell.

Davis, A. (2003): *Are Prisons Obsolete?*, New York: Seven Stories Press.

Davis, M. (2002): *Late Victorian Holocausts*, London: Verso.

—— (2006): *Planet of Slums*, London: Verso.

Day, R. (2005): *Gramsci is Dead*, London: Pluto.

De Angelis, M. (2000): 'Globalization, New Internationalism and the Zapatistas', pp. 9–35 in *Capital and Class*, Vol. 70.

De Sario, B. (2009): 'Lo sai che non si esce vivi dagli anni ottanta?', pp. 108–33 in *Interface*, Vol. 1 no. 2.

De Sousa Santos, B. (2003): 'The World Social Forum', paper available at <www.ces.fe.uc.pt/bss/documentos/wsf.pdf>.

—— (2006): *The Rise of the Global Left*, London: Zed.

Desai, R. (2004): 'From National Bourgeoisies to Rogues, Failures, and Bullies', pp. 169–85 in *Third World Quarterly*, Vol. 25 no. 1.

—— (2013): *Geopolitical Economy*, London: Pluto.

Dinerstein, A. (2002): 'The Battle of Buenos Aires', pp. 5–38 in *Historical Materialism*, Vol. 10 no. 4.

—— (2010): 'Autonomy in Latin America', pp. 356–66 in *Community Development Journal*, Vol. 45 no. 3.

——(2014): *Autonomous Organising in Latin America*, London: Palgrave Macmillan, forthcoming.

Dongfang, H. (2013): 'Han Dongfang discusses the fast emerging labour movement in China' <http://www.clb.org.hk/en/content/han-dongfang-discusses-fast-emerging-labour-movement-china>.

D'Souza, R. (2009): 'Sandwich Theory and Operation Green Hunt' <http://mrzine.monthlyreview.org/2009/dsouza171209.html>.

Dubouis, L. (2004): *Avengers of the New World*, Cambridge, MA: Harvard University Press.

Duffield, M. (2001): *Global Governance and the New Wars*, London: Zed.

—— (2007): *Development, Security and Unending War*, Cambridge: Polity.

Duménil, G. and Lévy, D. (2004): *Capital Resurgent*, Boston, MA: Harvard University Press.

—— (2011): *The Crisis of Neoliberalism*, Boston, MA: Harvard University Press.

Dwivedi, R. (2006): *Conflict and Collective Action*, New Delhi: Routledge.

Dyer-Witherford, N. (2004): '1844/2004/2044', pp. 3–25 in *Historical Materialism*, Vol. 12 no. 4.

Edsall, T. (1985): *The New Politics of Inequality*, New York: W.W. Norton.

Eschle, C., Flesher Fominaya, C., Motta, S. and Cox, L. (2011): 'Feminism, Women's Movements and Women in Movement', pp. 1–32 in *Interface*, Vol. 3 no. 2.

Esping-Andersen, G. (1990): *The Three Worlds of Welfare Capitalism*, Princeton, NJ: Princeton University Press.

Evans, P.B. (1995): *Embedded Autonomy*, Princeton, NJ: Princeton University Press.

Eyerman, R. and Jamison, A. (1991): *Social Movements*, Cambridge: Polity.

Fantasia, R. (1988): *Cultures of Solidarity*, Berkeley: University of California Press.

Féliz, M. (2012): 'Neo-Developmentalism', pp. 105–23 in *Historical Materialism*, Vol. 20 no. 2.

Fine, B. and Saad-Filho, A. (2004): *Marx's* Capital, London: Pluto.

Fischer, S. (2004): *Modernity Disavowed*, Durham, NC: Duke University Press.

Fischer, W. (1966): 'Social Tensions at Early Stages of Industrialization', pp. 64–83 in Comparative Studies in Society and History, Vol. 9 no. 1.

Flesher Fominaya, C. (2013): 'Movement Culture Continuity', in Flesher Fominaya, C. and Cox, L. (eds), *Understanding European Movements*, Abingdon: Routledge.

—— and Cox, L. (2013): *Understanding European*, Abingdon: Routledge.

Flett, K. (2006): *Chartism after 1848*, London: Merlin.

Foran, J. (ed.) (2003): *The Future of Revolutions*, London: Zed.

Foster, J.B. and Magdoff, F. (2009): *The Great Financial Crisis*, Kharagpur: Cornerstone.

Fracchia, J. (1991): 'Marx's Aufhebung of History and the Foundations of Historical-Materialistic Science', pp. 153–79 in *History and Theory*, Vol. 30 no. 2.

—— (2005): 'Beyond the Human–Nature Debate', pp. 33–62 in *Historical Materialism*, Vol. 13 no. 1.

Freire, P. (1972): *Pedagogy of the Oppressed*, New York: Herder and Herder.

Friedmann, H. (1982): 'The Political Economy of Food', pp. 248–86 in *American Journal of Sociology*, Vol. 88/Supplement – 'Marxist Inquiries'.

—— (2005): 'From Colonialism to Green Capitalism', pp. 227–64 in *Research in Rural Sociology and Development*, Vol. 11.

Fuster Morell, M. (2009): 'Action Research', pp. 21–45 in *Interface*, Vol. 1 no. 1.

Garciá-Guadilla, M.P. (2011): 'Urban Land Committees', in Smilde, D. and Hellinger, D. (eds): *Venezuela's Bolivarian Democracy*, Durham, NC: Duke University Press.

Genovese, E.O. (1976): *Roll, Jordan, Roll*, New York: Vintage.

—— (1979): *From Rebellion to Revolution*, Baton Rouge: Louisiana State University Press.

Geras, N. (1983): *Marx and Human Nature*, London: New Left Books.

—— (1995): 'Human Nature and Progress', pp. 151–60 in *New Left Review*, Vol. 213.

Gibson-Graham, J.K. (2006): *The End of Capitalism*, Minneapolis: University of Minnesota Press.

Giddens, A. (1979): *Central Problems in Social Theory*, London: Macmillan.

Gill, S. (1990): *American Hegemony and the Trilateral Commission*, Cambridge: Cambridge University Press.

—— (1995): 'Globalisation, Market Civilization, and Disciplinary Neoliberalism', pp. 399–423 in *Millennium*, Vol. 24 no. 3.

—— (2000): 'Towards a Postmodern Prince?', pp. 131–40 in *Millennium*, Vol. 29 no. 1.

—— (2003a): *Power and Resistance in the New World Order*, Basingstoke: Palgrave Macmillan.

—— (2003b): 'Grand Strategy and World Order', lecture delivered at Yale University in ISS's Grand Strategy Series, 20 April 2000, revised for publication 10 December 2003.

Gillan, M. (2010): 'Class, Voice and State', unpublished PhD dissertation, National University of Ireland, Maynooth.

—— and Cox, L. (2014): 'The Birth of Indymedia.ie', forthcoming in Meade, R. and Dukelow, F., *Defining Events*, Manchester: Manchester University Press.

Gilmore, R.W. (2007): *Golden Gulag*, Berkeley: University of California Press.

Gilroy, P. (1993): *The Black Atlantic*, London: Verso.

Giri, S. (2009): 'The Dangers Are Great, the Possibilities Immense' <http://mrzine.monthlyreview.org/2009/giri041109.html>.

Glyn, A., Hughes, A., Lipietz, A. and Singh, A. (1991): 'The Rise and Fall of the Golden Age', in Marglin, S.A. and Schor, J.B. (eds), *The Golden Age of Capitalism*, Oxford: Oxford University Press.

Gordon, U. (2007): *Anarchy Alive!*, London: Pluto.

Gottlieb, R. (1989): *An Anthology of Western Marxism*, Oxford: Oxford University Press.

Gowan, P. (2009): 'Crisis in the Heartland', pp. 5–29 in *New Left Review*, Vol. 55.

Gramsci, A. (1978): 'Some Aspects of the Southern Question', in *Selections from Political Writings (1921–1926)*, London: Lawrence and Wishart.

—— (1998): *Selections from the Prison Notebooks*, London: Lawrence and Wishart.

Green, D. (2003): *Silent Revolution*, New York: New York University Press.

Grugel, J. and Rigirozzi, P. (2012): 'Post-Neoliberalism in Latin America', pp. 1–21 in *Development and Change*, Vol. 43 no. 1.

Grumley, J. (1999): 'A Utopian Dialectic of Needs', pp. 53–72 in *Thesis Eleven*, Vol. 59.

Guo, X. (2001): 'Land Expropriation and Rural Conflict in China', pp. 422–39 in *The China Quarterly*, Vol. 166.

Gurney, J. (2012): *Brave Community*, Manchester: Manchester University Press.

Habermas, J. (1987): *The Theory of Communicative Action*, Cambridge: Polity Press.

Hall, B., Clover, D., Crowther, J. and Scandrett, E. (2012) (eds): *Learning and Education for a Better World*, Rotterdam: Sense.

Hall, S. (1983): 'The Great Moving Right Show', pp. 19–39 in Hall, S. and Jaques, M. (eds): *The Politics of Thatcherism*, London: Lawrence and Wishart.

—— (1989), 'Politics and Letters', in Eagleton, T. (ed.), *Raymond Williams*, Cambridge: Polity.

—— (1996): 'Encoding/Decoding', pp. 41–9, in Marris, P. and Thornham, S. (eds): *Media Studies*, Edinburgh: Edinburgh University Press.

Halperin, S. (2004): *War and Social Change in Modern Europe*, Cambridge: Cambridge University Press.

Hanley, B. and Millar, S. (2009): *The Lost Revolution*, London: Penguin.

Hardt, M. and Negri, T. (2000): *Empire*, Cambridge, MA: Harvard University Press.

Harman, C. (1998a): *Marxism and History*, London: Bookmarks.

—— (1998b): *The Fire Last Time*, London: Bookmarks.

Hart, G. (2002): *Disabling Globalization*, Berkeley: University of California Press.

Harvey, B. (2014): *Are we Paying for That?*, Dublin: Advocacy Initiative.

Harvey, D. (1985): *Consciousness and the Urban Experience*, Oxford: Basil Blackwell.

—— (1990): *The Condition of Postmodernity*, Oxford: Blackwell.

—— (1996): *Justice, Nature and the Geography of Difference*, Oxford: Blackwell.

—— (1999): *Limits to Capital*, London: Verso.

—— (2000): *Spaces of Hope*, Edinburgh: Edinburgh University Press.

—— (2001): *Spaces of Capital*, Edinburgh: Edinburgh University Press.

—— (2003): *The New Imperialism*, Oxford: Oxford University Press.

—— (2005): *A Brief History of Neoliberalism*, Oxford: Oxford University Press.

—— (2006): *Spaces of Global Capitalism*, London: Verso.

—— (2007): 'Neoliberalism as Creative Destruction', pp. 22–44 in *Annals of the American Academy of Political Science*, Vol. 610.

—— (2010): *A Companion to Marx's* Capital, London: Verso.

Heintz, J. and Balakrishnan, R. (2012): 'Debt, Power, and Crisis', pp. 387–409 in *American Quarterly*, Vol. 64 no. 3.

Helleiner, E. (1994): *States and the Reemergence of Global Finance*, Ithaca, NY: Cornell University Press.

Heller, A. (1976): *The Theory of Need in Marx*, London: Allison and Busby.

Heller, H. (2010): *The Birth of Capitalism*, London: Pluto.

Herman, S.N. (2014): *Taking Liberties*, New York: Oxford University Press.

Hesketh, C. and Morton, A.D. (2014): 'Spaces of Uneven Development and Class Struggle in Bolivia', pp. 149–69 in *Antipode*, Vol. 46 no. 1.

Hill, C. (1961): *The Century of Revolution*, Edinburgh: Thomas Nelson.

—— (1967): *Reformation to Industrial Revolution*, London: Weidenfeld and Nicolson.

—— (1980): 'A Bourgeois Revolution?', in Pockock, J.G.A. (ed.): *Three British Revolutions*, Princeton, NJ: Princeton University Press.

—— (1975 [1991]): *The World Turned Upside Down*, London: Penguin.

Hirtz, N.V. and Giacone, M.S. (2013): 'The Recovered Companies Workers' Struggle in Argentina', pp. 88–100 in *Latin American Perspectives*, Vol. 40 no. 4.

Hobsbawm, E.J. (1987): *The Age of Empire*, New York: Vintage.

—— (2004): *The Age of Capital*, New York: Abacus.

—— (2005): *The Age of Revolutions*, New York: Abacus.

Holloway, J. (1995): 'The Abyss Opens', pp. 69–91 in Bonefeld, W. and Holloway, J. (eds): *Global Capital, National State and the Politics of Money*, Basingstoke: Macmillan.

—— (2002): *Change the World without Taking Power*, London: Pluto.

Holstun, James (2002): *Ehud's Dagger*, London: Verso.

Hope, A. and Timmel, S. (1984): *Training for Transformation*, Gweru: Mambo.

Horton, M. and Freire, P. (1990): *We Make the Road by Walking*, Philadelphia, PA: Temple University Press.

Huber, E. and Stephens, J. (2012): *Democracy and the Left*, Chicago, IL: University of Chicago Press.

Humphrys, E. (2013): 'Organic Intellectuals in the Australian Global Justice Movement', in Barker, C. et al. (eds), *Marxism and Social Movements*, Leiden: Brill.

ILO (2014): *Global Employment Trends 2014*, Geneva: International Labour Office.

INCITE! Women of Color Against Violence (eds) (2009): *The Revolution will not be Funded*, Boston, MA: South End Press.

Inglis, T. (1998): *Lessons in Irish Sexuality*, Dublin: UCD Press.

Inman, P. (2014): 'Disposable incomes "will not rise for average family until 2015"' <http://www.theguardian.com/business/2014/feb/11/disposable-incomes-average-family-resolution-foundation>.

Ivins, C. (2013): *Inequality Matters* <http://www.oxfam.org/sites/www.oxfam.org/files/brics-inequality-fact-sheet-oxfam-03-14-2013_0.pdf>.

James, C.L.R. (2001): *The Black Jacobins*, London: Penguin.

Jasper, J.M. (1997): *The Art of Moral Protest*, Chicago, IL: University of Chicago Press.

Jay, M. (1984): *Marxism and Totality*. Cambridge: Polity.

Jayasuriya, K. (2006): *Statecraft, Welfare and the Politics of Inclusion*, Basingstoke: Palgrave.

Jessop, B. (1982): *The Capitalist State*, Oxford: Martin Robertson.

—— (1990): *State Theory*, Cambridge: Polity.

—— (2003): *The Future of the Capitalist State*, Cambridge: Polity.

—— (2008): *State Power*, Cambridge: Polity.

——, Bonnett, K., Bromley, S., and Ling, T. (1988): *Thatcherism*, Cambridge: Polity.

Jones, D.S. (2012): *Masters of the Universe*, Princeton, NJ: Princeton University Press.

Júlíusson, Á. and Helgason, M. (2013): 'The Roots of the Saucepan Revolution in Iceland', in Flesher Fominaya, F. and Cox, L. (eds), *Understanding European Movements*, Abingdon: Routledge.

Juris, J. (2008): *Networking Futures*, Durham, NC: Duke University Press.

Katsiaficas, G. (1987): *The Imagination of the New Left*, Boston, MA: South End Press.

—— (2006): *The Subversion of Politics*, Oakland, CA: AK.

Kaviraj, S. (1997): 'A Critique of the Passive Revolution', pp. 45–88 in P. Chatterjee, (ed.): *State and Politics in India*, Delhi: Oxford University Press.

Kellogg, P. (2007): *Regional Integration in Latin America*, pp. 187–209 in *New Political Economy*, Vol. 29 no. 2.

Kennedy, G. (2008): *Diggers, Levellers, and Agrarian Capitalism*, Lanham, MD: Lexington.

Kennemore, A. and Weeks, G. (2011): 'Twenty-First Century Socialism?', pp. 267–81 in *Bulletin of Latin American Research*, Vol. 30 no. 3.

Khagram, S. (2004): *Dams and Development*, Ithaca, NY: Cornell University Press.

Kiely, R. (2005): *The Clash of Globalisations*, Leiden: Brill.

—— (2007): *The New Political Economy of Development*, London: Palgrave Macmillan.

—— (2010): *Rethinking Imperialism*, Basingstoke: Palgrave.

Klimke, M. (2008): *1968 in Europe*, New York: Palgrave Macmillan.

Kohl, B. and Farthing, L. (2006): *Impasse in Bolivia*, London: Zed.

Kohli, A. (2004): *State-Directed Development*, Cambridge: Cambridge University Press.

Koopmans, R. (2004): 'Protest in Time and Space', in Snow, D. et al. (eds), *The Blackwell Companion to Social Movements*, Oxford: Blackwell.

Kotz, D. (2002): 'Globalization and Neoliberalism', pp. 64–79 in *Rethinking Marxism*, Vol. 14 no. 2.

——, T. McDonough and M. Reich (1994): *Social Structures of Accumulation*, Cambridge: Cambridge University Press.

Krinsky, J. (2009): *Free Labor*, Chicago, IL: University of Chicago Press.

Laclau, E. and Mouffe, C. (2001): *Hegemony and Socialist Strategy*, 2nd edn, London: Verso.

Lan, D. (1985): *Guns and Rain*, Berkeley: University of California Press.

Larrain, J. (1986): *A Reconstruction of Historical Materialism*, London: Allen and Unwin.

Lash, S. and Urry, J. (1987): *The End of Organized Capitalism*, Madison: University of Wisconsin Press.

Lazar, S. (2010): *El Alto, Rebel City*, Durham, NC: Duke University Press.

Lebowitz, M. (2003): *Beyond Capital*, Basingstoke: Palgrave Macmillan.

Lee, C.K. (2007): *Against the Law*, Berkeley: University of California Press.

——and Selden, M. (2008): 'Inequality and its Enemies in Revolutionary and Reform China', pp. 27–36 in *Economic and Political Weekly*, Vol. 43 no. 52.

Leonard, L. (2005): *Politics Inflamed*, Drogheda: Choice.

Levien, M. (2011): 'Special Economic Zones and Accumulation by Dispossession in India', pp. 454–83 in *Journal of Agrarian Change*, Vol. 11 no. 4.

—— (2012): 'The Land Question', pp. 933–69 in *Journal of Peasant Studies*, Vol. 39 nos 3–4.

—— (2013a): 'Regimes of Dispossession', pp. 381–407 in *Development and Change*, Vol. 44 no. 2.

—— (2013b): 'The Politics of Dispossession', pp. 351–94 in *Politics and Society*, Vol. 41 no. 3.

Li, L. and O'Brien, K. (1996): 'Villagers and Popular Resistance in Contemporary China', pp. 28–61 in *Modern China*, Vol. 22 no. 1.

Lichterman, P. (1996): *The Search for Political Community*, Cambridge: Cambridge University Press.

Linebaugh, P. (2006): *The London Hanged*, London: Verso.

—— and Rediker, M. (2000): *The Many-Headed Hydra*, London: Verso.

Lowrey, A. (2013): 'The Rich Get Richer Through the Recovery', *New York Times*, 10 September, available at <http://economix.blogs.nytimes.com/2013/09/10/the-rich-get-richer-through-the-recovery/?_php=true&_type=blogs&_r=0>.

Ludden, D. (2005): 'Development Regimes in South Asia', pp. 37–41 in *Economic and Political Weekly*, Vol. 40 no. 37.

Lukács, G. (1971): *History and Class Consciousness*, Cambridge, MA: MIT Press.

Lyder, A. (2005): *Pushers Out*, Victoria: Trafford.

Lynch, K. and McLaughlin, E. (1995): 'Caring Labour and Love Labour', in Clancy, P. et al. (eds), *Irish Society*, Dublin: Institute for Public Administration.

Lysgaard, S. (1985): *Arbeiderkollektivet*, Oslo: Universitetsforlaget.

Macintyre, S (1987): *A Proletarian Science*, London: Lawrence and Wishart.

Maeckelbergh, M. (2009): *The Will of the Many*, London: Pluto.

—— (2012): 'Horizontal Democracy Now', pp. 207–34 in *Interface*, Vol. 4 no. 1.

Mahmud, T. (2012): 'Debt and Discipline', pp. 469–94 in *American Quarterly*, Vol. 64 no. 3.

Mallon, F. (1995): *Peasant and Nation*, Berkeley: University of California Press.

Manji, F. and Ekine, S. (2011): *African Awakening*, Cape Town: Fahamu.

Mann, M. (2012): *The Sources of Social Power*, Cambridge: Cambridge University Press.

Manning, B. (1991): *The English People and the English Revolution*, London: Bookmarks.

—— (1996): *Aristocrats, Plebeians and Revolution in England*, London: Pluto.

Marx, K. (1970): *Critique of Hegel's* Philosophy of Right, Cambridge: Cambridge University Press.

—— (1977): *Critique of Hegel's 'Philosophy of Right'*, Cambridge University Press.

—— (1981a): *Economic and Philosophic Manuscripts of 1844*, London: Lawrence and Wishart.

—— (1981b): *Contribution to the Critique of Political Economy*, London: Lawrence and Wishart.

—— (1984): *The Eighteenth Brumaire of Louis Napoleon*, London: Lawrence and Wishart.

—— (1990): *Capital: A Critique of Political Economy* (Vol. 1), Harmondsworth: Penguin.

—— (1995): *The Poverty of Philosophy*, New York: Prometheus Books.

—— (1999): 'Theses on Feuerbach', pp. 123–5 in Marx, K. and Engels, F.: *The German Ideology*, London: Lawrence and Wishart.

—— and Engels, F. (1888): *The Communist Manifesto*, available at <https://www.marxists.org/archive/marx/works/1848/communist-manifesto/>.

—— (1974): *The German Ideology*, London: Lawrence and Wishart.

—— (1999): *The German Ideology*, London: Lawrence and Wishart.

Matellart, A. (2010): *The Globalization of Surveillance*, Cambridge: Polity.

Mattoni, A. (2012): *Media Practices and Protest Politics*, Farnham: Ashgate.

Mayo, P. (1999): *Gramsci, Freire and Adult Education*, London: Palgrave Macmillan.

McDonagh, B.A.K. (2009): 'Subverting the Ground', pp. 191–206 in *Agricultural History*, Vol. 57 no. 2.

—— (2013): 'Making and Breaking Property', pp. 32–56 in *History Workshop Journal*, Vol. 76 no. 1.

McIntyre, M. and Nast, H. (2011): 'Bio(necro)polis', pp. 1465–88 in *Antipode*, Vol. 43 no. 5.

McKay, G. (1996): *Senseless Acts of Beauty*, London: Verso.

McMichael, P. (1997): 'Rethinking Globalization', pp. 630–62 in *Review of International Political Economy*, Vol. 4 no. 4.

—— (2004): *Development and Social Change*, Thousand Oaks, CA: Pine Forge.

—— (2012): 'The Land Grab and Corporate Food Regime Restructuring', pp. 681–701 in *Journal of Peasant Studies*, Vol. 39 nos 3–4.

—— and Raynolds, L.T. (1994): 'Capitalism, Agriculture and the World Economy', in Sklair, L. (ed.): *Capitalism and Development*, London: Routledge.

McNally, D. (1988): *Political Economy and the Rise of Capitalism*, Berkeley: University of California Press.

—— (1993): *Against the Market*, London: Verso.

—— (1995): 'Language, History and Class Struggle', pp. 13–40 in *Monthly Review*, Vol. 47 no. 3.

—— (2001): *Bodies of Meaning*, New York: SUNY Press.

—— (2006): *Another World is Possible*, Winnipeg: Arbeiter Ring.

—— (2011): *Global Slump*, London: Merlin.

—— (2013): 'Unity of The Diverse', in Barker, C., Cox, L., Krinsky, J. and Nilsen, A.G. (eds): *Marxism and Social Movements*, Leiden: Brill.

Meisner, M. (1996): *The Deng Xiaoping Era*, New York: Hill and Wang.

Melucci, A. (1989): *Nomads of the Present*, London: Hutchinson.

Membretti, A. and Mudu, P. (2013): 'Where Global Meets Local', in Flesher Fominaya, C. and Cox, L. (eds), *Understanding European Movements*, Abingdon: Routledge.

Menon, N. and Nigam, A. (2007): *Power and Contestation: India Since 1989*, London: Zed Books.

Mills, C.W. (1962): *The Marxists*. New York: Dell.

Mirowski, P. and Plehwe, D. (2009): *The Road from Mont Pelerin*, Boston, MA: Harvard University Press.

Moody, T., Martin, F. and Byrne, F. (eds) (1991): *Early Modern Ireland 1534–1691*, Oxford: Oxford University Press.

Mooers, C. (2001): *The Making of Bourgeois Europe*, London: Verso.

Moore Jr., B. (1991): *Social Origins of Dictatorship and Democracy*, London: Penguin.

Moore, D.S. (1998): 'Subaltern Struggles and the Politics of Place', pp. 1–38 in *Cultural Anthropology*, Vol. 13 no. 3.

——(2000): 'The Crucible of Cultural Politics', pp. 654–89 in *American Ethnologist*, Vol. 26 no. 3.

Morais, L.M. and Saad-Filho, A. (2011): 'Brazil Beyond Lula', pp. 31–44 in *Latin American Perspectives*, Vol. 38 no. 2.

—— (2012): 'Neo-Developmentalism and the Challenges of Economic Policy-Making under Dilma Rouseff', pp. 789–98 in *Critical Sociology*, Vol. 38 no. 6.

Morena, E. (2013): 'Constructing a New Collective Identity for the Alterglobalization Movement', in Flesher Fominaya, C. and Cox, L. (eds), *Understanding European Movements*, Abingdon: Routledge.

Morton, A.D. (2005): 'The Age of Absolutism', pp. 495–517 in *Review of International Studies*, Vol. 31 no. 3.

——(2007) 'Waiting for Gramsci', pp. 597–621 in *Millennium*, Vol. 35, no. 3.

——(2007): *Unravelling Gramsci*, London: Pluto.

——(2011): *Revolution and State in Mexico*, Lanham, MD: Rowman and Littlefield.

Motta, S.C. (2008): 'The Chilean Socialist Party (PSCh)', pp. 303–27 in *British Journal of Politics and International Relations*, Vol. 10, no. 2.

——(2011): 'Populism's Achilles' Heel', pp. 28–46 in *Latin American Perspectives*, Vol. 38 no. 176.

——and Nilsen, A.G. (2011): 'Social Movements and/in the Postcolonial', in Motta, S.C. and Nilsen, A.G. (eds): *Social Movements in the Global South*, London: Palgrave Macmillan.

Müller, M.-M. (2012): 'The Rise of the Penal State in Latin America', pp. 57–76 in *Contemporary Justice Review*, Vol. 15 no. 1.

Mukherji, N. (2012): *The Maoists in India*, London: Pluto.

Murray, M. (2003): 'Waste Management in Ireland', unpublished PhD thesis, National University of Ireland, Maynooth.

Naples, N. (1998): *Grassroots Warriors*, New York: Routledge.

National Equality Panel (2010): *An Anatomy of Economic Inequality in the UK* <http://eprints.lse.ac.uk/28344/1/CASEreport60.pdf>.

Neeson, J.M. (1984): 'The Opponents of Enclosure in Eighteenth-Century Northamptonshire', pp. 114–39 in *Past and Present*, Vol. 105.

——(1993): *Commoners*, Cambridge: Cambridge University Press.

Neilson, D. and Stubbs, T. (2011): 'Relative Surplus Population and Uneven Development in the Neoliberal Era', pp. 435–53 in *Capital and Class*, Vol. 35 no. 3.

Nigam, A. (2010): 'The Rumour of Maoism' <http://www.india-seminar.com/2010/607/607_aditya_nigam.htm>.

Nilsen, A.G. (2007): 'History Does Nothing', pp. 1–30 in *Sosiologisk Årbok*, Vol. 1 no. 2.

——(2008a): Review of David McNally's *Against the Market*, pp. 147–50 in *Capital and Class*, Vol. 32 no. 1.

—— (2008b): 'Political Economy, Social Movements and State Power', pp. 303–30 in *Journal of Historical Sociology*, Vol. 21 nos 2–3.

—— (2009a): 'The Authors and the Actors of Their Own Drama', pp. 109–39 in *Capital and Class*, Vol. 33 no. 3.

—— (2009b): 'Autonome Domener eller Relasjonelle Praksiser?', pp. 126–66 in *Agora*, No. 1.

—— (2010): *Dispossession and Resistance in India*, London: Routledge.

—— (2012): 'Adivasis in and Against the State', pp. 251–82 in *Critical Asian Studies*, Vol. 44 no. 2.

—— (2013): 'Against the Current, From Below', in *Journal of Poverty*, Volume 17 issue 4.

—— (2015): 'Postcolonial Social Movements', in Ness, I. and Ba, S.M. (eds): *The Palgrave Encyclopedia of Imperialism and Anti-Imperialism*, New York: Palgrave Macmillan.

O'Malley, K. (2008): *Ireland, India and Empire*, Manchester: Manchester University Press.

O'Sullivan, E. (1999): *Transformative Learning*, London: Zed.

—— and O'Donnell, I. (2012): *Coercive Confinement in Ireland*, Manchester: Manchester University Press.

OECD (2008): *Growing Unequal?*, Paris: OECD Publishing.

—— (2011): *Divided We Stand*, Paris: OECD Publishing.

—— (2013): 'Crisis squeezes income and puts pressure on inequality and poverty' <http://www.oecd.org/social/soc/OECD2013-Inequality-and-Poverty-8p.pdf>.

Offe, C. (1984): *Contradictions of the Welfare State*, Cambridge, MA: MIT Press.

Ollman, B. (1993): *Dialectical Investigations*, London: Routledge.

Ortner, S. (1995): 'Resistance and the Problem of Ethnographic Refusal', pp. 173–93 in *Comparative Studies in Society and History*, Vol. 37 no. 1.

Overbeek, H. (1990): *Global Capitalism and National Decline*, London: Routledge.

—— and Van Der Pijl, K. (1993): 'Restructuring Capital and Restructuring Hegemony', pp. 1–27 in Overbeek, H. (ed.): *Restructuring Hegemony in the Global Political Economy*, London, Routledge.

Oxfam (2014): *Working for the Few* <http://www.oxfam.org/sites/www.oxfam.org/files/bp-working-for-few-political-capture-economic-inequality-200114-en.pdf>.

Padel, F. and Das, S. (2010): *Out of This Earth*, New Delhi: Orient Blackswan.

Panizza, F. (2009): *Contemporary Latin America*, London: Zed.

Pavone, C. (1991): *Una Guerra Civile*, Torino: Bollati Boringhieri.

Peck, J. (2001): *Workfare States*, New York: Guildford Press.

—— (2002): 'Political Economies of Scale', in *Economic Geography*, Vol. 78 no. 3.

—— (2010a): *Constructions of Neoliberal Reason*, London: Oxford University Press.

—— (2010b): 'Zombie Neoliberalism and the Ambidextrous State', pp. 104–10 in *Theoretical Criminology*, Vol. 14 no. 1.

—— (2011): 'Global Policy Models, Globalizing Poverty Management', pp. 165–81 in *Geography Compass*, Vol. 5 no. 4.

—— and Tickell, A. (2002): 'Neoliberalizing Space', pp. 380–404 in *Antipode*, Vol. 34 no. 3.

——, Theodore, N. and Brenner, N. (2012): 'Neoliberalism Resurgent?', pp. 265–88 in *South Atlantic Quarterly*, Vol. 111 no. 2.

Peet, R. (2007): *Geography of Power*, London: Zed.

—— and Watts, M. (1993): 'Liberation Ecology', pp. 1–45 in Peet, R. and Watts, M. (eds): *Liberation Ecologies*, London: Routledge.

Peluso, N.L. (1992): *Rich Forests, Poor People*, Berkeley: University of California Press.

Perreault, T. (2010): 'Dispossession by Accumulation?', pp. 1050–69 in *Antipode*, Vol. 45 no. 5.

Petras, J. and Veltmeyer, H. (2001): *Globalization Unmasked*, Delhi: Madhyam.

—— (2005): *Social Movements and State Power*, London: Pluto.

—— (2009): *What's Left in Latin America?, Farnham: Ashgate.*

—— (2013): *Social Movements in Latin America*, Basingstoke: Palgrave Macmillan.

Piven, F.F. and Cloward, R.A. (1977): *Poor People's Movements*, New York: Vintage.

—— (1982): *The New Class War*, New York: Pantheon.

Polanyi, K. (2001): *The Great Transformation*, Boston, MA: Beacon.

Polet, François and CETRI (eds) (2003): *Globalizing Resistance*, London: Pluto.

Poulantzas, N. (1978): *State, Power, Socialism*, London: Verso.

Powell, F. and Geoghegan, M. (2004): *The Politics of Community Development*, Dublin: Farmar.

Pradella, L. (2013): 'Imperialism and Capitalist Development in Marx's *Capital*', pp. 117–47 in *Historical Materialism*, Vol. 21 no. 2.

Prashad, V. (2007): *The Darker Nations*, New Delhi: Leftword.

—— (2012): *The Poorer Nations*, London: Verso.

Prevost, G., Campos, C.O. and Vanden, H.E. (eds) (2012): *Social Movements and Leftist Governments in Latin America*, London: Zed.

Prichard, A., Kinna, R., Pinta, S. and Berry, D. (eds), (2012): *Libertarian Socialism*, Houndmills: Palgrave.

Punch, M, (2009): 'Contested Urban Environments', pp. 83–107 in *Interface*, Vol. 1 no. 2.

Ramesh, R. (2011): 'Income inequality growing faster in UK than any other rich country, says OECD' <http://www.theguardian.com/society/2011/dec/05/income-inequality-growing-faster-uk>.

Ramnath, M. (2011): *Decolonizing Anarchism*, Oakland, CA: AK Press.

Rankin, K. (2001): 'Governing Development', pp. 18–37 in *Economy and Society*, Vol. 30 no. 1.

Raschke, J. (1985): *Soziale Bewegungen*, Frankfurt: Campus.

—— (1993): *Die Grünen*, Köln: Bund-Verlag.

Rees, J. (1998): *The Algebra of Revolution*, London: Routledge.

Regan, J. (1999): *The Irish Counter-Revolution, 1921–1936*, Dublin: Gill and Macmillan.

Rigirozzi, P. (2012): *The Rise of Post-Hegemonic Regionalism*, New York: Springer.

Rivat, E. (2013): 'The Continuity of Transnational Protest', in Flesher Fominaya, C. and Cox, L. (eds), *Understanding European Movements*, Abingdon: Routledge.

Robinson, C. (2000): *Black Marxism: The Making of the Black Radical Tradition*, Chapel Hill: University of North Carolina Press.

Robinson, W.I. (1996): *Promoting Polyarchy*, Cambridge: Cambridge University Press.

—— (2004): *A Theory of Global Capitalism*, Baltimore, MD: John Hopkins University Press.

Romanos, E. (2013): 'Collective Learning Processes within Social Movements', in Flesher Fominaya, C. and Cox, L. (eds), *Understanding European Movements*, Abingdon: Routledge.

Rooke, M. (2003): 'The Dialectic of Labour and Human Emancipation', pp. 76–98 in Bonefeld, W. and Visquerra, S.T. (eds): *What is to be Done?*, e-book available at <www.endpage.org>.

Roseberry, W. (1989): *Anthropologies and Histories*, New Brunswick, NJ: Rutgers University Press.

—— (1995): 'Hegemony, Power, and Languages of Contention', pp. 71–84 in Wilmsen, E.N. and McAllister, P. (eds): *The Politics of Difference*, Chicago, IL: University of Chicago Press.

Roy, A. (2010): Walking With the Comrades <http://www.outlookindia.com/article.aspx?264738-1>.

Ruggie, J. (1982): 'International Regimes, Transactions, and Change', pp. 379–415 in *International Organization*, Vol. 36 no. 2.

Rupert, M. (1990): 'Producing Hegemony', pp. 427–56 in *International Studies Quarterly*, Vol. 34 no. 4.

Sader, E. (2011): *The New Mole*, London: Verso.

Samara, T.R. (2010): 'Order and Security in the City', pp. 637–55 in *Ethnic and Racial Studies*, Vol. 33 no. 4.

Sampat, P. (2010): 'Special Economic Zones in India', pp. 166–82 in *City and Society*, Vol. 22 no. 2.

Sangvai, S. (2000): *The River and Life*, Mumbai: Earthcare.

Sarkar, S. (1997): *Writing Social History*, Delhi: Oxford University Press.

Saville, J. (1994): *The Consolidation of the Capitalist State*, London: Pluto.

Sayer, D. (1987): *The Violence of Abstraction*, London: Blackwell.

Schaefer, T. (2009): 'Engaging Modernity', pp. 397–413 in *Third World Quarterly*, Vol. 30 no. 2.

Schaumberg, H. (2008): 'In Search of Alternatives', pp. 368–87 in *Bulletin of Latin American Research*, Vol. 27 no. 3.

Scholl, C. (2013): *Two Sides of a Barricade*, New York: SUNY Press.

Scott, J.C. (1985): *Weapons of the Weak*, New Haven, CT: Yale University Press.

—— (1990): *Domination and the Arts of Resistance*, New Haven, CT: Yale University Press.

Selden, M. (1993): *The Political Economy of Chinese Development*, New York: M.E. Sharpe.

Sen, J. (1999): 'A World to Win, But Whose World is it Anyway?', in Foster, J.W. and Anand, A. (eds): *Whose World is it Anyway?*, Ottawa: United Nations Association in Canada.

—— and Waterman, P. (2012): *World Social Forum*, New Delhi: OpenWord.

Sethi, N. (2013): 'Majority of Orissa villages reject Vedanta bauxite mining project' <http://www.livemint.com/Companies/TbDsogtW2GI364AyW8YThN/Majority-of-village-councils-reject-Vedantas-bauxite-mining.html>.

Sewell, W.H. (1992): 'A Theory of Structure', pp. 1–29 in *American Journal of Sociology*, Vol. 98 no. 1.

—— (1996): 'Historical Events as Transformation of Structures', pp. 841–81 in *Theory and Society*, Volume 25 no. 6.

Shihade, M., Flesher Fominaya, C. and Cox, L. (2012): 'The Season of Revolution', pp. 1–16 in *Interface*, Vol. 4 no. 1.

Silver, B.J. (1995): 'World-Scale Patterns of Labor-Capital Conflict', pp. 155–92 in *Review*, Vol. 18 no. 1.

—— (2003): *Forces of Labour*, Cambridge: Cambridge University Press.

—— and Slater, E. (1999): 'The Social Origins of World Hegemonies', in Arrighi, G. and Silver, B. (eds): *Chaos and Governance in the World System*, Minneapolis: University of Minnesota Press.

Sitrin, M. (2012): *Everyday Revolutions*, London: Zed.

Skocpol, T. (1979), *States and Social Revolutions*, Cambridge: Cambridge University Press.

Smith, G.A. (2011): 'Selective Hegemony and Beyond', pp. 2–38 in *Identities*, Vol. 18 no. 1.

Smith, N. (1990): *Uneven Development*, Oxford: Blackwell.

—— (2005): *The Endgame of Globalization*, London: Routledge.

Soederberg, S. (2012): 'The Mexican Debtfare State', pp. 561–75 in *Globalizations*, Vol. 9 no. 4.

Sohn-Rehtel, A. (1978): *Intellectual and Manual Labour*, London: Macmillan.

Sotiris, P. (2013): 'Reading Revolt as Deviance', pp. 47–77 in *Interface*, Vol. 5 no. 2.

Starhawk (1988): *Truth or Dare*, San Francisco, CA: Harper.

Starr, A. (2001): *Naming the Enemy*, London: Zed.

Ste. Croix, G.E.M. (1981): *The Class Struggle in the Ancient Greek World*, London: Duckworth.

Stedile, J. (2007): 'The Neoliberal Agrarian Model in Brazil' <http://monthlyreview.org/2007/02/01/the-neoliberal-agrarian-model-in-brazil>.

Steinberg, M.W. (1999): 'The Talk and Back Talk of Collective Action', pp. 736–80 in *American Journal of Sociology*, Vol. 105 no. 3.

Sundar, N. (1997): *Subalterns and Sovereigns*, Oxford: Oxford University Press.

—— (2012): 'Insurgency, Counter-insurgency, and Democracy in Central India', in Jeffrey, R., Sen, R. and Singh, P. (eds): *More Than Maoism*, New Delhi: Manohar.

Swyngedouw, E. (2002): 'Dispossessing H_2O', pp. 81–98 in *Capitalism, Nature, Socialism*, Vol. 16 no. 1.

Szolucha, A. (2013): 'No Stable Ground', pp. 18–38 in *Interface*, Vol. 5 no. 2.

Taylor, M. (2006): *From Pinochet to the 'Third Way'*, London: Pluto.

—— (2009): 'Displacing Insecurity in a Divided World', pp. 147–62 in *Third World Quarterly*, Vol. 30 no. 1.

—— (2012): 'The Antinomies of "Financial Inclusion"', pp. 601–10 in *Journal of Agrarian Change*, Vol. 12 no. 4.

Thompson, E.P. (1963): *The Making of the English Working Class*, Harmondsworth: Penguin.

—— (1975): *Whigs and Hunters*, New York: Pantheon.

—— (1978): *The Poverty of Theory and Other Essays*, London: Merlin Press.

—— (1993): *Customs in Common*, London: Penguin.

—— (1995): *The Poverty of Theory*, London: Merlin.

—— (1998): *Witness Against the Beast*, Cambridge: Cambridge University Press.

Thompson, W. (1997): *The Left in History*, London: Pluto.

Tilly, C. (1996): *European Revolutions*, New York: Wiley Blackwell.

Tormey, S. (2001): *Agnes Heller*, Manchester: Manchester University Press.

Touraine, A. (1981): *The Voice and the Eye*, Cambridge: Cambridge University Press.

—— (1985): 'An Introduction to the Study of Social Movements', pp. 749–87 in *Social Research*, Vol. 52.

Tovey, H. (1993): 'Environmentalism in Ireland', pp. 413–30 in *International Sociology*, Vol. 8 no. 4.

Tsui, E. (2012): 'China Pushes Minimum Wage Rises' <http://www.ft.com/intl/cms/s/0/847b0990-36a2-11e1-9ca3-00144feabdc0.html#axzz2vP6b5g2P>.

Udall, L. (1995): 'The International Narmada Campaign', pp. 201–27 in Fisher, W.F. (ed.): *Towards Sustainable Development?*, London: M.E. Sharpe.

UNDP (1999): *Human Development Report 1999*, New York: Oxford University Press.

—— (2000): *Human Development Report 2000*, New York: Oxford University Press.

—— (2013): *Human Development Report 2013: The Rise of the South*, New York: United Nations Development Programme.

—— (2014): *Humanity Divided*, New York: United Nations Development Programme.

Van der Pijl, K. (1998): *Transnational Classes and International Relation*, London: Routledge.

Vester, M. (1975): *Die Entstehung des Proletariats als Lernprozess*, Frankfurt (M): Europäische Verlagsanstalt.

Vološinov, V.N. (1986): *Marxism and the Philosophy of Language*, London: Seminar.

Wacquant, L.C. (2004): *Urban Outcasts*, Cambridge: Polity.

——(2008): 'The Militarization of Urban Marginality', pp. 56–74 in *International Political Sociology*, Vol. 2 no. 1.

——(2009): *Punishing the Poor*, Durham, NC: Duke University Press.

Wade, R. (1990): *Governing the Market*, Princeton, NJ: Princeton University Press.

Wainwright, H. (1994): *Arguments for a New Left*, Oxford: Blackwell.

Walby, S. (1991): *Theorizing Patriarchy*, New York: Wiley-Blackwell.

Walker, K.L. (2006): '"Gangster capitalism" and Peasant Protest in China', pp. 1–33 in *Journal of Peasant Studies*, Vol. 33 no. 1.

—— (2008): 'From Covert to Overt', pp. 462–88 in *Journal of Agrarian Change*, Vol. 8 nos 2–3.

Wallerstein, I. (1989): '1968: Revolution in the World-System', pp. 431–49 in *Theory and Society*, Vol. 18 no. 4.

——(1990): 'Anti-Systemic Movements', in Amin, S., Arrighi, G., Frank, A.G. and Wallerstein, I. (eds): *Transforming the Revolution*, New York: Monthly Review.

——(2006): 'The Curve of American Power', pp. 77–94 in *New Left Review*, Vol. 40.

——(2011): *The Modern World-System*, Berkeley: University of California Press.

Walton, J. and Seddon, D. (1994): *Free Markets and Food Riots*, Oxford: Blackwell.

Watts, M. (2001): '1968 and All That ...', pp. 157–88 in *Progress in Human Geography*, Vol. 25 no. 2.

Webber, J. (2011): *From Rebellion to Reform in Bolivia*, Chicago, IL: Haymarket.

——(2012a): *Red October*, Chicago, IL: Haymarket.

West, E. and Nelson, F. (2013): 'The Strange Death of the British Middle Class', *Spectator*, available at <http://www.spectator.co.uk/features/9000951/the-missing-middle/>.

——(2012b): 'Revolution against "progress"' <http://www.isj.org.uk/?id=780>.

Weyland, K., Madrid. R.L. and Hunter, W. (2010): *Leftist Governments in Latin America*, Cambridge: Cambridge University Press.

Whitehead, J. (2010): *Development and Dispossession in the Narmada Valley*, New Delhi: Pearson Education.

Wilkin, P. (2000): 'Solidarity in a Global Age', pp. 20–65 in *Journal of World-systems Research*, Vol. VI no. 1.

Williams, R. (1965): *The Long Revolution*. Harmondsworth: Penguin.

——(1977): *Marxism and Literature*, Oxford: Oxford University Press.

——(1983): *Towards 2000*, London: Chatto and Windus.

——(1989): *Resources of Hope*, London: Verso.

Wilpert, G. (2007): *Changing Venezuela*, London: Verso.

Wolf, E.R. (1982): *Europe and the People Without History*, Berkeley: University of California Press.

Wolford, W. (2010): *This Land is Ours Now*, Durham, NC: Duke University Press.

Wood, A. (2001): *Riot, Rebellion and Popular Politics in Early Modern England*, Basingstoke: Palgrave.

——(2007a): *The Politics of Social Conflict*, Cambridge: Cambridge University Press.

—— (2007b): *The 1549 Rebellions and the Making of Early Modern England*, Cambridge: Cambridge University Press.

Wood, E.M. (2002): *The Origin of Capitalism: A Longer View*, London: Verso.

Wood, L. (2007): 'Breaking the Wave', pp. 377–88 in *Mobilization*, Vol. 12 no. 4.

—— (2012): *Direct Action, Deliberation and Diffusion*, Cambridge: Cambridge University Press.

—— (2014): *Crisis and Control*, London: Pluto.

Woodman, J. (2014): 'India's Rejection of Vedanta's Bauxite Mine is a Victory for Tribal Rights' <http://www.theguardian.com/global-development/poverty-matters/2014/jan/14/india-rejection-vedanta-mine-victory-tribal-rights>.

Wright, A.L. and Wolford, W. (2003): *To Inherit the Earth*, Berkeley, CA: Food First.

Wylde, C. (2013): 'The Developmental State is Dead, Long Live the Developmental Regime!', in *Journal of International Relations and Development*, advance online publication: <http://www.palgrave-journals.com/jird/journal/vaop/ncurrent/abs/jird201232a.html>.

Ytterstad, A. (2012): 'Norwegian Climate Change Policy in the Media, unpublished PhD dissertation, Oslo and Akershus University College.

Zagato, A. (2012): Community Development in Dublin', unpublished PhD dissertation, National University of Ireland Maynooth.

Zibechi, R. (2010): *Dispersing Power*, Oakland, CA: AK.

—— (2012): *Territories In Resistance*, Oakland, CA: AK Press.

Zinn, H. (1999): *Marx in Soho*, Boston, MA: South End Press.

Index